D1504627

Praise for *Social eCommerce*

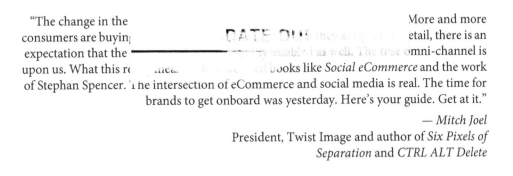

"The change in the [...] consumers are buyin[...] expectation that the [...] upon us. What this r[...] [...]ea[...] [...]ooks like *Social eCommerce* and the work of Stephan Spencer. The intersection of eCommerce and social media is real. The time for brands to get onboard was yesterday. Here's your guide. Get at it."

More and more [...] etail, there is an [...]mni-channel is

— *Mitch Joel*
President, Twist Image and author of *Six Pixels of Separation* and *CTRL ALT Delete*

"How does Stephan Spencer have the ability to predict the future? Here's a person who knows what's hot even before it's luke warm. Over the past twelve years, our executive team has followed his advice, learned from his counterintuitive insights and reaped the benefits of creating a brand that now has authority, influence and exactly the positioning we want in our market space. The lesson is to listen, gain understanding and act upon his incredible insights."

— *Steve Spangler*
Speaker Hall of Fame inductee, Emmy award–winning television personality, Guinness World Record holder, bestselling author, founder of *SteveSpanglerScience.com*

"Stephan Spencer's new book is a must-read for anyone interested in doing business on the Web."

— *John Chow*
Super Affiliate, author of *Make Money Online: Roadmap of a Dot Com Mogul*

"*Social eCommerce* represents an easy-to-read, yet highly actionable guide to generating ecommerce transactions by building relationships with people through social media. This book effectively dispels gimmicks, while providing a treasure trove of insider tips and strategies to help you turn social engagements into leads, transactions, and profits. Buy a copy for yourself and your staff, as this book will deliver 1,000x return on investment."

— *Kristopher B. Jones*
Best-selling author of *Search Engine Optimization: Your Visual Blueprint to Effective Internet Marketing*, Chairman of Internet Marketing Ninjas

"Social media is rapidly changing the way brands monetize and engage with their audience online. Spencer not only examines every facet of social media, but he also delivers quality case studies and guidance in each new chapter for you to implement into your business or brand!"

— *Zac Johnson*
Super affiliate, blogger at *ZacJohnson.com*

"Here's my guidance for the world's greatest social media strategy: Inform, entertain, provide utility. Simple, right? It is, but it takes a clear strategy, a structured process, and the right people. Stephan, Jimmy, and Jennifer show you how in this book."

— *Avinash Kaushik*
Author of *Web Analytics 2.0* and *Web Analytics: An Hour A Day* (Sybex)

"It's finally here—the definitive guide that every online entrepreneur should read if they want to be successful in the age of social media. Simply brilliant."

— *Jeni Larson Hott*
Seven-figure blogger

"Authors Stephan Spencer and Jimmy Harding set the record straight—and give you a solid network for representing yourself properly and authentically in the world of SEO and social media. Get past mindless self-promotionand focus on the channels that matter to your company and to your customers."

— *Kelly Goto*
Founder of gotomedia, co-author of *Web ReDesign 2.0: Workflow that Works*

"This book is a must-read for both handling day-to-day social media and online marketing activities for an ecommerce website as well as directors of online marketing. It provides a great wealth of information in both strategy and tactics for anyone dealing with social ecommerce. I will be adding this book to our must-read books for all of our team."

— *Khalid Saleh*
Author of *Conversion Optimization: The Art and Science of Converting Prospects to Customers*, founder & CEO of Invesp

"Stephan Spencer has applied his years of experience and thought leadership in online marketing to the social media world. This book is filled with clear fundamentals that anyone can take and use, whether it be the founder of a start-up firm or the CMO of a large enterprise. Social media is here to stay as a critical component of any company's marketing plans, and Stephan helps us understand how to use it to our advantage, while having fun every step of the way!"

— *Toni Sikes*
Founder and CEO, CODAworx

"Most books on marketing suffer from one or two problems. Either they're laundry lists of piecemeal tactics, or they present one solution for every situation. What's so refreshing and valuable about *Social eCommerce* is the combination of a single overarching social strategy and a tailored approach for many different applications. Follow the prescriptions outlined in this book and you'll stand out as fascinating, ethical, and valuable."

— *Howard Jacobson*
Co-author of *Whole: Rethinking the Science of Nutrition*,
co-author of *Google AdWords for Dummies*

"*Social eCommerce* is not just another social media tip sheet on setting up profiles and getting 'likes'—it's a way to build key business relationships and extend and connect your brand to new and existing customers. Stephan has a unique point of view in the field of search engine optimization and social media and provides a blueprint for your social strategy."

— *Tony Hsieh*
NY Times bestselling author of *Delivering Happiness*,
CEO of Zappos.com

"*Social eCommerce* is a buzzword without meaning for many. But for Stephan, it's a path to amazing marketshare and revenue. The simple how-to approach of explaining what works, what to do, and where to go is about right for everyone trying to get handle on how to use social media to drive ecommerce. As a person who makes his living on education, I can confidently say…this is the real deal, period."

— *Aaron Kahlow*
CEO and founder of Online Marketing Institute

"You're smart and want to leverage social media for ecommerce, right? Here are 100+ ideas and examples from one of the industry's finest. You should follow Stephan's tips and make more money!"

— *Chris Goward*
Author of *You Should Test That!*, Founder, WiderFunnel
Marketing Optimization

"For the better part of a decade, I have been talking about social media with Stephan and he is one of the few people who really understands the blend between SEO and social media, and how it related to commerce, specifically ecommerce. With *Social eCommerce*, Stephan demonstrates that effective blend step by step, so that anyone can improve their social media efforts and improve success."

— *Brent Csutoras*
Social Media Strategist and Founder of Kairay Media

"Understanding social media can help you skyrocket your business to success; inversely, ignoring it completely can cause you major cause major pitfalls when crisis arises. Stephan has done an amazing job of outlining what companies should due to maximize on the ever changing social media landscape, and avoid the pitfalls."

— *Dave Snyder*
CEO of CopyPress

"Stephan is one of the leading ecommerce experts in the world— his book is a priceless resource."

— *Gokul Rajaram*
Product Engineering Lead, Square; former Product Director,
Ads at Facebook; and former Product Director,
AdSense at Google

"If you only buy one book on social ecommerce, this should be it. It takes a lot to keep my attention and this book (surprisingly) did it. It's good. Damn good actually. Chockfull of proven tips and tricks to help you build a social ecommerce program, you'll learn about the different networks and how to master them; how to market physical goods, info products, and even events; how to design and test ads on Facebook; and how to build a reputation management program (which everyone needs and very few companies have). There's also BONUS advice on hiring experts to help you if you don't want to do it all yourself; promoting a book; and conducting solid influencer outreach campaigns. It's the ONLY book you'll need on social ecommerce, written by folks who've actually done it."

— *Amy Africa*
CEO of Eight by Eight

"The best business books deliver equal parts of two things: a look to the future and a roadmap for how to navigate it. *Social eCommerce* fulfills that mission beautifully."

— *Ann Handley*
Chief Content Officer at MarketingProfs,
author of *Content Rules and Everybody Writes*

"*Social eCommerce* is one of the most comprehensive books I've read on the entire social media puzzle. From understanding the different pieces to putting them all together so you can get results in your brand and business, this book covers it all! Stephan definitely made sure this book is the bible for today's social media and commerce world!"

— *Com Mirza*
The $500M man with 26 companies in 7 countries with over
10 million customers, serial entrepreneur and venture capitalist

"If you aren't skilled in social media strategies, you're stuck in the 20th century. Stephan is exactly the teacher you need to succeed from here out. Get this book or be sorry you didn't."

— *Chris Hurn*
Author of *The Entrepreneur's Secret to Creating Wealth: How the Smartest Business Owners Build Their Fortunes*

Social eCommerce

Stephan Spencer, Jimmy Harding, and Jennifer Sheahan

Beijing · Cambridge · Farnham · Köln · Sebastopol · Tokyo

Social eCommerce

by Stephan Spencer, Jimmy Harding, and Jennifer Sheahan

Published by O'Reilly Media, Inc., 1005 Gravenstein Highway North, Sebastopol, CA 95472.

O'Reilly books may be purchased for educational, business, or sales promotional use. Online editions are also available for most titles (*http://safaribooksonline.com*). For more information, contact our corporate/institutional sales department: 800-998-9938 or *corporate@oreilly.com*.

Editor: Mary Treseler	**Indexer:** WordCo Indexing Services
Production Editor: Melanie Yarbrough	**Cover Designer:** Karen Montgomery
Copyeditor: Rachel Monaghan	**Interior Designer:** David Futato
Technical Editor: Rob Woods	**Illustrator:** Rebecca Demarest
Proofreader: Kiel Van Horn	

August 2014:   First Edition

Revision History for the First Edition:

2014-07-30:   First release

See *http://oreilly.com/catalog/errata.csp?isbn=9781449366360* for release details.

ISBN: 978-1-449-36636-0

[LSI]

Table of Contents

Foreword

With commerce, there isn't just one pathway to success. Nonetheless, all indicators point to the incredible importance of having a solid and interactive online presence. Even locally, people are using search engines to find information and social media as a barometer of the public's opinion. Many companies are being forced to compete with online retailers or risk obliteration.

I've witnessed firsthand the potential of social media marketing to boost sales and to improve conversion. In my case, I've had multiple occasions where one single well-planned event drove massive traffic and significantly boosted my audience.

I consider myself a serial entrepreneur. I've built many companies over the last decade, three of which I have sold, and currently am CEO of ShoeMoney Media Group and The PAR Program, Inc. In January of 2013, I wrote my own book titled *Nothing's Changed But My Change—The ShoeMoney Story*, which has sold hundreds of thousands of copies to date. But what I am probably most known for is my *ShoeMoney.com* blog (*http://shoemoney.com*), which reaches millions of people per month.

But in the beginning, I admit to you that I was very ignorant of social media, which is really ironic, since it has become such a pivotal part of my brand building and ecommerce strategy. When I started working with Stephan, he already had a thriving search engine optimization (SEO) business. This was the 2000s, when SEO was still in its early phases. My brand was in need of a refresh. Stephan suggested an idea that I still consider innovative. He proposed having a contest to design my new business card. In turn, the contest would be sponsored by his client, Overnight Prints. The winning designer would win a lifetime supply of business cards, but more importantly, exposure on a highly read blog.

We launched the contest, and it immediately took off like a rocket. I had a solid following at the time, so between those readers, interest from followers of Overnight Prints, and various designers who had heard about the contest through social media, hundreds of designs flooded in.

Social media played a pivotal role in the promotion of the contest and in designers asking for votes from their networks, friends, and family. The contest was structured such that designs with enough votes went on to become finalists, and from there I would pick the winner.

One of my crowning achievements as an online entrepreneur was when I was named "The Most Influential Person on the Internet" by *Fast Company Magazine* in 2010. It was based on online voting from 1.63 million individuals. More on that in Fast Company (*http://bit.ly/1nolYVS*).

However, I didn't become an overnight success. Many years of hard work got me to the position where I could influence so many people online. Social media may not be directly relatable to the bottom line, but make no mistake, social media drives business value as a vehicle for influence. Nowadays, it is an essential ingredient to building a brand. Not only did Overnight Prints go from nowhere to position two for the keyword "business cards" in Google and a boost in business, but the positive exposure they received from the contest cannot be easily quantified in terms of sales or conversions. Instead, it is a priceless strategy move that has the possibility of taking a business into the future. Doing one specific action for search engine optimization or social media marketing will not bring success. But with a creative strategy over time, you will find profit. Especially when you find ways to do it with minimal overhead. In the contest, Overnight Prints only had to provide business cards to the winner, a deal that for a printing company, was a minimal cost.

Soon after the partnership and contest, I signed up with ad.ly (*http://ad.ly/*), a social media company that partners big businesses with high-profile social media users. I had already garnered 100,000 Twitter followers, so I started receiving offers from very large brands, including Kmart, Walmart, and Universal Studios. I couldn't believe these companies were offering me thousands of dollars per tweet, but the value must have been there for them or they wouldn't have done it.

It was only once I launched my own ecommerce products that I truly understood the value that social media brings to ecommerce—when done right. What I love most about this book is the authors not only peel back the curtain into their methodology, but also give you a step-by-step plan and strategy to ensure social media success for your company.

—Jeremy Schoemaker, Founder and CEO of ShoeMoney Media Group and author of
Nothing's Changed But My Change: The ShoeMoney Story, 2014

Preface

We've taught a lot of people how to be more successful on the Web. The definitions of "the Web" and "success" have changed a lot over the years, but many of the low-level principles and theories remain the same. We dreamed up this book as a way to communicate those concepts to our friends, colleagues, and clients (current and future). Our goal was to create the definitive guide to selling things on social media. In support of that, we agreed to take a radical, personalized approach.

One strategy does not fit all businesses. If you're trying to establish a successful social media presence for your local restaurant, you're going to use different tactics than Coca-Cola uses for its worldwide branding efforts. Or if you're really good at restaurant marketing but now want to get into selling ebooks or custom guitars, you'll find that a lot of your "guaranteed" tactics no longer work in a different context. Some of them even seem to make things worse for you. We understand that perfectly!

In order for a strategy to be effective, it must have three components: intention, context, and tactics. Most books on this subject assume the intention, give a broad context ("Sell ALL the things!"), and concentrate on good tactics. Sun Tzu said in *The Art of War* that tactics without strategy is the noise before defeat; this applies equally in war and ecommerce. There are a lot of tactics in this book, but they are presented with a context in mind. The idea is to form or modify a marketing strategy that includes (or concentrates on, depending on your situation) social media. We accomplish this by being outcome-focused instead of activity-focused. Instead of checking off activities from a list, you work toward objectives that lead to a goal, such as "Increase event ticket sales by 25% from social media sources." If you accomplish the goal early, then there's no need to continue with the to-do list. Instead, you can focus on a new goal.

The Web is constantly evolving to be more dynamic. Lately, that means being more social—that is, having more interactive elements and offering more ways to share and connect with other people. As a result, old ecommerce tactics must similarly evolve if you expect your online business to survive in the social era. Traditionally, if you were in the ecommerce business, you bought pay-per-click (CPC, or cost per click) or pay-per-view (CPM, or cost per mille) ads on a big advertising network like Google Ad-Words, DoubleClick, or some other advertising network. Then you'd optimize your site for search engine traffic (SEO) so that you can get more visitors for free over time. These tactics are still valid and important, but over time they have gotten more expensive, more complex, and, in some cases, less effective, and they don't represent a comprehensive strategy.

When you market your online business through social media, you reach people at a time and place when they aren't expecting it. You're selling in context. Your customers have their guard down. They're not looking for something to buy right now, they're enjoying what their friends, family, and colleagues are doing. That's precisely why social ecommerce is so effective, but it's also why you need to be wise in how you go about it. It's easy to take a few shortcuts. Then you run the risk of being seen as a ruthless, self-interested marketer who only cares about sales. If this is how you're perceived, you'll at best have wasted your time, and at worst you'll have destroyed your reputation.

Social media represents a much more intimate connection between businesses (or brands) and customers. When you follow a brand page on Facebook, you may be the first to know about a new product, or get a special discount, or connect to other people who like this brand and share stories or advice. Before social media, this kind of interaction was impossible on anything other than a hyperlocal scale, and rarely happened outside of conferences, conventions, and international launch events for big companies.

So it's big, it's important, it's powerful…and it's cheap! That is, if you have some time to spend building your social media presence. Even if you have to pay someone to do it for you, it's probably still less expensive than traditional advertising. There are still old-school CPC and CPM advertising behemoths out there that demand a five-figure minimum upfront investment with no guarantee of conversion rate or sales numbers. Such anxiety! You've no idea if that will be successful for you. With a good social media strategy, you can reach a lot of people, but more importantly you can more easily reach people who are more likely to either buy or help spread the word, and you don't need to write a check at the start. Or even at the finish, though there really isn't a finish, because—as you will learn in this book—social media is a long-term strategy that requires vigilance and maintenance. It isn't hard work (it can even be fun!), and it can be outsourced to qualified professionals, firms, or even other people at your company. After all, in this day and age, everyone is familiar with at least one social media network from a personal perspective.

Social Media Defined

When you think of "social media," what comes to mind? Facebook? Discussion forums? There are a lot of sites that describe themselves as a social network or social media site, and some attempt to use cute marketing terms to describe themselves as something beyond that. This is the definition of social media that we are using in this book:

Any site or online service that, as an integral part of its functionality, allows and encourages social interaction such as commenting, voting, discussion, and sharing/bookmarking.

With that in mind, you may find that social media is a broader topic than you realized. By our definition, YouTube, Yelp, Craigslist, and StumbleUpon are social media. That doesn't mean that you can use the same tactics across all social media sites and get the same results. Each site or network has its own rules of engagement, barriers to entry, and level of commitment required for users to achieve results.

Social Media Myths

There are plenty of rumors about social media that sabotage people's marketing efforts before they even begin. Before you write off social media as ineffective or a silly fad, check your assumptions against this list:

Most people still make purchasing decisions through offline word-of-mouth.
> Actually, this is true, but that doesn't mean that social media isn't a part of the conversation. One of the problems with calculating social media's *return on investment* (ROI) is that something further down the chain of communication gets the credit for the sale. People hear about something online—usually through social media—and then go and discuss it with family and friends offline. Social media starts the conversation that leads to the sale.

My product isn't exciting enough to get new customers on Facebook or Twitter.
> Something must make your product successful, right? There must be something extraordinary about what you're selling; otherwise, no one would buy it. The competition would have obliterated you before you even got off the ground. Your brand must be remarkable before it can be successfully shared online. It doesn't have to be the best, or the most unique; there just has to be something about it worth talking about. Most of the people who have failed in social media marketing skip the "remarkable" step. They want to sell their product, so they set up an ad campaign on Facebook, it doesn't work, and they give up. What they should be doing instead is asking what makes their product remarkable, then focusing on spreading the word about these unique qualities through an ad campaign. *Social eCommerce* will show you how to do that.

Social media is for teenagers and geeks.
> If I put up a social media page for my company, our customers will think we aren't serious. It's almost certain that all of your customers are on some kind of social network—Facebook, Twitter, YouTube, LinkedIn, Google+. How would interacting with them and sharing things with them on these sites reduce your credibility? In 2013, according to the Pew Research Center (*http://pewinternet.org*), some 73% of online adults were using a social networking site of some kind, and that percentage increases each year. Look at the businesses running the biggest social networks. Do

you think that Google isn't a serious company? A more valid concern would be appearing to be out of touch with modern technology because you aren't on social media.

If I put up a Facebook page or Twitter account, Internet trolls will attack me. Upset customers will completely destroy us with untrue public comments.

This is why it is important to be present, to control the conversation from the very beginning. When you have an established social media presence, you have your finger on the pulse. Getting into social media will not enable people to say anything that they can't already. Anyone can get on Twitter and flame you, whether you have a presence there or not. If you don't have a Facebook page for your business, someone else can create one and cause plenty of damage. Isn't it better to be in control of your presence on social networks, rather than let other people lead the conversation about your company and products?

All right, so Facebook is huge. Twitter is huge. So were Friendster and MySpace. I'd rather wait until the next big thing starts, and get in on it early.

Getting in early is overrated. Getting in today is what is most important for you and your customers. Yes, it's possible that something will come along and eclipse Facebook, Twitter, and other major sites. However, the industry has learned from the failures of its predecessors, and there is a lot more money and corporate structure behind today's social networks. The fact of the matter is that today's big sites are, well, big *today*. You can capitalize on them *today*. Why would you wait to make more money when you can do it now with no penalty?

To do this right, I have to outsource it.

It depends on your skill set and the amount of time you have to dedicate to social media, but there is no good reason why you can't cover at least the basics in-house. If you have several employees, they can all help in some way, under the guidance of a good social media policy. This work requires knowledge (this book!), time, and dedication. If your company is large, consider hiring an expert to help you create your initial strategy, and then your internal team can take over once the strategy is in place. Outsourcing is certainly an option, but it's not a requirement by any means.

I don't have time for social media.

After you've established your social media presence (which does require some upfront time and effort), it takes only a small amount of time to maintain it. Once the framework is in place, and you have a content plan, you just have to ensure you're posting new content, replying to customers, and being sociable. A tweet here, a Facebook post there, a blog post about your new product features to link from all of your social media sites. If you don't even have a few minutes a day to spare, then this is something that an employee could easily do, or you can outsource it to a qualified professional.

I've already set up a Facebook page for my business, so I'm "done."

Your social media efforts are "done" like your kitchen is "clean." If it's ever true, it certainly doesn't stay that way for long. Your website is never "done"; it should always be evolving to meet current needs and support current methods and technologies. Likewise, your social media presence is a continuous process of engagement, improvement, and growth.

I attended a seminar that told me all the secret tricks for social media, so I've got this handled.

Perhaps so…or perhaps not. Some or all of that advice may have been good, but again we say that tactics are not the whole solution. You might have heard or seen surefire tactics that work for businesses completely unrelated to yours, or for companies that have a vastly higher budget and dedicated staff, or are in an entirely different market. Context is everything; we've gone to a lot of effort in this book to keep you in the context that applies to you. Has anyone ever given you "secret tricks" for parenting, weight loss, or financial investment? Did those isolated tactics solve all of your problems? Finally, be aware that even the "secret" tricks and tactics for social media that work today will not, most likely, work tomorrow. Lots of "tricks" intended to game the system on Facebook get squashed when Facebook tweaks its algorithm regarding what gets visibility.

The Three Categories of eCommerce

Social media and ecommerce are both broad categories that span many industries. The typical approach is to concentrate on individual tactics and give broad advice that isn't specific to any market, industry, or strategy. We've decided to take it in a different direction. Wherever possible, we have provided specific advice that applies directly to your situation.

Basically, there are three categories for all ecommerce business:

- You're selling something locally, like a sole-proprietor shop, law office, or restaurant.
- You're selling something physical or digital that requires some kind of fulfillment, with wide distribution.
- You're selling something one-off, like an event, convention, or course.

In the first two categories, you need a long-term community to have real success. However, there are a lot of things that you do only once, like a coaching course, seminar, class, concert, or holiday event. In these instances, you don't necessarily need a long-term community, you just need to establish your authority in the field.

If you put all businesses into one of these categories, you can easily form a successful strategy composed of tactics that will actually work. However, at the core, there are certain things that you're going to do on all of the social networks in which you participate. If you decide to create a YouTube video, the same principles apply to creating and promoting the video no matter who you are or what you're selling. There are certain best and worst practices that apply to Facebook, Twitter, Google+, and Pinterest as well. What you actually post there is what's different among the three main categories, but how you establish your professional presence is more or less universal. Accordingly, *Social eCommerce* starts out by explaining all of the major social networks, what they're good for, and the basic rules of engagement. You're then directed to Chapter 3, Chapter 4, or Chapter 5 to help you form a strategy specific to your industry.

Living Up to Your Sales Potential

A lot of businesses try to succeed without social media. It's easier to pay for advertising and traditional marketing and leave it at that. There is a ceiling to this practice, though, and it is lowering as time goes on. With enough money, you will max out on those efforts; you'll reach a point where CPC and CPM ads cannot go any further. Your leads potential will not be able to go any further without social media. We've seen this happen with a lot of our clients over the years. In order to scale, they need innovative and creative ways to reach new markets, and we help them do that through social media.

Over the past several years, social media has taken over the Web's traffic and attention. YouTube is now the second most popular search engine. Facebook has more than 1 billion users. This is not just for geeks and teenagers; whomever your customers or prospects are, you can reach them through social media.

It is not expensive to experiment with social media marketing. Advertising on social media—Facebook, mostly—does require a small amount of money at first, but it isn't much of a risk.

Beyond the Ads: Social Media's Unique Opportunities

Social media enables you to reach customers in a better context than other forms of online communication. Facebook ads, for instance, represent an "impulse buy" opportunity; your customer didn't go to Facebook to buy something, but while he's there, he might buy your product or service. It's a lot like the checkout aisle at the grocery store —it's stuff you didn't plan on buying, but very well might. Social media marketing catches your customers off guard when they're not looking for information or anything to buy.

Most businesses, whether they are involved in ecommerce or not, have their own websites and social media accounts on LinkedIn, Facebook, Pinterest, and Twitter to promote their organization. Having accounts and posting messages to them is not a strategy, though, and if you don't have a strategy, you could do more harm than good.

Still Not Convinced?

If you're in the ecommerce business, go take a look at your competitors' social media presence. Whatever they are doing is probably making them money. On a large enough scale, your industry's sales are capped and zero-sum, so every dollar that doesn't go to you goes to a competitor.

If you're not in the ecommerce business, your competitors may have no social media presence. For instance, if you're starting a plumbing business, your competitors might have a website but no Facebook page or Twitter account. This is an open field for you because you'll have 100% of the social media front. Someone who needs a plumber and goes to the Web to find one is going to find you and be able to identify with and connect with you more easily. You aren't just a phone number and a mailing address in the industrial district; you're now a real person on Facebook who interacts with customers and seems accountable for good service.

Maybe you've already tried and failed at social media marketing. Perhaps you've set up some accounts, posted some messages, and gotten zero response from anyone. Then you let the accounts go dormant, or don't use them often enough to reap any significant benefit. A business that posts only the occasional comment about a new product on its Facebook page, or the occasional tweet about its services, isn't likely to generate the desired amount of momentum or interest, particularly if each of these updates has to do with selling something.

Although it can be rather slow when you're just getting started, the process of gaining fans and likes and increased group members can and will inevitably build momentum if you regularly offer interesting content. For example, using Facebook to post funny, controversial, or interesting content that triggers comments and replies from your fans or gets them to share and repost your content will in turn attract people from outside your circle of fans, which can increase your number of fans and promote your message even further.

Many businesses' social media pages go stale because their owners think every post should be exclusively related to the individual business or about its services and products. However, it's strongly advised to tie interesting quotes, pictures, and other types of content into aspects that are more loosely related to the business in either a humorous or serious way. This will generate more attention than a simple product update. Most people don't really want to read product marketing material; they just want content that is interesting. You can tie your products into that, but there's a careful balance between serving your purposes and satisfying the interests and curiosities of your fans and followers. We'll explain this in more detail throughout the book.

There are a lot of business owners who avoid social media to prevent the potential waste of time. Although it's true that there are people who spend far too much time on social media sites recreationally, if you instead use them in a systematic way with a goal in mind, you can get considerable benefit from the time you spend. If you're overwhelmed by the vast social media landscape, then just concentrate on the three most relevant social networks; we explain which ones are best for you in Chapter 1.

Last, if you're relying on traditional "organic" search traffic or search advertising to drive your sales, then you're going to have to get into social media sooner or later. Search engines are paying much more attention to social signals as a sign of authority, trust, and quality. If you don't have a social media presence, you're going to become less and less relevant in search results in the future.

Let's Get Started

It's important to understand the social media basics. By the time you're done with Chapter 1, you will have a basic social media strategy, an excellent understanding of relevant social networks, and some ideas for what to post and how often to post it. Let's get to it!

Conventions Used in This Book

The following typographical conventions are used in this book:

Italic
Indicates new terms, URLs, email addresses, filenames, and file extensions.

`Constant width`
Used for program listings, as well as within paragraphs to refer to program elements such as variable or function names, databases, data types, environment variables, statements, and keywords.

`Constant width bold`
Shows commands or other text that should be typed literally by the user.

`Constant width italic`
Shows text that should be replaced with user-supplied values or by values determined by context.

 This element signifies a tip or suggestion.

This element signifies a general note.

This element indicates a warning or caution.

Safari® Books Online

 *Safari Books Online* is an on-demand digital library that delivers expert content in both book and video form from the world's leading authors in technology and business.

Technology professionals, software developers, web designers, and business and creative professionals use Safari Books Online as their primary resource for research, problem solving, learning, and certification training.

Safari Books Online offers a range of product mixes and pricing programs for organizations, government agencies, and individuals. Subscribers have access to thousands of books, training videos, and prepublication manuscripts in one fully searchable database from publishers like O'Reilly Media, Prentice Hall Professional, Addison-Wesley Professional, Microsoft Press, Sams, Que, Peachpit Press, Focal Press, Cisco Press, John Wiley & Sons, Syngress, Morgan Kaufmann, IBM Redbooks, Packt, Adobe Press, FT Press, Apress, Manning, New Riders, McGraw-Hill, Jones & Bartlett, Course Technology, and dozens more. For more information about Safari Books Online, please visit us online.

How to Contact Us

Please address comments and questions concerning this book to the publisher:

O'Reilly Media, Inc.
1005 Gravenstein Highway North
Sebastopol, CA 95472
800-998-9938 (in the United States or Canada)
707-829-0515 (international or local)
707-829-0104 (fax)

We have a web page for this book, where we list errata, examples, and any additional information. You can access this page at *http://oreil.ly/1nSIadQ*.

To comment or ask technical questions about this book, send email to *bookques tions@oreilly.com*.

For more information about our books, courses, conferences, and news, see our website at *http://www.oreilly.com*.

Find us on Facebook: *http://facebook.com/oreilly*

Follow us on Twitter: *http://twitter.com/oreillymedia*

Watch us on YouTube: *http://www.youtube.com/oreillymedia*

Acknowledgments

First of all, a big thanks to our technical editors Jem Matzan and Rob Woods. We also would like to thank reviewers Carolyn Ketchum, Jill Kocher, Jai Rawat, Michelle Corteggiano, and Augustin Delaporte. Also much appreciation to our case study contributors: Michael Geneles, Alex Gophstein, Robert Irvine, Lee Lucier, Taki Moore, Jamie Salvatori, Chris Hurn, Robert G. Allen, Ted Miller III, Zac Johnson, and Kurt Shuster. Thanks to our foreword author, Jeremy Schoemaker, a.k.a., "Shoemoney." And finally, a big thanks to our industry friends for their various contributions and guidance: Amy Africa, Brent Csutoras, Rand Fishkin, and Jeff Martin.

CHAPTER 1

The Social Media Landscape

It's impossible to list every social network that exists. New ones are popping up all the time. Some of them fail quickly and disappear, while others fail slowly and linger for years. The sites that are on top right now were at one time niche networks that spent a lot of time in the second tier before overtaking their rivals. Within the span of only a few years, the mighty have fallen and even mightier have risen to take their place. Social media is a volatile industry.

This chapter is intended to categorize social networks not based on size, but on their value to you as someone who is selling something online. The smaller and emerging social networks are almost certainly a waste of your time and money—from a business perspective, anyway. From a personal perspective, feel free to explore the Web and sign up for whatever interests you. Making money off of social media participation is a completely different game.

Tier 1 Social Networks

If you have limited resources, then don't concern yourself with smaller social networks; just concentrate on the sites that are actually going to make money for you. The three sites explained in the following subsections are the most important now and in the near future, though each of them is good for something different. If you can branch out to all of them, great; if not, then pick the one that will have the most benefit to you and begin to map out your strategy. If you aren't sure which site to concentrate on, the next few chapters will help you sort that out.

Twitter

Twitter is a microblogging site that asks participants: "What are you doing right now?" Indeed, most of the communication on Twitter is of the "what I'm doing right now" variety. That is to say, it's pretty mundane, and the 140-character limit forces some interesting language shortcuts. However, Twitter's tagline is only a suggestion, not a rule. As you participate more on Twitter, you'll discover that the most successful and popular users have a strategy for releasing small but interesting bits of information.

Microblogging is the practice of making frequent, short, unedited, unrefined message posts. This is not limited to Twitter—you could easily do the same thing on Facebook, Google+, LinkedIn, and Instagram—but it is the most popular and profitable platform dedicated to this task. Twitter users refer to these posts as *tweets*.

Typical tweets tend not to question reality or pontificate on lofty topics such as ethics, religion, or politics, nor do they dare ponder the ironies of the universe. Twitter microbloggers merely write something quick (140 characters or fewer) to explain what they're doing. You should explore Twitter for an hour or two and find active users, just to see how they use the site. You can see someone's whole day play out for you, one sentence at a time.

When you mention someone in a tweet who has a Twitter account, the protocol is to include his or her username with an @ in front. For example, you might send out an update like "Checking out Twitter at the suggestion of @sspencer." (And if I'm *following* you on Twitter, I'll see that you mentioned me; I can also search for my username and see everyone who's mentioned me recently.) If you want to talk about a certain topic in which other people might be interested, you can put a # symbol before it. This is called a *hashtag*, and it turns a word or amalgamated short phrase into a topic that can easily become its own community. For instance, if you are attending the SXSW conference and are microblogging about your experiences there, you would include #sxsw somewhere in your tweet so that other people who are interested in that topic can more easily find tweets relating to it. Twitter (*http://twitter.com*) offers documentation that covers all of its features; we won't duplicate that effort here.

Twitter starts with sending out updates, but it doesn't end there. You can also use it to engage in conversations with other Twitter users, almost as if using an instant messenger client. Granted, some of it is idle banter, but fascinating discussions can take place on Twitter in this way.

For instance, what does that person do when he sees your tweet mentioning him? It's not unusual for him to respond to your tweet by posting his own tweet publicly as a reply. If you are following him, then he could alternatively send a response privately by *direct message*, but Twitter users rarely do that.

Many businesspeople use Twitter to share links to interesting web pages with their friends or colleagues, to meet or keep in touch with industry contacts, or to promote blog posts. A significant number also use Twitter to engage in dialogue with customers/prospects. This isn't something you can jump into and figure out quickly, though; it takes knowledge and skill to use Twitter effectively.

Even if you don't intend to use Twitter much for marketing, you should still establish a Twitter account so that you can track conversations that mention your brand. The Notifications tab in Twitter shows you all of the tweets that include your username, but you should make an effort to look up related hashtags as well.

Twitter "espionage" is one of the easiest ways to gain insight into your target market, to see what the individuals it comprises are talking about, and what they're sharing with their peers. You can use Twitter's search functions to look up what people are saying about you, your company, your products, and your competition. You can also see what your customers' other interests are on Twitter—information that can help you to really fine-tune your marketing campaign.

Twitter's website (*http://twitter.com*) is not the only way to interact with the service. There are several other options: instant message services, text messages, web browser extensions, and standalone Twitter clients. You can also set up an RSS feed that will deliver relevant tweets to other, non-Twitter-specific tools. Two Twitter management tools that we recommend are Hootsuite (*http://www.hootsuite.com*) and Tweetdeck (*http://tweetdeck.twitter.com*).

Aside from marketing and sales, Twitter is great for networking at industry events such as conferences and trade shows. By following that conference's hashtag (and related hashtags), you can see what other conference-goers are up to, and learn about parties and various other related events that aren't on the official schedule.

Like many online services, Twitter can also become a distraction and a time-sink if you actively follow the tweets of a large number of Twitter users. So exercise caution when you start using the Follow feature to subscribe to folks' Twitter streams.

Related to Twitter is Vine (*http://www.vine.co*). With Vine, you create short, looping videos that you can post directly to your Twitter feed. Any serious Twitter strategy should consider including Vine videos in some way. Nordstrom partnered with top 100 Vine user Zach King to create a series of sponsored Vines that featured department stores and closets. The Vines were then featured on Zach King's Vine feed, Nordstrom's Vine feed, and hosted on Vine sharing websites across the Internet to achieve a sizeable amount of views.

Facebook

Odds are very good that you already have a personal Facebook account. There are more than 1 billion Facebook accounts. That's a seventh of the world's entire population!

At first it may seem strange to try to use Facebook to sell anything. Maybe you've already tried and failed miserably, probably by posting some kind of ad to your personal Facebook timeline. If that's what you did, whether you realize it or not, you've spammed your friends, family, and colleagues. It's extremely poor form to do this.

In sociology there are concepts of "place." Your first place is your home; your second place is your office (assuming you work outside of your home). However, one of the essential ingredients in both a healthy community and a healthy social life is the "third place." That's the social environment outside of your home where you gather with other people for things non-work-related. There is a decent explanation of it on Wikipedia (*http://en.wikipedia.org/wiki/Third_place*).

The Web has digital third places because today's society is inherently more mobile and transient. In that, Facebook is the clear frontrunner in terms of number of active members, ability to share, ability to connect, and accessibility to targeted advertising. That last point is what makes Facebook a top-tier social network as a sales and marketing tool.

Facebook enables you to share just about anything, from raw information (such as your age, birthdate, or relationship status) to messages of varying length, to photos and videos. Virtually every other major app, service, or site connects to Facebook in some way so that you can share what you are doing in those apps (such as what song you are listening to in your music player, or what movie you just paid to stream, or what item you just bought from a store). Many sites and apps outsource their login procedure to Facebook, requiring you to have a Facebook account just to sign up.

For business use, the first thing you do to branch out from personal Facebook behavior is to create a page for your business. Make it professional and friendly. Explain your business—not in cold, boring marketing terms, but in more social and interesting ways. Think of your "elevator pitch." What do you tell people about your business when you have to communicate it in less than 30 seconds? Your Facebook page should be more like your elevator pitches than your press releases.

Secondly, you have promotion options available to you through Facebook Ads. You can either promote your page (get more likes) or promote a certain post that you've made. We have a whole chapter dedicated to ad design later in the book. For now, just start with the Facebook page and think about the kind of content that you can post there.

And post you must! Every day you should post something that is interesting and shareable. Don't start just yet; for right now, just think about the subjects you can post about, who will write the posts (you or someone who works with/for you), who will monitor the site for replies and other feedback, and the best time of day to publish your posts. This is just an initial plan; some of this will need to change later on once you've got a page, content, and ads up and running.

Also think about how much you want to spend on a daily basis. Facebook Ads is designed to enable daily spending limits, so determine the budget you want to dedicate to promoting your page accordingly. You may need only $5 or $10 per day, though it may take some ramp-up time to build a community around your brand.

LinkedIn

You probably think of LinkedIn for professional networking, but this social network's potential goes well beyond that. The company has nearly two dozen products aimed at everything from recruiting to advertising. It even has its own conference. Not that networking with other professionals and potential clients isn't important; it's just that LinkedIn can deliver so much more, provided you have the budget and the right product, service, or event to sell.

LinkedIn was developed in 2003, and has been growing rapidly since then. It is a perfect place for professionals around the globe to search for jobs, employees, joint venture partners, and compatible business partners.

Small-business owners like us need help and support. We need contacts, connections, groups, and networks that help us get further than we would on our own. People in our networks can provide information, advice, support, and help. Sometimes, we can make connections that can double or triple our business.

The best results come when you know exactly what your objectives are, and you are presenting to exactly the right audience. You can achieve this by designing targeted messages delivered to targeted groups of people. In the past, this was a costly exercise with tons of research, trial and error, and wasted money. With LinkedIn, this process is fast, easy, and cheap.

LinkedIn is best for these kinds of businesses:

- Those that are building a community
- Those that are searching for sales, connections, joint venture (JV) partners, and investors
- Those that want traffic to their blog, website, or social media profiles
- Those that are searching for jobs/employees
- Those that are promoting a product/service/event

Your LinkedIn profile is an integral part of your marketing. The power lies in your ability to easily connect with like-minded business professionals. If someone views your profile, and your only connections are your mother and your husband, that person may get the impression that you're not very well connected. Aim for a solid group of relevant contacts, all linked to you and your business. No profile is complete without a recommendation or two, so encourage your clients and customers to write recommendations for you, and provide valuable recommendations for others when asked.

You should also set up a page for your company (this is different than your personal LinkedIn profile). To do this, you must first have at least a few connections, and your personal profile must be complete. Company pages offer public information about your business, and function much the same as Facebook pages. You can use your company page to post company status updates, advertise jobs, interact with employees, and promote valuable articles or resources on your website.

To make the most of LinkedIn, use all of the tools and features that are relevant to your industry to your advantage. Use the LinkedIn search feature to find people and groups in your industry, and potential customers. Search for your biggest competitors, or a similar business in your market. Take a close look at what they are doing well, and where they could improve.

LinkedIn is particularly good for advertising B2B (business-to-business) products, services, and events. If you have a line of kids' toys, a series of novels, or music festival tickets to sell, this is probably going to cost you a lot of money and get you nowhere. People go to LinkedIn for professional reasons, so you should speak to their professional lives with everything you do there. Be wary of the cost of LinkedIn ads, though. We've seen it cost two to four times as much as a Facebook ad campaign with a similar reach. If you have a big budget and a national or international appeal, and your product is delivered digitally (software, IT solutions, change management consultations), then LinkedIn ads are worth experimenting with. The most successful advertising on LinkedIn involves creating an ad that sends traffic to a targeted landing page to collect opt-in leads. You've got to provide good, relevant content here, such as a short video or a really good short article.

One thing LinkedIn is very good for is finding people to fill difficult-to-find job openings. You can do this through the LinkedIn Jobs service, or through clever digging on your own. If you're in search of a job, LinkedIn is also a great place to look for one, especially if you've expanded your professional network to the point that you can find a first- or second-degree contact at the company you want to work for. Then you're just two emails or phone calls away from a personal connection who can get you an interview.

LinkedIn recommends that you connect only with people whom you actually know. In general, this is a good idea for your personal account on any social media site, but LinkedIn intentionally straddles the boundary between personal and professional.

There are people who flagrantly disregard this recommendation; they are called *LinkedIn Open Networkers* (LIONs). LIONs will connect with just about anyone reflexively, just to build their network. If you connect to one or two of these people, you can greatly expand the reach of your job postings. You can find a list of the most popular open networkers on TopLinked.com (*http://toplinked.com*).

You can push the boundaries of LinkedIn's connection recommendation without going over the top. It will help increase your company's, brand's, or individual professional exposure with LinkedIn by searching for relevant companies and people in your field, then connecting with them. When you contact them, include a personal note with your request; explain how you met, describe where you know them from, or mention your reasons for connecting with them.

Unless you pay for a monthly Premium subscription, LinkedIn allows you to send InMail (in-network messaging) only to people with whom you're already connected. That means if you want to contact a particular engineer for a job opening you have, you can't contact her directly unless you pay for LinkedIn Premium on a subscription basis. The best way around this is to search other social media sites for her name and contact her there. You can prevent this from happening to you by adding your email address to your LinkedIn profile headline. Or, just spring for Premium, keeping in mind that this gets you only five free InMail responses per month.

There is a decent amount of community participation on LinkedIn. You can post a question to LinkedIn Answers that serves your own purposes, and get some great responses. For instance, you might find people to hire this way instead of posting a job listing. Your question can be posed as a thinly veiled job advert, or you can subtly market your services and products by asking people what their preferred solution in your industry is, or what technologies in your field they are interested in playing with. Always add value to the community with the anticipated answers.

If you really want to go the extra mile, get a URL specifically for your LinkedIn profile, and redirect it there. This can be easier to remember than your LinkedIn profile URL, and is useful for business cards, your website, and email signature.

Tier 2 Social Networks

We define a "tier 2" social network in terms not of traffic or reach, but of how easily you can make money by participating. Certainly, a site with a ton of traffic is going to lead to some kind of success, but how much will it cost you to achieve that (in terms of time and money)? A second-tier site may have tremendous value for certain industries and businesses, and little to no value for others.

Sites can move from tier 2 to 1 pretty easily over a relatively short amount of time. No site starts out in the first tier.

Google+

If any social network ever started out with a superior advantage, it was Google+. With industry examples to follow, the support of one of the world's smartest technology companies, and an almost unlimited pool of resources from which to draw, Google+ was launched with high expectations.

Despite all that, it is really a "distant third" in terms of the top social networks. It hasn't been around for nearly as long as Facebook or Twitter, but it has a significant membership that includes many celebrities and politicians. *Star Trek* actor William Shatner, for instance, has an enormous Google+ following—so much so that he's pushed the limits of the service. Barack Obama had a campaign presence on Google+, and even did a "hangout" (video chat) that drew a huge audience.

Google+ is a direct competitor of Facebook, and both companies have taken this battle very seriously.

If you have a Google profile, then you have a Google+ account, even if you never post anything to it. One of the benefits of having a Google+ page is authorship credit for all articles, videos, and blog posts that Google has in its index that it can positively identify as having been written by you. Google offers step-by-step instructions on how to claim authorship (*https://plus.google.com/authorship*). However, Google may have thrown in the towel with the departure of Vic Gundotra, previous head of Google+.

YouTube

You probably don't think of YouTube as a social network, but sharing, rating, and commenting on videos is certainly a social activity. You probably also didn't think of YouTube as a search engine, but in terms of the overall volume of search queries, it's second only to Google.

YouTube is an excellent "supplemental network" for a campaign focused on a more monetizeable social media site. Unless you're selling a video, show, movie, or song, YouTube may not make sense as the social network to concentrate on. Certainly though, use YouTube as a way to enhance your main marketing efforts.

There's nothing that you can't make a video for. It may not be obvious at first, but if you think about the industry, the product, and your customers, you can come up with some ideas for good videos. Like everything else, you want to create compelling content that reinforces the message of your brand.

By the nature of its social networking capabilities—which show the most viewed videos, favorites, channels, likes/dislikes, comments, and video replies—YouTube is a far more effective venue for posting videos than your corporate website, if you want your videos to spread virally. Therefore, videos should be on YouTube as well as embedded on your company website.

It's all about the content, though. If your video content is mediocre, it doesn't matter how much you optimize it; it won't become popular. Nor should it. Mediocre content doesn't deserve the rankings or the attention.

It's not enough to post a great video; you also must know how to take advantage of the social nature of YouTube. As with all other social networks, you need to build up friends and subscribers on YouTube so you can leverage them to increase your video's reach.

Don't get too caught up in achieving a certain number of views, a certain number of links to the video, or a certain ranking in the YouTube search results. What matters is the impact the video has on the bottom line. Quick and easy videos to make are how-to or FAQs; these not only offer customers additional information but can impact your conversion rates as well.

Case Study: Will It Blend? Yes It Will!

One of the most well-known viral video campaigns by an online merchant is Blendtec's "Will It Blend?" This series of videos showed various household objects being run through a Blendtec blender, including marbles, rake handles, light bulbs, golf clubs, and iPads.

How did the campaign come about? Blendtec's founder/CEO Tom Dickson likes to run nonstandard things through its blenders to test out their strength, according to George Wright, Blendtec's former marketing director. After watching Dickson test a blender by jamming a 2" × 2" piece of wood in it, Wright had the idea to post those demonstrations of "extreme blending" online.

Dickson and Wright went to work creating the videos in the fall of 2006, starting with five "Don't Try This at Home Blending" videos. They built a companion microsite to go with it—WillItBlend.com (*http://willitblend.com*)—and sent an email to all employees to spread the word about the videos and the site.

They then emailed their customer base and asked for suggestions on things to blend. Not only did emails pour in, so did calls from the media. The campaign was covered by the *Today Show*, *iVillage Live*, *Newsweek*, *Playboy*, and the *New York Times*.

Blendtec had a surprisingly low budget. The company did have an on-staff video producer and webmaster, so development of the first five videos ran just $50 to $100, including buying the domain name, a couple of rakes, some marbles, and few other supplies. It was proof positive that viral video marketing can be done on a shoestring budget.

Wright advises companies wishing to get into YouTube marketing to focus on something fun, but don't try to force it. It really should be something worth watching.

Wright's second piece of advice is to clearly demonstrate the product. For Blendtec, it was initially about branding, but after the brand awareness has been established, there has to be a need and a catalyst to compel viewers to solve the problem. A consumer watching a blender chop up a rake handle would likely conclude that this blender would do a pretty good job at blending ice as well.

As a result of the videos, Blendtec saw a dramatic increase in sales of both consumer and commercial blenders. The "Will It Blend?" campaign targeted the home market, and web sales were more than four times greater than the previous top-selling month. All other channels have seen big increases as well.

Pinterest

According to Experian Hitwise, as of the publication of this book, Pinterest is the third most popular social network in terms of traffic.

You're likely already dabbling in using Pinterest to drive traffic to your ecommerce site. Perhaps you have the basics down: adding "Pin it" buttons to your product pages, and creating neatly organized boards for your customers and potential customers to browse through. What you may be missing is an overall strategy for how Pinterest can not only increase your traffic and engagement, but generate sales as well.

As with all social networks, engagement comes first. There is no valid path to quick and easy sales, especially on Pinterest. That doesn't mean that there aren't ways to capitalize on Pinterest's highly loyal user base of more than 70 million people (as of July 2013).

Unlike other social networks, Pinterest is primarily product-based. For this reason, it has surpassed Facebook and Twitter in terms of generating referrals to product-based ecommerce sites. According to Adam Audette of Rimm-Kaufman Group, Pinterest converts 22% more than Facebook does. Additionally, Pinterest users spend 60% more than Facebook users do. And unlike Facebook and Twitter posts, pinned images tend to have a long lifecycle. Whereas tweets and Facebook posts may generate a lot of discussion and interaction when first posted, pinned images may resurface with much fanfare, weeks or even months later.

The virality of a pin on Facebook should also not be underestimated. Once a user authorizes Facebook integration, his pins can be automatically published to his Facebook timeline. This integration with Facebook greatly increases the viral effect of pinning. You can also connect your Pinterest account to Twitter so that your new pins are cross-posted along with the Twitter hashtags that you're targeting (though Pinterest treats hashtags like normal words, so if you're not cross-posting or encouraging others to tweet your pins, don't bother with the hashtags on Pinterest).

Many ecommerce businesses are also using Pinterest as a way to do cost-effective, low-risk market research. By pinning a product (in some cases, even before it's launched), business owners can gauge interest levels in the product, and even ask for feedback or votes.

As shown in "Case Study: Will It Blend? Yes It Will!" on page 9, increased interest in your products will ultimately lead to increased sales.

Food photos do very well on Pinterest, especially for cookbooks and restaurants, and to appeal to people with specific dietary preferences or limitations.

If you're selling some kind of service, Pinterest is a much more difficult site on which to capitalize. Unless you can think of some interesting and unique ways to represent your business with graphics, the time spent curating photos on Pinterest should probably be redirected to sites that can more effectively engage with potential subscribers.

Figure 1-1 demonstrates a successful way that a salon represents its service with imagery.

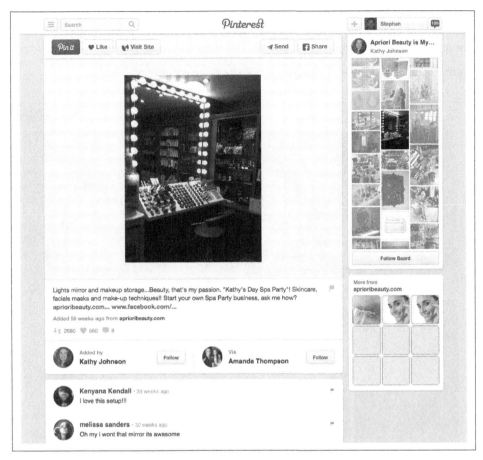

Figure 1-1. A salon posts a picture of its new Hollywood-style mirror on Pinterest

Tumblr

Tumblr is one of those social networks that, although not as inherently useful for ecommerce as some others, can be tremendously useful for *certain types* of ecommerce businesses. It certainly has a lot of reach and a high level of engagement:

- There are more than 100 million Tumblr blogs.
- Almost half of Tumblr users are between the ages of 18 and 34.
- The average user stays on Tumblr for 14 minutes each visit; the average Facebook user spends only 12.5 minutes.

A Tumblr blog can be set up in a few minutes, but there is no option to self-host, which makes customization much trickier. Altering themes, widgets, and plug-ins often means heavy code editing, making major changes unfeasible. However, there are commercial options that enable businesses to easily customize Tumblr for ecommerce, such as Shopify (*http://www.shopify.com*) and BlkDot (*http://theblkdot.com*).

Figure 1-2 is an example of an ecommerce site done entirely on Tumblr.

Figure 1-2. A Tumblr-based ecommerce site

Once you've decided to use Tumblr for your ecommerce business, it's not hard to get the hang of using it. Regardless of whether you plan to actually sell on Tumblr or simply use it as another method of marketing your business, here are some fundamental tips:

Set up your Tumblr blog right the first time.
    The process of setting up a Tumblog is extremely simple. However, once created, it can be difficult to delete. Of key importance at this stage is choosing a name that accurately represents your business or brand. You'll likely want to immediately redirect your Tumblr blog to a custom domain. So, for example, rather than having them access your blog by going to *http://socialecommercebook.tumblr.com*, you'll send your visitors directly to *http://socialecommercebook.com*.

Post good, Tumblr-friendly content.

Once the basics of your blog are set up, you can start posting. You can post an image, video, link, or quote. If you don't want to have to log into your Tumblr dashboard to post content, you can install and use a Tumblr app (such as the Tumblr bookmarklet) that allows you to post and share content from any sites you're visiting. When you post something, make sure you use tags. This will enable other Tumblr users to search for and find your posts using tag-based keywords. Lastly, post content that speaks to your customers, whether it's inspirational images, quotes, or some other evocative content that will generate discussion. The most successful brands on Tumblr post images of all kinds, not just photos of their own products.

Connect with other Tumblr users.

As with any social network, connecting with and following others is the key to success on Tumblr. Start by searching for posts related to your products or business, and like or reply to them. If there's something you particularly like, you can *reblog* a post, which essentially reposts it to your own feed with attribution given to the original poster. You can also track down people who are influential in your niche and follow them, ensuring you stay connected with what's going on in your industry.

Use Disqus to enable commenting.

Part of what makes Tumblr so simple to use is that it doesn't include any extra features. That doesn't mean you shouldn't add whatever you need; one thing you should definitely add to your blog is a user comment function. One of the best ways you can expand your reach as an ecommerce business and increase engagement on your Tumblr blog is to actively encourage commenting. Although commenting isn't native to Tumblr, it's easy to implement via Disqus (*http://disqus.com*). Once Disqus is installed, commenting will be automatically enabled. In the absence of comments (there are many large ecommerce Tumblr blogs that don't have commenting enabled), you'll simply see "notes," which is a list of all the people who have "liked" or reblogged your posts.

Although there's much that can be said about effectively using Tumblr for your ecommerce business, the essential first step is deciding whether Tumblr is right for you. For businesses with access to high-quality, inspirational imagery, and the ability to post engaging, humorous, or pithy commentary, Tumblr can be an excellent addition to a solid marketing strategy.

Tier 3 Social Networks

Tier 3 is reserved for sites that are popular and interesting, but not particularly profitable for most people. With the right monetization strategy, a third-tier site can easily make the leap to a second- or top-tier social network.

reddit

reddit (yes, it's a lowercase *r*) is a social link aggregation and discussion site, organized into topical communities that are self-organized and independently moderated. There are millions of visitors each day, and reddit has hosted Ask Me Anything interviews from many celebrities and a few politicians, including Barack Obama.

So it's got a lot of traffic, a lot of users, and a lot of discussion. Sounds like a great place to be if you have something to sell, right? Not necessarily. You must be a member of reddit in order to advertise there. It isn't difficult to create an account, but the targeting is not very good because there is little capacity for users to provide revealing demographic data about themselves. In general, ad results seem to be less than stellar for any product or service that doesn't specifically appeal to self-described "geeks," and redditors are generally hostile toward self-promotion of any kind. If you try to guerrilla market by posting links to your site or Facebook page or anything that looks remotely promotional, redditors will slap you down very, very hard.

If you have high-quality photos of some action shots of your products or related topics, you might host them on imgur (see "imgur" on page 15) and post links to appropriate photo-oriented subreddits (such as */r/pics* or */r/earthporn*). They must be valid photos in their own right, not just marketing materials. Even if you're successful, it will be difficult or impossible to convert that attention into sales because reddit and imgur don't provide an easy way to link to your site without it being called out as spam.

The only consistent, reliable, and ethical strategy for marketing on reddit that we're aware of is giving away free products or samples on */r/freebies*. Offer a certain number of free giveaway items or samples, and hope that your product appeals to some of the communities on reddit. If you're successful, you might focus some reddit ads on the subreddits that find the freebies most appealing.

In general, reddit is a site you should be aware of and familiar with. If you want to try to participate there, you must give yourself some time to learn the site and the *reddiquette* (*http://www.reddit.com/wiki/reddiquette*) before attempting to contribute any material related to your business.

Regardless of how you choose to participate, one thing you probably do not want to do is reveal your real name and contact information. If you become disfavored on reddit at some point in the future, this information can be used to terrorize and threaten you in person, over the phone, and certainly over the Internet. Women are particularly vulnerable to cyberbullying on reddit, and should avoid revealing their name and gender when participating there. *Doxxing*, revealing another redditor's real-life identity, is against reddiquette and hopefully will never happen to you.

imgur

imgur (yes, it's all lowercase, like reddit) is a social photo-sharing site that offers community voting and commenting on pictures. It was originally created by a redditor who was fed up with spammy, limited, and slow free photo-sharing sites. For most of its existence, imgur has been closely associated with reddit, but it has reached the point where it offers much of reddit's core functionality in terms of voting and commenting.

If you intend to have both a reddit and an imgur account, and you want to use imgur for photo hosting and sharing outside of reddit, then you should register different usernames on both sites. If you use the same username (or if you use the same username on reddit that you do on any other social network), then you risk revealing your identity and contact information.

imgur has few rules; you can post pretty much anything there privately, but if you share something publicly that is illegal or copyrighted by someone else, it can be reported and taken down.

While imgur is an interesting photo-sharing site with a lot of traffic, its content is mostly temporary and ephemeral, whereas Pinterest is about curating collections of high-quality images over time, and Instagram is much more personal and stylized. It could be a good social network if you're planning to focus on viral photo content. *Memes* (pictures combined with words, in the style of Meme Generator (*http://memegenera tor.net*) and quick meme (*http://quickmeme.com*), and which we'll cover in more detail later in this book), however, are best left to meme-generation sites.

Quora

Quora is a place to ask questions, and hopefully get responses from experts in the Quora community. It doesn't offer much of a direct advertising benefit, but you can do a lot of inexpensive research here. If you're trying to figure out what the most important questions and issues are for your as-yet-unreached prospects, Quora is an excellent place to start.

The community is pretty big, and includes a lot of tech celebrities. If your question doesn't gain much traction on its own merit, you can pay a fee to try to get an expert to offer some comments.

It may also raise your professional profile to provide answers on Quora. You can make limited use of your Quora byline to mention your business or product; if your answers are highly ranked, everyone who reads that question will see your byline and your insightful response.

Instagram

While Pinterest focuses on collections of curated pictures uploaded and modified through a desktop computer, Instagram primarily relies on mobile devices with integrated cameras. That means that it tends to include more candid, less curated photos. Instagram has built-in photo filters, and restricts the picture size to a prescribed square size; you might find this entertaining or constricting, depending on your attitude toward photography and how you share it socially. Instagram is also a bit more one-directional than Pinterest; it's much easier to share other people's pins than it is to pass around someone's Instagram posts.

Visual content has begun to dominate the Web. More and more people prefer visual content such as videos, images, and infographics to replace, or to break up, a wall of text —and for good reason. You can potentially communicate a lot more information in a shorter amount of time with one good picture than with a typical text-only company blog post. Instagram makes it incredibly easy for other users to share that graphical content, and thus increase your brand and product visibility online.

Once you have an account set up, here are some ideas to get you successfully started on converting visitors and leads with Instagram:

Showcase new products.
> Providing visitors, leads, and customers with "sneak peeks" of your upcoming hot new products only on Instagram will give a sense of exclusivity (and who doesn't like to feel like a VIP?). If you announce on your other social media sites like Facebook and Twitter that you have a special new "sneak peek" announcement on Instagram, your Followers number is sure to increase.

Showcase current products.
> Not only can Instagram enable you to show everyone how to use your product and showcase its features and benefits, but if you have some creative uses for your products, it's ideal for sharing those as well. Keep an eye on your other social media sites to learn how customers are using your products, and share their ideas—and make sure you give those customers a shout-out on Instagram. That's a great first step to creating a brand loyalist!

Give behind-the-scenes shots.
> To take pictures of one's company in action is to build trust among visitors, leads, and customers. Take snapshots of your employees having fun at work, packing and shipping orders, or receiving a new shipment of stock. Show everyone how you roll —Instagram allows you to engage people like never before.

These are just a few ideas for using Instagram to help build your business. No matter what images or themes you create on the site, however, be sure that you provide context for the images and include #hashtags to help categorize them as you're posting.

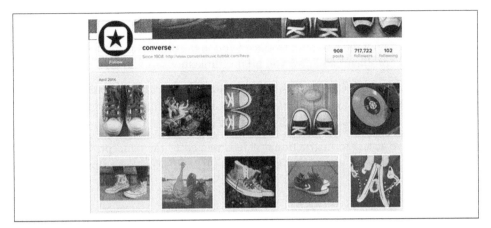

Figure 1-3. Converse's Instagram page combines colorful pictures of shoes with art and flashy graphics

Figure 1-3 shows how Converse creates brand loyalty with creative images on Instagram.

Niche Social Networks

In a few other chapters, we explain niche social networks and how to best use them. However, there may be niche social networks that we've never heard of, or that apply to your specific industry, product, or field. By all means, look for them!

For instance, if you are selling products or services for pets, there is Dogster and Catster. If you're selling books, there is Goodreads, LibraryThing, RedRoom, and Shelfari. Are you selling products that appeal to artists? Then deviantART is the social network for you.

If you don't know of any niche social networks for your industry, ask some of your colleagues or friendly competitors where they're spending their time online.

If there aren't any niche social networks in the modern sense—sites like Facebook, for instance (which used to be a niche social network for college students)—then there are probably forums and/or groups on larger sites. For instance, LinkedIn has many groups that people can join, each with its own discussions and events.

Summary

While you've probably heard of most of the social networks in this chapter, hopefully you learned something new about each in terms of how it can be useful to your business.

You probably also learned about a few lesser or niche social networks that could be useful to your overall social media strategy. There are a few more that we'll discuss in other chapters, and some of the ones that we mentioned only quickly here will be explained later in the proper context.

In essence, this is Act One: we've introduced you to the characters. In the next chapter, we'll frame the "problem" and how you might think about solving it.

Head over to the *Social eCommerce* site (*http://www.socialcommercebook.com*) to post your burning questions to us authors, and for access to exclusive offers, discounts, and coupon codes on various social media tools and services.

To get exclusive access to instructional videos related to the concepts in the chapter, simply send a text with your email address to *+1(213)947-9990* and prepare to have your mind blown!

CHAPTER 2

Basic Social Media Strategy

If you're struggling to make sales on social media, it's not the channel that is to blame, but the strategy you've developed (or haven't developed). To convert prospects on Facebook, Twitter, LinkedIn, or any other social network, you need compelling content delivered systematically. Be interesting. Be remarkable.

From there, you need to give prospects a reason to convert—and an opportunity to engage with you further. This is how you can align your sales with your social media efforts.

The approach to using social media is different from other types of marketing. Without the right planning, you can find yourself quickly getting frustrated. This chapter helps you form a valid, basic strategy for the most important social networks.

We'll also help you to establish goals. Without those, you've got nothing solid to work toward. You might think that your only goal is to reach as many people as you can to raise awareness about what you're offering. However, just planning on getting the word out and attracting the maximum number of followers with a platform such as Facebook won't necessarily guarantee increased growth and revenue. Selecting one site blindly and dumping money into it is a bad idea, but so is trying to spread equally blind efforts across multiple sites. There are numerous social networks, and it's impossible to incorporate all of them into your plans. Even if you could, it would be a waste of time and money, since many of them won't advance your goals.

Too many marketers tragically underestimate the work involved with getting the best results from using social media. A quality social media marketing plan will improve your ability to effectively manage the campaign and provide a way for you to measure your resulting progress. By the end of this chapter, you'll have a good foundation for a social media marketing plan.

Understand Who You Are and Why You Do It

In order to form a successful, actionable social media sales and marketing strategy, you must understand your business from a customer's perspective. That might seem silly to you at first—after all, you already have products and customers. Obviously whatever you're doing is working, right?

It's hard to argue with success. On the other hand, it's also hard to design a highly targeted marketing campaign without truly understanding what makes your company, your brand, and your product, service, or event unique. Traditional marketing isn't really targeted. An ad in a newspaper reaches newspaper readers; the publisher probably has a vague idea of subscriber demographics, but it isn't possible to display the ad only to readers who fit the right criteria. The same is true with billboards, radio ads, and so on; the best you can do is generalize the audience and your customer base and look for a good match.

Even online advertising in CPC or CPM ads on search engines, blogs, and news sites is broadly targeted because it's tough—from a legal and technical standpoint—to collect much data on readers or visitors.

Social media is totally different. Since everyone who signs up on a social network gives myriad details about themselves, each site automatically starts out with the ability to do specific ad targeting. Even if someone puts in only her age and gender, those two data points are a huge advantage in targeted advertising, assuming you know who you're selling to. As each member interacts with other members and participates in discussions and clicks voting buttons, joins groups, or excludes herself from certain parts of the site, she (perhaps unwittingly) offers a treasure trove of behavioral and personal preference data to social networks. Over time, this data is collected and organized in such a way that every participant can be specifically targeted according to her lifestyle and preferences. This enables you to do extremely fine-grained ad targeting. On a social network like Facebook that has a population measured in a double-digit percentage of the planet's population, even the most fine-grained targeting can reach thousands of prequalified sales leads.

The catch is, if you don't understand your product/service/event's fine-grained demographics, then you won't know whom to target. Worse, you won't know how to appeal to that audience even if you do reach it. Therefore, a superior social media sales and marketing strategy starts with knowing your company, your brand, and whatever you are selling *really* well. If you're already at this point, then go ahead and skip to the next section.

So how do you find out these valuable hidden details? Well, you should probably start with your own company and employees, and perhaps your customers as well; just ask them their opinions and take some notes. Consider getting on the phone with and talking to some current customers. Develop a set of questions designed to elicit both specific responses as well as freeform feedback. Beyond that, though, the answer is: use social media!

In order to leverage social media to give you better insights for ad targeting, you must first determine what the most important questions are in your industry. What big problems are there? What problems do you solve that your competitors don't? What are your customers' (and more importantly, prospects) chief concerns?

Whatever the questions are, make note of them, and ask them on social media. Some good sites for asking questions and getting good user participation are:

- Twitter (only if you have enough followers to get decent responses)
- Yahoo Answers
- Quora
- reddit (the askreddit subreddit, usually)

If you're well established on other social networks, go ahead and ask there, too.

The answers that you receive, and the demographics of the people who respond, are useful in a variety of ways:

- Ad targeting
- FAQ content on your website
- Social media posts
- Quotes or bullet points for traditional marketing materials

Set and Meet Goals

You cannot improve what you don't measure. If you have an existing social media presence and want to improve its effectiveness, then you must measure your current baseline, and then think of some realistic goals. Here are some ideas (replace the numbers with some that are realistic for your business and industry):

- Get to 1,000 Facebook likes
- Gain 15 new Twitter followers per day
- Increase social media sales leads by 10%
- Have 20 customers interact with you publicly through social media
- Solve 10 customer complaints posted on Twitter
- Get an invitation to speak at a conference

- Get mentioned in two press articles or posts on popular blogs

It's important that your goal is realistic. If you are in a niche industry and expect to gain 10,000 Facebook likes, you're probably going to fail. When you are just starting out in social media, set easy, measurable goals for yourself until you gain more experience. Know your limits before you push them.

If you're starting out with nothing in terms of social media presence, then your initial goals should be a bit different. First, aim to identify the social networks that are relevant to you. Then join them and customize them. Once you're established, *then* set some initial targets for how many likes or followers or the level of engagement you want to achieve. Again, start with something easily and cheaply achieved, then move upward from there.

When you meet your goal, immediately plan a new one based on your current success. If you set a goal of 50 Facebook likes within one month and end up reaching it within a week, then try for 200 before the month is up.

You can also choose goals that conform to a budget. For instance, if you are spending $10 per day on Facebook ads and getting about 100 new likes per day, try doubling that money and see if you can double your likes. If not, scale back. Find the sweet spot. Or if your budget is low, concentrate on tactics that will help you meet your engagement or sales goal without buying more ads.

Have a Scalability Plan

It's nice to dream about "good problems to have," such as a level of success that you cannot keep up with. Regardless of how realistic you believe your chances are for out-of-control success in ecommerce, the only way to prevent those dreams from turning into nightmares is to have at least a basic plan for how you can scale up to meet demand. By "nightmares," we mean that one of your products or marketing efforts becomes viral overnight and you go from fulfilling 10 orders per day to having your web store crash due to load, your email inbox fill up with more than a thousand orders and presales questions, and angry comments about your poor customer service on Twitter.

There are three "good problems to have" scenarios to plan for: unexpected big orders, a sudden long-term increase in sales, and seasonal or holiday increases.

A Sudden Big Order

Let's say you have a part-time business buying small-time wholesale boxes of electronics parts and assembling specialized computing devices. There are a lot of companies that do this with system-on-board devices like the Raspberry Pi. But then all of a sudden an industrial railroad consulting company wants to buy 500 of your devices to integrate into railroad car safety monitoring equipment. Your website says that orders usually ship within three days of payment, and you have a flat-rate shipping fee that barely covers the cost of shipping in the continental U.S.—and 20 of the orders need to be shipped to Alaska at double the cost, which erases all profit from those orders. There's no way you can fulfill this order on your own, according to the terms you've specified. Even a basic scalability plan would have prevented the stress of dealing with this mess.

Your Viral Efforts Accidentally Worked

Welcome to the Internet! Your viral product video has just hit the front page of reddit and has been tweeted, shared, and blogged about more times than you can keep track of, and you're not even done with your first cup of coffee. The cute, custom-made kids' dolls you make full-time in your retirement are suddenly in demand. You can only make one per week at best, but there is now a backlog of 300 orders, and more are coming in every minute. There are actually so many orders that you cannot calculate how far into the future it would take to fulfill even half of them.

This scenario isn't complete fiction; it's based on a real story that happened to Child's Own, a small business that made dolls from children's drawings. As shown in Figure 2-1, the owner actually asked people to stop sharing her site on social media because she had no hope of keeping up with demand: *http://www.childsown.com/ 2012/02/07/oy/*.

It's So Popular That No One Goes There Anymore

It's great to have a local business that has so many customers that there's a line out the door, but be careful that you don't develop a reputation for being so busy that customers decide it isn't worth the hassle. Extremely popular, exclusive, upscale New York City restaurants can turn people away without batting an eyelash, but you can't.

For local businesses, scalability plans should involve:

- Extending store hours
- Temporary increase in staff
- Temporary expansion (into the parking lot, the stockroom or loading dock, a nearby empty storefront, or temporary space in a mall kiosk or seasonal storefront)
- Permanent expansion in the form of a second or third location

This shouldn't be too much different than your ordinary scalability planning for seasonal rushes.

Figure 2-1. Child's Own had a great product, but no ability to scale production

Prevention and Planning

The first thing you should do is ensure that you aren't making claims that you cannot back up. Specify in your terms of service, in your ads, and on the ordering page that orders over a certain amount will take longer to ship.

Check your shipping policies and your shipping price calculation algorithms to make sure that you're accounting correctly for the areas and countries that you serve. There are several parts of the U.S. that are not serviced by certain FedEx, UPS, and U.S. mail services such as overnight, Saturday delivery, or ground shipping. Don't allow an order to complete if it has an invalid shipping service selected.

Limit your inventory quantity so that orders cannot be completed beyond a certain threshold. If you choose this path, you should definitely provide a simple "notify me" opt-in email form so that you can try to regain this sale when you are prepared to fulfill more orders.

If you need to assemble a physical good, create simple instructions (in the form of a manual, video, or presentation) for assembling, testing, packing, and shipping a product. This will enable you to quickly train a temporary employee.

Ask family and friends if and when they might be available to help with a sudden swell in orders, and figure out how much you can pay for their help. Beyond that, you should also contact some local temporary staffing agencies to see what they may be able to provide in terms of short-term, short-notice labor.

Prepare an ad that you can post to local newspapers, ad services, and job listing services. If you ever need to use it, you'll have good ad copy ready to paste into a form.

Ensure that your website is hosted on a server that can handle increased load, or can scale dynamically with load. If you are on a cheap hosting plan that doesn't allow for heavy traffic, contact your service provider to figure out how you can upgrade your hosting service on short notice. It may turn out that you will have to change your hosting plan or switch to a more agile hosting provider in order to get proper scalability. Definitely make sure that you aren't going to be charged high fees for going over a certain bandwidth threshold. If you're not particularly technical and are having difficulty understanding what we're talking about in this paragraph, you should enlist the help of a competent system administrator or web developer.

Define Your Presence

The first thing you must do on every social media site is define a username or namespace for your company. This is often part of the URL, such as on Tumblr where your username becomes a subdomain—for example, *http://socialcommercebook.tumblr.com*. Or sometimes it's a directory off of the main URL, such as on Facebook: *http://www.facebook.com/socialcommercebook*.

Not all social networks have this feature. LinkedIn profile URLs, for instance, do contain your name, but with a bunch of "alphabet soup" as well. If you are working with a social network that does this, then you may find some utility in buying a domain name (they're cheap—$15 a year or so, depending on how far into the future you reserve them).

You can also redirect certain directories on your corporate site to specific social networks. For instance, if you wanted to do a cheap (essentially free, if you have full control over your corporate website) vanity URL to go to your LinkedIn profile, you could redirect this to it: *http://www.<example.com>/linkedin/* (where *<example.com>* is your site).

If you are serious about increasing your fans/friends/followers, you can get a specialized domain name that specifically encourages liking or following. For example, *FBjen.com*.

Watch out for trademark violations, though. Not only is the word *Facebook* a corporate trademark, but *FB* is as well. This may not be a problem depending on where you live and the details of your own trademarks. If you don't have an intellectual property attorney available to check this out for you, then avoid anything with questionable legality.

White Hat Versus Black Hat

In the online world, there are tactics that are considered ethical, or *white hat*, and tactics that are considered unethical, or *black hat*. If you aren't sure, or if a particular technique is transitioning from one to the other, it could be considered *grey hat*. You absolutely want to stay away from black hat tactics. They are unethical for a reason, and the admins and stewards of social networks will punish you harshly and in many cases permanently for attempting to use them.

Black Hat Examples

Read the terms of service for the social network you're participating in. The dos and don'ts are pretty clearly laid out there—or at least, the general sense of "good and evil" is explained.

If there is any question as to whether a particular tactic is white hat or black hat, just ask yourself this: "Does this misrepresent the amount and depth of actual sharing that is taking place?" If it does, then don't do it. Here are some specific examples of known black hat techniques:

Buying friends, fans, and followers.
> Facebook has already cracked down on this by deleting fake accounts and removing fraudulent likes and fans. Not only is this a waste of money due to your bought friends being deleted, but it's also pretty embarrassing to get caught doing this. Twitter doesn't have such strict rules, so it's much more common to find people buying followers on Twitter, or using bots to follow other people with the hope that they'll be followed back. Just because Twitter allows it doesn't mean you should do it; imagine how embarrassed you'd be if your friends, family, coworkers, employees, and customers found out that your followers number were falsely inflated.

Buying Amazon or Yelp reviews.
> This became a famous and successful black hat tactic a while ago, and several businesses sprang up to capitalize on it. However, in late 2012 Amazon cracked down on the fake review industry, removing fraudulent accounts and deleting fake reviews. A number of new features have been implemented to combat fake reviews, including review ratings, verified purchase tagging, and a quick link to a reviewer's history. Yelp recently found and eliminated fake reviews on a large scale as well. The FTC cracked down on 19 companies creating fake reviews in September 2013 for total fines amounting to $350,000. Among the companies were Swam Media

Group (a gentleman's club franchise) and US Coachways, Inc. (a bus charter company). Again: you will be caught, you will be embarrassed, you will look petty and desperate, and you will wish you hadn't done this.

Fraudulent Google AdSense clicks.
If you display Google AdSense ad units anywhere on any of your sites, and you click on them to gain revenue, you will feel the wrath of Google. That doesn't mean mere suspension of your AdSense account; it means complete suspension or deletion of your entire Google profile. You could permanently lose access to Google Drive, Gmail, Picasa, and Google+.

Buying (or selling) links on your web page or social media pages.
No one would notice if you bought or sold just one link. However, that's not how link buying/selling typically works. A black hat SEO company will want to buy links on as many sites as possible. This is easily picked up by spam-catching algorithms of the search engines. If you buy or sell links for SEO purposes, you'll pay the price.

Editing Wikipedia articles.
You are traceable on Wikipedia. All it takes is one suspicious editor to look into the revision history of a Wikipedia page to get your account banned and your page deleted. This also applies to editing other articles to mention your product, brand, or company. There are a lot of ways you can be caught, such as through your IP address. Don't be concerned with trying to hide your identity or origin—just don't edit Wikipedia for marketing or self-promotion purposes.

White Hat Examples

It's impossible to define every white hat technique, since anything that is not specifically unethical is almost always perfectly acceptable. If you're encouraging people to share and participate, you aren't breaking any stated or implied rules; this is how social networks are supposed to work.

Having been intimately involved in the social networking space for many years now, we've heard more than a few misconceptions related to using social media for business. Here are some things that people think are bad practices, but actually aren't:

Asking for Facebook likes or Yelp reviews.
How else would you jumpstart your product or company page, other than by asking your personal friends, family members, and colleagues to follow your page? It's not a good idea to repeatedly spam for likes or follows, but not because it's unethical—it's just annoying.

Buying Facebook ads that increase your likes.
Of course it isn't against Facebook's policies to pay it for ads that promote your page! We have a whole chapter dedicated to that practice in this book.

Outsourcing social media posting/management.

You don't have to be the person who posts to any of your social media sites—even your own personal pages. While many social networks have a Terms of Service clause that bars you from registering under someone else's identity, there are no rules against having someone else post, comment, or reply for you. Having said that, the most authentic, passionate, and consistent voice you'll find for your business is your own. If you do decide to outsource your social media, be sure you're available to field expert-level questions, and that whoever's monitoring and managing your social media profiles has a clear understanding of your business, including your goals, values, and the "personality" of your brand.

Social media monitoring.

Many businesses make a point of monitoring what social media users are saying about their brand or products. Some people feel that this is privacy infringement, though social networks do not have rules against it. Although this is an area where businesses need to tread carefully, paying attention to conversations in your industry can build deeper connections with both current and potential customers. Although most Internet users know that businesses are listening to what they have to say online, a majority believe that brands should respond only to online comments made directly to them. Being aware of what people are saying about your brand and products is a critical (and totally legit) part of a marketing strategy, but be careful about how you use that information—not because it's against any laws or site terms, but because it makes your followers and customers more comfortable.

How Black Hat Tactics Hurt You

Having too few fans of your business seems a bit like having a social gathering with too few guests. As the desire for social proof grows, so too can the desire to buy Facebook fans or Amazon reviews. That purchase will cost you a lot more than you're anticipating.

If you are wrestling with this idea, think about a friend who is looking for a meaningful relationship. How effective would it be to purchase escort services to find a date? OK, it would certainly be one of the easiest, fastest ideas, and perhaps in the short term it may appear as if our single friend sure knows a lot of women who are interested in him personally. But hiring services to give the appearance of popularity most likely will not lead to any kind of long-term relationship. The same is true with Facebook.

Relationships cultivated on Facebook are the true value indicator; they are what make it worth your time and money. In fact, buying fans removes one of the great functions of Facebook: its natural filter. If you are strategic about your efforts, your fans will join you because they are interested in your business. They are qualified leads, not anonymous and nonparticipatory numbers. In fact, a 2010 study by Chadwick Martin Bailey and iModerate Research Technologies revealed that over 50% of Facebook fans were more likely to buy and recommend products and services that they had engaged with on Facebook.

If you try to demonstrate your social proof by buying fans, you are clouding your ability to read what your customers actually want. When you send out a fan-only promotion and a certain percentage respond, your statistics will be skewed because of your inflated fan base. That's just the beginning of troubles you could encounter with purchasing fans.

You are not the only one who notices the sudden increase in likes or followers. Having fans who are not interacting with your business page can negatively affect your visibility. Facebook's algorithm determines what information will make it into News Feeds, and the affinity score is part of that equation. The affinity score is based on the number of interactions you have with your fans. As fans interact with your page by commenting or sharing information, your affinity score is positively impacted. The more fans you have engaging with your page and content, the greater your chances are to appear in future News Feeds. If you decide to buy Facebook fans, they will most likely not be interacting with you, and therefore will reduce your affinity score. In an effort to boost your social proof, you could actually make your updates and links disappear from the News Feeds of your true fans.

For people who are looking for quick results, legitimate paid traffic can be the perfect social proof boost. If you have not done so, consider a Facebook ad campaign. By creating an extremely targeted ad campaign on Facebook, you can attract the kind of fans who will gain value from your business.

Shy away from short-term strategies. Remember that your social media plan is not a sprint, it's a marathon. There are valid white hat techniques for getting a quick boost, but buying fans isn't worth the time, the money, or the buyer's remorse.

Integrate Social Media into a Larger Campaign

You probably already have some kind of marketing program that is funded and working, whether or not it includes online resources. So how do you add social media to that? What do you do about budgeting and resource distribution? The details of this situation can be overwhelming, so start simple: focus on an upcoming holiday and create a campaign that offers a holiday special. This is a paradigm that you're already familiar with as a consumer and an entrepreneur, and the fundamentals are the same as with other marketing methods, so you can safely gain a lot of experience in creating ads and campaigns and measuring success.

Before jumping into any campaign or spending any money on ads, be sure to read Chapter 6 so that you have a firm understanding of how to create and monitor ads on social media.

Holiday sales can apply to any industry, product, and service. Even if you are selling tickets to an event, you can sell advance tickets as part of a holiday promotion. Here are some general tips and guidelines for using a social media holiday campaign as a way to begin integrating social media into an existing marketing effort:

Design a promotion, contest, or offer.
>Choose something easy and fun for your promotion. If this is memorable and re-markable, then you're far more likely to gain traction on Facebook. If you're having difficulty coming up with an idea, then aim for something simple, such as a "like this video" post, a news update, a behind-the-scenes photo album, or a sneak peek of a new product.

Create a custom landing page on Facebook.
>Facebook should almost always be the core of your social media marketing strategy. Beyond your corporate page (and possibly also product pages), you can create a custom Facebook landing page for this holiday campaign. Not only does this in-crease conversions for people who are using Facebook, it also adds another layer of metrics (through Facebook's page visitor stats) beyond what is provided by the advertiser—even if that advertiser is Facebook.

Use tracking links for all Facebook posts, ads, and promotions.
>This data is going to come in handy later. It may be worth the time and expense to set up a Bit.ly link to both shorten the URL and track the traffic generated by your post (there are many other sites that will just shorten the URL, if that's all you're after). This is especially important when sales/conversions are your goal.

Post a related photo/video on your Facebook page with a one-sentence description.
>Create a photo to promote your contest/offer and post it to your company's Face-book page. A screenshot of a video works wonderfully because the "play button" icon in its center encourages people to click the photo and engage with your post. In terms of the text content, keep it short and simple. If you have more to say, add it in a comment below the post. Shorter is better on social media. Short, choppy sentences work best.

Use the "Boost post" feature for simpler, easier post promotions, such as targeting more of your fans.
>This ensures that your fans get to see your post in a crowded and active activity stream. That means that they're more likely to like, comment, and share. Only a single digit percentage of fans see your posts without paid promotion. Because this

is a special promotion (not an everyday post) and you're looking for a sales boost, pull out all the stops.

Create a Promoted Post.
In the Ads Manager on Facebook, you can create a Promoted Post to promote this post in a different way. Use clever targeting to ensure a strong message-to-market match. You can promote this to fans only, but you can also set up a targeted demographic if this post will appeal to people outside your current group of fans.

Continue to post once or twice per day.
Regular posts increase engagement and will boost traffic before the holidays. Out of ideas? Try these: helpful hints, tips, recipes, photos, videos, family traditions, questions, and surveys. Have fun with your posts, reply to everyone who comments or shares, and hit the Like button on their comments. Delete/ban/block anyone who harasses you, and encourage your existing fans with thoughtful replies and comments.

When your holiday campaign is complete, you'll have engagement data to examine and costs to analyze. Determine what was most effective, and use that to rethink your overall marketing strategy inclusive of social media.

Make Your Website More Social

There are lots of ways to make your site more social. First, you must consider what sort of site it is and what makes sense in terms of engagement. Then you must consider the three types of social interaction: following/liking, sharing, and commenting.

Like/Follow Buttons

Traditional corporate websites don't usually offer much interaction for visitors—perhaps some kind of opt-in or lead qualification form, but beyond that there is rarely anything interactive. More social-savvy companies will add some social media interaction buttons that enable you to like or follow the corporate page or account. It's always a good idea to have a Facebook Like button and a Twitter Follow button, assuming you've got well-curated accounts on each. If you are sufficiently invested in a niche social network, and it has a good button that follows this paradigm, then it usually makes sense to add that to your site as well.

However, when you're adding social media buttons to a corporate site, be careful that you don't go overboard. Too many buttons leads to clutter in the site design, and can discourage interaction. Good social media buttons are obvious as to what site they represent, and are easy to interact with. These should also be social networks that you're actively participating on; you don't want to lead your customers and prospects to a social network that has no content on it.

Share Buttons

And then there are *share* buttons, which automate the process of posting a link to a visitor's personal social media page, or to a social news or discussion site. In general, share buttons are of very little value for corporate content. If the content is not interesting, then don't offer to share it. Certainly don't offer to share it in an automated and generic way as part of your site navigation.

There is usually a wide array of options for share buttons and widgets. Some social networks have an option for a link that you can use with or without your own graphics; some set the baseline a little higher than that, and offer buttons that have a small icon that represents the social network's logo. Then there are larger buttons, and buttons with dynamic content such as the number of shares or comments that this page has received.

Show the buttons with numbers only if you have, or reasonably expect to quickly have, a significant number of shares. If your buttons show that you have zero shares, then you're going to look like a loser.

If you have a blog or some other content-heavy site, share buttons and small widgets may make more sense than on a static corporate site. However, most visitors have their own preferred methods of submitting links to social news and discussion sites, so if you add too many social media share buttons, visitors are unlikely to use most of them and the buttons will just clutter up your navigation.

Content sites are also a good use case for the small widgets that show the number of shares this page has received. If you're promoting your site decently, the number shouldn't ever be at zero, so there's not much risk of looking weak. New visitors who find your content through social media or social news sites are late to the party, so they'll see a ton of social proof when they arrive at your content. That may well encourage them to like/follow/friend you and become a regular visitor.

Liking something on Facebook or following a site or company on Twitter isn't just a way for customers and prospects to stay up to date; it's also a kind of vote. They're telling their friends and colleagues that they publicly acknowledge their admiration for your company, brand, product, or content.

Sometimes it's just silly to include a particular social media button, such as when you have a Pin It button on a page with no real graphics to pin. If there's something that people want to share photos of, put the button there. However, the content on the page with the Pin It button must be worthy of being pinned. On the other hand, putting up a link to your Pinterest boards can help you get more followers on Pinterest, even on pages where you don't have any graphics. A classy way to add pinning functionality is with a "Pin It" hover button that appears only when a cursor is placed over the image. This is easily accomplished on your WordPress blog with the Pinterest Pin It Button for Images plug-in (*http://bit.ly/1m0cHCm*).

Figure 2-2. An example of a good social media widget

In our opinion, the worst of the worst are the widgets (defined in the next section) that act as collections of share buttons for a large number of social networks. When you mouse over one of these widgets, it automatically pulls out into a larger area of the screen, which covers up your content or navigation and in general annoys the heck out of your visitors. We recommend that you never use these kinds of add-ons for your site.

Widgets

A *widget* is more than just a graphical link to a social network; it actually provides a window into what's there. In terms of engagement, widgets are sort of a combination of the *like/follow* and *share* paradigms. So, again, make sure that you have a decent presence on any site for which you're using a widget.

Good widgets are dynamic and interactive, and show some content from the site to which they lead. The Pinterest widget shows thumbnails from your board, for instance (the first image you submit to a board is the default thumbnail, but you may want to change this manually if you have a better idea for a thumbnail image later). There are many kinds of widgets that can show avatars of your fans, comments from your pages, and other related content. Figure 2-2 shows an interesting, engaging, and unobtrusive Facebook widget that can be easily integrated into a blog or website.

This figure shows a good use of a widget. It displays both a high number of likes, and it shows mini-avatars of other people on Facebook who have liked this page. It shows both social proof and relevancy.

Cross-Posting

Cross-posting is submitting content to one online location and then having that service automatically distribute it to all other social network accounts belonging to the user. The benefit of this is obvious: your post reaches a larger number of viewers. A service such as Hootsuite (*http://hootsuite.com*) will manage and measure your engagement with social networks. It can schedule messages and tweets, track brand mentions, and analyze social media traffic. Note, however, that while cross-posting can save time, posts that you publish using third-party applications (particularly with Facebook) can get less visibility than those you manually post to Facebook.

Adding Comments

If you don't want to direct all feedback and user interaction to social media, you can integrate a third-party comment system into your website. Most content management systems have plug-ins or extensions that add this functionality seamlessly. If possible, that's probably the option you should take, so long as your webmaster, sysadmin, and web designer agree.

There are also third-party comment solutions that are easily implemented on a per-page or sitewide basis. Two that we confidently recommend are:

Bazaar Voice (http://www.bazaarvoice.com)
> Offers various feedback tracking systems, including an Amazon-like review system that you can integrate into your ecommerce site

Disqus (http://disqus.com)
> A full-featured open source comment system that can be integrated easily into any site

Again, solutions like these don't always make sense for corporate websites. For ecommerce and content sites, however, they are a must-have.

Another option is to integrate Facebook, Twitter, or Google+ comments into your site. Every comment posted through one of these plug-ins will show up on the social network that is hosting it. A lot of people aren't comfortable with this, so unless you have a thriving social media community around your business or brand already in place, it's probably not going to help you to directly integrate a social media–based comment system.

Customize Your Channel

Regardless of which social media sites you participate in and how you are using them, you must customize your pages on those sites and make them distinctive. Use your logo, your colors, your graphics, your fonts—customize everything. Make your social media pages look like they are natural extensions of your official website.

Here are some examples of well-customized pages:

- *https://twitter.com/sspencer*
- *https://www.facebook.com/TheJimmyHarding/*
- *http://www.linkedin.com/company/ibm/*
- *http://universalhorrorfilms.tumblr.com/*
- *http://www.youtube.com/user/GibsonGuitarCorp/*

Some social sites allow more customization than others. Whatever sites you're participating on, you should push customization to the limits. Also, this is something you should have a professional designer do, if you have the budget or staff for it. It's not enough to just look *different*; it also has to look *professional*.

Listen to the Conversation, Then Join In

Upon entering the social media realm, your first instinct may be to announce your amazing, finely crafted, heartfelt marketing messages to the entire universe. Or maybe you did that before you bought this book, and are now digging yourself out of an avalanche of failure. In any case, this is a bad tactic.

Social media is about conversation, connection, and sharing. Sharing, mind you, is a two (or more)-sided relationship. If you're blasting out your marketing messages, that's pretty one-sided, and it's not what people are on social media to consume. There are some exceptions to this—such as extremely famous celebrities who might post messages about their new album or television show—but they already have a very large captive audience that is used to listening without interacting. Even then, the audience is interacting with one another, so there is still a discussion taking place. You aren't a celebrity with a huge following, though, so your audience sees you as an equal, and expects more interactive social media behavior from you.

So how do you turn your marketing instincts into worthwhile social media habits? By participating in the conversation, by providing shareable material, and by connecting with people who are interested in topics that are related to your industry. Don't dive in right now, though—this chapter is about creating a strategy. The execution of specific tactics comes later.

Start with the connection part. Make a list of all of the famous people in your industry, past and present. Thought leaders, CEOs, inventors, and competitors are all good examples. Ask yourself how the people on your list would use the social networks that you've targeted, or take a look and see if they have accounts on those sites. The people who are following your list of industry leaders are the same people who are likely to follow you. Your participation strategy should be:

1. Observe the state of the conversation as it is now.
2. Begin participating in the conversation.
3. Build a community.
4. Start working your marketing into your normal social media routine.

You don't need an audience; you need a community. The easiest way to build a community around your brand is to create a dialogue with your customers.

Like a party with no attendees, a social media page with posts that don't have comments from followers is creepy and embarrassing. Nobody wants to be the sole commenter. You could comment on your own posts (perhaps from your personal account), but that might also look silly. Consider getting some friends to post a few comments on posts that you make early in your page's history so that newcomers will see a little bit of social proof and find an easier way into the conversation.

Customer Outreach

Communication on social media should always be two-way. Ideally, you should get a lot more back than you give out; for each post you make, there should be many comments, shares/retweets, and likes. It may take some time to build up your community if you are just now starting from scratch, but once you get rolling it should be a fun and interesting dialogue.

It's easy to focus just on what you post and how it is received, especially if you're a data wonk. You can pore over the metrics and try to improve your engagement constantly, and never spend one moment considering what people are actually saying when they are interacting with your company's social media pages. That is a big mistake.

Social media is the perfect platform for *customer outreach*—getting feedback from customers, answering questions from prospects, and connecting with bloggers and influencers with the hope that they'll be interested in your stuff and help promote it to their followers.

This is pretty easy to do if you're on only one or two social networks. Once you get to three, though, it can become much more difficult to manage. That's why there are tools for social media monitoring. There are a lot of sites and programs that do this, though most of them are specific to Twitter, or cover only the big social networks. Here are some examples that we think are worth your consideration:

- *TalkWalker* (*http://talkwalker.com*)
- *social mention* (*http://socialmention.com*)
- *Trackur* (*http://trackur.com*)
- *Twillow* (*http://twillow.net*)

These can also be great resources for keyword research when you are looking for ideas for new posts and blog content. For influencer outreach consider Pitchbox (*http://pitch box.com*), a toolset that works with the online influencers who can boost your search rankings if they link to you.

Twitter and Snapchat as Customer Service Tools

You can take the conversation to the next level by using social media as a customer service tool. Whenever someone complains about your brand, company, or product on social media, reply positively and publicly so that potential customers see that you're concerned about solving customer problems.

Some companies are apprehensive about having social media play a role in their customer service strategy. They're afraid that if a complaint is aired publicly, it could damage an otherwise excellent reputation. However, when managed professionally, negative comments have a tremendous *positive* impact on your public reputation.

Twitter, in particular, is excellent for identifying and resolving issues quickly while showing that you are respectful of your customer feedback and active in maintaining customer satisfaction. If you do happen to receive a negative tweet, be sure that you:

- Respond quickly.
- Be sincere, honest, and transparent.
- Provide solutions to the complaint.
- Provide a personal email address (not a generic "customer service department" email).
- Don't take it personally.

Another great customer service tool is Snapchat (a mobile app for Android and iOS that enables you to take a photo with your tablet or phone, and share it with a select number of people on a temporary basis). None of the photos are stored unless the sender chooses to save them; Snapchat photos are intended to be ephemeral and candid.

So how do you use this app for customer service? If a customer receives a product that is damaged, defective, or otherwise "not as advertised," Snapchat is a much more reliable and speedy way to directly see a picture of the problem.

Social Media for the Socially Challenged

Social media comes easily and naturally to extroverted people. Introverted people and perfectionists, however, can have a difficult time coming up with things to say. Being social is difficult for some people, even online where there is some degree of anonymity. That doesn't mean that successful social media marketing is only for the highly social.

Regardless of social ability, you must have a strong interest in whatever you are selling, and you have to want to sell it. If you don't have that kind of passion for your product, you can't expect to inspire it in others.

Don't write content with your friends in mind. Instead, write for an audience of people who are interested in the topic you're covering. The quicker you get out of your circle of friends and family—the people who care about *you*, not *your art or business*—and into the land of interested prospects, the better. Get to the people who are interested in this topic. Speak to the people who care about what you want to say. Join groups for people who are interested in what you're doing.

Does it have to be you who posts to your social media pages? Are you the only person who can post? Perhaps your spouse, employee, marketing manager—someone you know and trust who is better suited to the task—can do it for you, with some guidance.

You can also outsource the work to a good social media marketing firm. You'll still have to be involved on some level, but you won't have to worry about the content of daily posts. Just provide previous blog posts, videos, press releases, your product planning calendar, branding guidelines, and overall marketing strategy to your social media firm, and it can mine that for content.

If you're the only person who can reasonably post to social media, plan out your posts ahead of time so that you don't have to deal with writer's block on a daily basis; see "30 Days of Conversation Starters" on page 39 and modify it for your industry. You can even sit down and create several days of posts and schedule them ahead of time, assuming you are posting to a site that allows this (most do).

Get Ideas for New Content

You've probably got a bunch of ideas for social media content right off the bat. Eventually, though, it gets tougher to think of new things. Here are some common fallback topics for social media posts:

- Requests for feedback or opinion about products or events

- Free giveaways
- Fun images of your product
- Famous quotes relevant to your business

If you're truly out of ideas after considering this list, then head to Yahoo Answers, LinkedIn, and/or Quora and ask some questions relevant to your industry.

In the absence of new content, you can keep the conversation going by retweeting positive tweets from followers and tweeting friendly replies to negative feedback. Using mentions (@ on Facebook or Twitter, and + on Google+), you can reach a lot of people quickly.

You can also search for good articles, photos, and videos that you already know are somewhat popular. If there's a tie-in to your business or industry, that's even better! reddit is an excellent source for quality content links, as are all of the major social bookmarking and social news sites (Popurls, Flipboard, Delicious, StumbleUpon—pick one you like and start looking for good links).

---

30 Days of Conversation Starters

Here's a content plan that we sometimes use as a template for clients. The idea is to script out the first month's worth of content with the intention of jumpstarting a new community and forming good social media habits to keep you going:

1. Share a photo behind the scenes at your business, factory, or office.
2. Link to timely news story that could impact your fans.
3. Ask your fans for questions that haven't been answered.
4. As the saying goes, "Leaders are readers." Ask your fans what they are reading.
5. Post a frequently asked question that you receive, and answer it.
6. Post a how-to video that solves a problem for your target audience.
7. Take a snapshot of your favorite "working remotely" place, and ask your fans where they enjoy working when not in an office.
8. Share a cool quote (on a picture) that will be of value to your fans. Ask them to click Like if they agree.
9. Ask, "What are your biggest issues, concerns, problems with __?" (insert something related to your business).
10. Ask your fans to fill in the blank for a question like, "The goal I would most like to achieve is __."
11. Announce a deal that is available only to this specific social network, three days in advance, and ask followers to watch for details.

---

12. Ask whether your fans love or hate something timely and controversial in your market.

13. Ask, "Considering our services (or product)?" and then add a testimonial from a recent happy customer. Also, post a quick reminder about tomorrow's deal.

14. Launch your site-specific sale or deal, and give it a short deadline. Promote one of your products at a discount.

15. Share a blog post or status update posted by one of your faithful fans.

16. Ask a non-business-related question that almost anyone could answer—for example, "I need a terrific brownie recipe. Any suggestions?"

17. Have people describe, in a few words, their dream __ (the word in the blank depends on your market).

18. Give two choices for your fans, such as: "Work from home or an office?"

19. Ask, "Who is the best __?" Fill in the blank with a word that connects to your market. For instance: "Who is your best kind of client?" Or you could ask for a recommendation: "Who is the best expert for SEO?"

20. Ask, "What makes a business/service/restaurant [whatever applies to your company] successful?"

21. Ask, "When buying __ [a word connected to your market], what means the most to you? What do you care about?"

22. Post "Click Like if you love __!" (Choose a word connected to your business.)

23. Ask for help. Post a question related to your business or something fun that your audience could answer; for example, "I need help getting good examples of Facebook ads for a local business. Has anyone spotted one lately? If so, what made it great? What stood out?"

24. Ask, "Do you think this is true?" Then post a quote. For example: "Do you think this is true? 'Success is going from failure to failure without losing your enthusiasm.' — Winston Churchill."

25. Ask, "What are your favorite __?" (insert: podcasts, magazines, YouTube videos, fan pages, etc.).

26. Ask, "What do you think about __? Love it or hate it?" (Choose any topic related to your industry.)

27. Offer a hot tip that will be extremely valuable to your fans. If one of your fans recommended it, tag and publicly thank that person.

28. Ask, "Who wins: _ or _?" (Example: "Who wins: GPS or your sense of direction?")

29. Post "Have you checked us out on __?" (Insert other social media platform with link.) For example: "Have you checked us out on Pinterest [add link to Pinterest address]?" or "Are you following us on Twitter [add link to Twitter address]?"

30. Ask a question that relates to a recent, popular blog post, then link to the blog post in the first comment.

Content Marketing

If you're writing blog posts or articles on a content site or a corporate blog, then you've got a different set of variables to consider. Writing Twitter posts is one thing; writing 500- to 1,000-word blog posts is another. Again, this doesn't have to be you doing the writing. Blog posts and even magazine articles are easily outsourced to ghostwriters, though good writers are typically not cheap. Mediocre writers abound in communities like Odesk and textbroker, so be discerning. You need an outstanding writer to create outstanding content.

Your goal should always be "to be linked to from everywhere." You want your blog posts to be popular so that a lot of people will visit your site, become aware of your company and what it offers, and hopefully choose to follow you on social networks.

The key to writing great blog posts that have viral appeal is to write for the people who obsessively link to things. That means writing for teenage alpha-geeks who have little patience for literary fluff, viciously attack anything that looks like a sales ploy, and prefer short and easily quoted material. Make your blog post easily scannable by breaking up the paragraphs appropriately, and using lists whenever possible. In fact, if you can, make everything a list. It's long been a trick of tabloid publishing—even before the Web—to put a number and a superlative in the headline to attract readers who are glancing at the cover only for a few seconds. The word *amazing* is particularly good for headlines, but overusing it will look ridiculous, so save it for when you really need it. The Moz blog published the results of a fascinating study (*http://bit.ly/TX4A2R*) done by Conductor that measured how well headlines resonate with readers. Of the sample, 36% preferred headlines with a number, which is staggering next to the only 21% who chose the reader addressing style ("You Need to See ") and 17% who chose how-to headlines.

Examples of engaging link bait headlines are:

- Top 6 Weirdest Things About Dog Food
- The 3 Incredible Things Bears Do That You Should Too
- 5 Things Your Spouse Is Hiding from You
- 12 Most Amazing Photos Ever Taken of Hamburgers

Brian Clark on content marketing blog Copyblogger published statistics that 8 out of 10 people will read a headline, but only 2 out of 10 will read the article. This is how important headlines are. Some sites that really get that and are great for inspiration are Huffington Post, Upworthy, Buzzfeed, and Viralnova. In real life, say you are waiting in the checkout line at a grocery store and you see an issue of *Cosmopolitan*. The headlines are consistently juicy and exciting, and make you want to open the magazine right there in line. These are the type of headlines you should strive for. Additionally, David Snyder of content marketing firm CopyPress is quick to state on his blog that "content drives traffic," pointing to the same publications to watch such as *Huffington Post*, *Vice*, and *CBSi*, where publishers are looking to diversify revenue streams by constantly tweaking those headlines and lead-in photos, looking for the perfect hook. Look not just at the headlines and images of the hook, but their positioning on-page, and how sharing elements are baked into the landing page content to encourage further promotion.

Pack your article with quotable phrases and interesting but small graphics. If you have the skills and time, infographics are a good addition to an article. Or, if you're really talented with graphics (or have access to someone who is), a large infographic can be link bait all on its own.

If you need some specific examples of good viral posts, look at the front page of reddit and Techmeme. The articles linked to on these sites *are* what is popular on the Internet today. These are social news sites; they curate newsworthy stories through community voting and discussion.

In terms of submitting links to social news sites, there aren't usually solid rules against it. However, if you're seen as a self-promoter, you will be exposed and downvoted. In some cases you may be blacklisted; community moderators determine what is and is not allowed to be posted, so you are at their mercy in terms of what is right and wrong.

It's perfectly all right—and encouraged!—to post links to your blog on your social network accounts, though. If you've built up a decent-sized community, someone therein will submit your blog post to social news sites all on his own.

Create Apps

Social media apps are important because they have different functions. A Contest app allows you to collect names and emails so that you can do email marketing. Then there are other apps that connect social platforms. For instance, Twitter and YouTube will show up on your Facebook page. It's not that apps aren't good, it's that you need to advertise in order to get your content shown—so you'd run ads to your app, not your page.

The drawback with many apps is that they aren't mobile friendly. Contestdomination.com (*http://contestdomination.com*) is a Facebook app that does provide a separate link to promote to mobile users.

Facebook offers the most prominent and technologically capable application platform, but many other social networks have some kind of API that can be used to create an app or extension. There is usually good documentation on social network app platforms and APIs, and tutorials and examples as well, but if you're serious about a highly professional online appearance, then this isn't something you should do yourself unless you have a strong background in software development. Even then, it's still better to give this task to someone who is already familiar with the platform you're publishing on.

Some popular app development firms are:

- App Development (*http://appdevelopment.com*)
- SocialCubix (*http://socialcubix.com*)
- ConvoSpark (*http://convospark.com*)
- ideavate (*http://ideavate.com*)
- AES Connect (*http://aesconnect.com*)
- ShortStack (*http://shortstack.com*)

You can also try your luck on Elance (*http://elance.com*) or oDesk (*http://odesk.com*).

If you're targeting Facebook, you're probably better off going directly to Facebook's Preferred Marketing Developer (PMD) program. This is a community of top app developers with social media marketing experience.

Real-Life Q&A: Facebook Apps

Q: How much does it usually cost to outsource app development (a range of figures)?

A: The numbers can be all over the map. Facebook app costs can range from as little as $60 to as high as $50,000 depending on your idea and what you want the app to do.

To answer this question in more detail, we need to take a look at what is involved in developing, marketing, and maintaining a Facebook app. While there are a variety of models used to price application outsourcing services, the most prevalent model involves the following components:

- A fixed monthly charge for application support
- A fixed monthly charge for a baseline number of application enhancement hours (typically included as part of the fixed fee for application support), with authorized incremental hours charged on a time and materials basis
- A framework for pricing significant development work on a project-by-project basis on a fixed fee, capped time and materials, or straight time and materials basis

Some developers want to be paid by the hour, and some prefer to be paid per project. The more accurately you can describe the project to the developer, the more accurately he can estimate the price.

For example, Bahndr, by Blue Label Labs, is a $30,000 social game built from scratch with completely custom graphics; it could have cost double that had the project been given to a larger shop.

On top of this, you can expect to spend $8,000–$30,000 on QA testing, depending on the app. The more changes you need to make, the more you will need to spend for your programmers to get rid of any bugs and improve usability.

Beyond development, there are costs associated with getting your app into relevant online stores and marketplaces:

- *Launching the app:* $99 on the App Store, $25 to register on Google Play
- *Infrastructure, servers, and other backend support:* $100–$200/month
- *Social media integration:* $500–$1,500
- *In-app purchasing:* $1,000–$4,000
- *Game Center:* $1,000
- *Marketing:* $1,000–$3,000 on initial marketing campaigns

Table 2-1 gives some ballpark estimates for different types of apps.

Table 2-1. Estimation for different apps

	Deployment/storage	Development time	Expected cost	Example
Simple local app	Everything is installed to the device.	Two to four weeks	$1,500–$4,000	C-Life (helps you track and manage prescriptions).
Database app	Data is stored on a server/database.	Four to eight weeks	$8,000–$50,000	Mime-Me (a fun social app based on charades).
Enterprise app	Integration with corporate backends; data is stored on device and on a server.	Three to six months	At least $50,000, or $150,000 and up for more complex apps	Oracle Business Indicators (mobile access to business intelligence and performance), Cisco WebEx Meetings (mobile web conferencing), TripIt (travel organizer).
Game	N/A	Depends on the type of game	$10,000–$250,000	Freelancer (*http://freelancer.com*) lists a range of app developer rates of $15–$30 per hour. The average cost of a small Facebook app, as of May 2014, was $58; a typical Facebook app cost $520.

Calculate ROI

Anyone who invests funds into social media advertising must know how to correctly measure the social media return on investment that she earns and if needed, alter her strategy to increase the resulting figure.

Plan to start with a small amount of money so that you can form a safe baseline. For example, advertising with Facebook will allow you to decide how much money you want to spend on advertising per day. If you're just starting out, having a daily limit that's relatively low (around $10) is a good idea.

Calculating ROI is fairly easy if you're trying to directly sell a product or service because all that's needed is for you to calculate how much money you earn each day through your advertisement. For example, if you've sold two $90 items on a certain day, and you needed to spend $10 to do so, you've gained an $80 profit. Therefore, for every $10 you spend, you make $80. This will probably scale linearly up to a certain point; we recommend you double a successful ad investment, and continue to do so until you reach the point of diminishing returns. Then scale back to the sweet spot.

When It's More Difficult to Work Out ROI

If your actual goal is to acquire more fans or followers (building your community) instead of directly making product or service sales, calculating your ROI can be more tricky because your return on investment is more long term than short term.

What this means is that if you manage to gain 1,000 followers after investing $35 on advertising, your earnings will amount to zero in the beginning. However, if you develop actual relationships with your followers, in the months ahead your number of followers could increase as friends of your followers start following you as well, and a good amount of these followers could begin purchasing your products.

If you're trying to increase your number of followers, you still need to keep an eye on the activities happening on your chosen social media site. For example, if you're advertising on Facebook, and your daily advertising investment is $10, and there's only a handful of visitors liking your page, your ROI is probably pretty low. If that happens, you'll have to rethink your approach. If, however, your $10 gets you several hundred likes, you could be on to something; keep these fans engaged and interested, and your ROI could end up being reasonably high.

Making Social Media Advertising Work for Your Business

Be prepared to put forth a lot of hard work to make your advertising efforts successful. It's pointless to get fans if you don't plan to give them anything in return. Simply posting affiliate product links, however, is a sure-fire way to quickly lose followers.

Once your page has Likes, be sure to keep your audience engaged! Post images, challenging questions, and interesting comments, and be an eager participant in conversations. Click Like on your fans' pages and comments, too! If you can successfully build solid relationships with your fans, your ROI will most likely be high.

Real-Life Q&A: Metrics and ROI

Q: There are so many tools for measuring demographics and other metrics. You've mentioned a few so far in this book. Some of them cost a lot of money, but seem like they might be useful. What tools should I really be using, with so many to choose from?

A: Start with the free stuff. Maybe that's all you'll ever need, and maybe you'll hit a limitation at some point and need to switch to a commercial alternative. Facebook and YouTube have free metrics built into their services. Use those to their full extent. Google Analytics is both free and effective, and can be implemented on a number of different websites. You can nab a ton of great information from this tool that most other web analytics packages provide only at a price.

Q: Is there any basic analytics advice you can give someone who makes a lot of mistakes? I'm, uh, asking for my friend.

A: The problem with measuring social media success, and why it's often so difficult for business owners and marketers, is that we look at it in social media terms rather than in business terms. One of the top mistakes that businesses make is focusing on indirect successes like how many followers, fans, and shares they have, when really they need to be looking at the same old metrics that they use in traditional marketing: revenue, cost, and sales volume.

Q: All right, I've set up some analytics, and I'm now flooded with data. What should I look for among all these charts and percentages?

A: There are some metrics that marketers and business owners tend to pick up on and know that they have to measure, like the number of visitors you're getting from social media and customer conversions. But there are other metrics that you should be looking at too:

- Lead conversions (both hard and soft conversions)
- Cost per lead
- Cost per click
- Cost per inbound link
- Cost per site visit

Q: What is *segmenting* social media leads?

A: Segmenting your leads is basically taking the leads you have and separating them into groups. Segmentation allows for more exact and effective targeting, and enables you to send unique messages. For instance, you can segment by social behavior, geography, and website interactions.

Q: Do I need to segment social media leads?

A: Yes! If you want to run an effective online marketing campaign, and if you want to be able to accurately go about measuring your social media ROI, then you need to segment those leads. Segmenting your leads allows you to know not only what their motivators and problems are, but also what sort of content you need to produce and post to social media in order to move them along the sales cycle and increase conversions.

Don't Break the Rules

How do you make sure that, as a business, you're generating meaningful engagement with your customers? That in the conversation, your business is coming across as social media savvy? There are three social media rules that businesses often violate.

Think Before You Share

The Internet never forgets. Social media may feel casual, intimate, and temporary, but your posts, comments, hashtags, likes, and images can be indexed, cached, and accessed forever. Deleting something makes it only slightly less easy to find.

Approach social media content like any other aspect of your business communications: professionally, and with a plan. Engage appropriately with your customers. If someone writes an angry rant about your product on your Facebook page, it's an opportunity to demonstrate to other potential customers the value your business places on customer service. Social media is not the place to respond with an angry insult.

Don't Flood the Feed

A common complaint about businesses on social media is their tendency to flood the feed. This means mass postings, updates, or tweets that overwhelm a user's feed, and lead very quickly to unfollowing, removing, or blocking your posts. Updating regularly is important to keep people engaged, but putting 10 posts about sales, new products, or other news up at once is a fast way to turn them off.

Attribute, Attribute, Attribute

While a lot of people are happy to share their work, and Creative Commons licensing is more and more widespread, this doesn't mean it's OK to use people's work without attribution—especially if you're a business. Nothing will anger people faster than using their words, images, or other creative work without asking permission or properly attributing the work.

This is a big problem on Pinterest, for example, and the site has created an "attribution statement" for specific websites, such as Etsy and Flickr, to try to address it. It's good business practice to show that you understand the importance of this, and give the creators credit where appropriate.

Summary

By this point you're probably champing at the bit. Whatever mysteries you harbored about social media marketing have just been fed with fresh clues, and you're ready to start taking action right now. You've scribbled down some ballpark figures for goals and spending, and you've got some great ideas for Facebook posts and how you're going to customize your Twitter account.

Hang on, though—remember what we said about tactics without strategy? While blindly applying some of the cool tricks we've talked about in this chapter will probably give you some kind of improvement over your current condition, you are in danger of hitting a wall of failure and frustration after your initial efforts fail to meet your expectations. That's why we've designed the following three chapters to funnel your efforts into productive strategies that will help your business. It's extremely important to use the right tool for the job. It's also important to be patient and roll out a social media marketing plan from a place of calm, educated determination.

Continue on to Chapter 3 if your business is selling physical goods through a website.

If you are selling a service or something that doesn't have to be shipped or delivered in person, then head directly to Chapter 4.

If you have a local storefront or restaurant, Chapter 5 was written specifically for you.

Head over to the *Social eCommerce* site (*http://www.socialecommercebook.com*) for more Q&A and to post your own burning questions!

You'll also have access to exclusive offers, discounts, and coupon codes on various social media tools and services.

To get exclusive access to instructional videos related to the concepts in the chapter, simply send a text with your email address to *+1(213)947-9990* and we'll send you some awesome links!

CHAPTER 3

Marketing Strategy: Physical Goods

In the beginning of this book, we said that a successful strategy has three components: intention, context, and tactics. This is why we have separated the sale of physical goods —things that have to be stocked, pulled, packed, shipped, and warrantied—from the sale of other sorts of things. There is a much higher barrier to entry for a physical sale compared with other categories. A click on a link can put an item and a quantity into a shopping cart, but the customer has to type in a lot of extra information to complete the sale. When you put it into the proper perspective, it's easy to see why a "physical goods" ecommerce business wouldn't want to use tactics designed for local businesses or service providers.

A strong, competent social media presence will give you a competitive advantage that separates you from your competitors. This is especially important in industries that sell goods with long life cycles, such as tools and appliances. We've spoken to people at marketing conferences who have very expensive, high-margin, niche-market, highly reliable products that they sell to customers on a 10-year sales cycle. Losing one customer is a significant problem for the whole company. Those are extreme cases, but the sentiment applies across the physical goods market segment: you've got to have the right alignment of intention, context, and tactics to complete the sale.

Physical Goods That Do Well on Social Media

No matter what you're selling, a good social media presence will help you in some way —direct sales, customer service, or brand awareness. In our combined experience, though, companies in or closely related to the following industries see a much more significant sales increase through social media:

- Merchandise linked to bands, TV shows, movies, celebrities, and other pop culture/ entertainment categories
- Tickets to events

- Limited-edition items
- Auction sites (local, traditional auctions are more like local events or services, and require a different strategy)
- Supplies featured in videos/training programs
- Children's items
- Specific problem solvers that can't be found in stores easily
- Specialist equipment
- Pet supplies: food, treats, beds, toys
- Craft supplies: plans, materials, kits, training
- DVD sets: personal development, unique or difficult-to-find items

Basically, anything that someone can't easily go out to a store nearby and pick up locally, or something that has to be highly customized, is going to do well with a good social media strategy.

Let's restate that for emphasis:

> Hard-to-find and/or hard-to-get items, both of which get lots of search traffic and motivated consumer interest on the Internet, represent major business opportunities in ecommerce. Companies that focus on the hard-to-find and hard-to-get will have an easy time increasing sales through social media marketing.

The Right Intent

Being successful on social media means engaging people with interesting content. You must start with this mindset; if you don't, you'll default to "sales mode," and be ignored by the people you're spending time and money to reach. Social media is where people go to hang out and have fun with their friends. That makes it a bad environment for selling stuff; everyone is focused on the content (the messages, photos, and links to interesting things), not the sales pitches. Sales pitches are not usually shareable or interesting to people who just want to have a good time, unless your pitch is so over-the-top that people enjoy making fun of it (think Billy Mays and the ShamWow Guy). So the focus here is developing shareable content while reducing the salesy-sounding stuff. Here are some guidelines for staying in the right frame of mind:

Bigger isn't better.
> You don't need tons of fans to make sales. Social media engagement is definitely a "quality over quantity" situation. Overlook the vanity metrics: likes, fans, friends, and followers. Instead, focus on the actions that drive sales.

Incorporate ratings and reviews on your sales pages.
Make them prominent. This is an excellent way to get simple, introductory engagement.

Reward people for referrals and recommendations.
Figure out why your current customers recommend you, and start using this information to assist with your sales follow-ups.

Ask for the testimonial ASAP.
Get that review while the positive experience is still fresh in the customer's mind—not months later.

Engage.
Look for a problem you can solve and a question you can answer, and send a relevant, helpful response.

Listen.
Look for buying signals: questions, concerns, and complaints.

Be authentic.
Show the real you with photos of yourself, your staff, and your office. Show that you're a real business by posting videos of your office or warehouse.

Your site is your home.
Facebook "storefronts" are generally not successful; people prefer to purchase on your website. When people view your content, they view it in their News Feed; they rarely go back to your storefront.

Converting Leads into Customers

Hopefully you didn't expect to just sign up on Facebook, post a few marketing messages, and kick back to watch the orders pour in. If so, if our advice up to this point hasn't sunk in then now's the time to sober up.

You have to do more than post stuff to social media. That serves a purpose and it is important, but it's not the whole plan. To turn more friends and fans into customers, you've got to create plenty of content to support the sales process. That means how-to guides, videos, case studies of success stories, newsletters, updates, niche landing pages, in-person events, conference attendance coverage and reports, blog posts, and podcasts. This is called education-based marketing.

One of the mistakes that businesses make when entering the social network realm is that they overfocus on indirect successes like how many followers, fans, and shares they have. Beware! The same criteria apply in the social network marketing world as in the traditional marketing, brick-and-mortar world: *revenue, cost,* and *sales volume.* Social media is often looked at as being different and special when compared to traditional marketing, but the basic theory and most of the intention behind the practice are actually quite similar. Think about how you've successfully taken "cold" leads and turned them into "warm" leads in the past, through other channels. Identify the key triggers and steps you took to convert them, then think about how you can transfer that to social media. Here are some basic tips:

Build an email list.
> Pay once; promote forever for free. Since someone's already bought from you once, that makes that person an excellent target for your new products, events, advice, and feedback. Practically every successful ecommerce business does this.

Make it easy for people to purchase.
> PayPal and other checkout services will help get you more sales because your customers will already have an account set up. All they have to do is sign in and complete the sale. You also won't have the added security concerns with handling and potentially storing credit card data and personal information.

Link directly to the item's sales page whenever possible.
> Sometimes the best landing page is the product page, assuming it has good navigation and is easy to perform a low-effort sale for your visitors.

Provide incentives.
> Offer discounts for customers who write reviews (on social media, Yelp, or your product page), or for people who like/friend/follow your page. Be careful not to cross the ethical line of requesting that people write positive reviews.

Forming a Superior Strategy

Now that you've established proper context and intention for the sale of physical goods on social media, it's time to commit to a plan. Use this list as a framework for your strategy:

Prepare your landing pages_. Don't start marketing until your sales infrastructure is ready. Make sure all of your ducks are in a row on your online store.

Set goals and checkpoints.
> How many sales and/or referrals is it reasonable to expect from your social media work? This is a hard question to answer accurately. Try to choose a conservative estimate so that you aren't discouraged with sluggish results. Some markets can be slow to reach, and will take more effort over a longer period of time.

Make a content plan.
> We published a good content plan in Chapter 2 that you can easily adapt for your market. You must have some kind of plan for how things are going to play out. For instance, it does no good to offer an amazing deal if you just set up your Facebook

page 10 minutes ago. You need an audience first, and then you need some engagement, and *then* you can push it over the edge with a special offer.

Establish a presence.
Identify the social networks that you're prepared to maintain a presence on and set up your pages there. Make sure it's fully customized and has a good account name that represents you properly.

Build a "starter" audience.
Advertise and promote your social media pages to build an audience. Only you can determine how much is a good minimum target. It may be 500 Twitter followers, or 1,000 Facebook likes. This is just the beginning—what you jumpstart your social media marketing effort with. This number is not the endgame goal. You should have some good starter content to post as well; this might be a good time to release some of your supporting material—the how-to guides and other ancillary marketing materials that you will offer on a permanent or long-term basis.

Execute your content plan.
Start posting on the schedule that you've laid out for yourself. Your content plan might allow for a minimal audience at first, so you don't necessarily have to wait until you have your target "starter" audience in order to start posting.

Increase engagement.
Now that you're up and running, the stats and feedback should have some hints as to what kind of content is and is not working. Streamline your efforts, adjust your content plan, and advertise and promote to gain maximum engagement (not maximum likes/fans—you only want good leads at this point).

Site-Specific Tactics

Now that you have a plan, you must identify tactics to help you achieve it. We've already covered the basics in the previous chapter, but now we're going to get more specific for your industry segment.

When it comes to selling physical goods, there are few social media boundaries. Which networks will give you the most return for your time and money is more about the kind of things you are selling. LinkedIn, for instance, is probably going to be a total loser for you if you're selling custom poker chips. If you're selling a revolutionary new kind of office chair, however, it might yield some results.

Facebook

Facebook should be your go-to social network for advertising physical goods. The ads are usually inexpensive, the audience is gigantic and diverse, you can easily target a specific market, and it's easy to announce promotions.

Some products are sold through a long-term sales process, and others are impulse buys. Figure out which one your product is—this may be different online than it is in a physical storefront—and modify your strategy to account for it. If it's over the impulse buy threshold (if visitors have to research or think about it, or invest a lot of cash), then you're better off getting an opt-in to build your list and reconnect with them later. Simple, inexpensive, no-brainer purchases are within the impulse buy limits and can be sold directly very effectively. If you're selling many different products, it will take some work to determine the threshold for your customers. If it's over the threshold, then direct your Facebook ad to an opt-in landing page that starts the sales process with a good initial message and a quick and simple name and email collection form; if it's under the threshold, then it's an impulse buy, and you should direct the click to the ecommerce product page for that item.

Regardless of which path you take, don't change your tracking code or analytics. You still want to know how people are finding you and what they're doing while they're on your site.

Twitter

Twitter is useful for customer service and brand/product awareness, but it isn't much of an advertising platform. If you have a decent number of followers, Twitter is great for announcing sales, new products, deals (if you want to track Twitter referrals, make a special "Twitter only" deal), coupons, and specials. For selling physical goods, Twitter is a secondary network. It's worth participating, but the benefits are indirect.

YouTube

YouTube does offer advertising, and it is worth your while to do a preliminary ad campaign through sponsored videos and in-video ads. It's going to be more expensive than Facebook, but you definitely want to keep YouTube in mind as an advertising platform once things get rolling.

Nothing you post on Twitter will ever go viral and make thousands of sales for you. A good video, however, can do exactly that.

YouTube was practically made for product demos. It's almost impossible to talk about the benefit of YouTube without slipping into "case study" mode, which we've already done with Blendtec earlier in this book. There are hundreds of great examples out there, but one that comes immediately to mind for the subject of physical goods ecommerce direct sales is Pro Guitar Shop (*http://bit.ly/U6v95R*). The store's frontman, Andy, posts videos that expertly demonstrate guitars, effects pedals, and amps. Occasionally he'll also post a video showing how to play famous classic rock songs, featuring equipment that Pro Guitar Shop sells. The store also advertises its contests and giveaways in its YouTube videos to drive traffic back to the store site. The contests are, of course, opt-ins for the weekly email newsletter. It's a brilliantly planned and executed marketing operation. As of the publication of this book, Pro Guitar Shop had more than 100,000 subscribers on YouTube.

This is how one privately owned storefront in Oregon can compete with huge national chains like Guitar Center and Sam Ash. In many instances these stores sell the same equipment at the same prices, and have the same manufacturer-sponsored sales at the same times. All other things being equal, social media engagement and good content can end up being the deciding factor for someone with cash to spend.

Instagram

Instagram is hugely popular, and it would be foolish to ignore it. On the other hand, it's difficult for some businesses to figure out how to use it effectively. It can be great way to get some buzz going around your brand. The catch is—as with any marketing effort —that you need to figure out why you're using it, determine what theme or message you're hoping to convey with your content, and then continually engage with other Instagram users.

Unlike other social networking sites, Instagram doesn't offer a separate type of account for business. It's also not web-based; it's an app for smartphones and tablets. You can only sign up for an account on an iPhone, iPad, or Android device.

Ford Motor Company has a great Instagram page, shown in Figure 3-1.

If you've determined that Instagram is useful to you and you are committed to making it a part of your overall strategy, the first step is to establish an account and get the app onto your devices.

Next, connect your account to your other ecommerce social media profiles, like Twitter and Facebook. Connecting your social media accounts will allow you to easily find others to follow on Instagram. It will also allow for easy cross-network sharing of your photos.

Unlike some other social networks, you can and should start posting content right away, but don't neglect community building. You ultimately need followers on Instagram in order to succeed there, but people aren't going to follow an account with no pictures. So what's a good amount of starter content? Perhaps 5 to 10 good, shareable images— or more, if you've got a lot of material to work with. Your instinct is probably to post photos of your products, and that's fine; it's a good idea. Just don't get locked into think-ing that this is the only kind of photo that you can or should share. Change things up, keep things fresh, and constantly ask yourself what images speak to your brand's per-sonality. Here are a few ideas for types of photos you could post:

Figure 3-1. Instagram web profile for Ford (http://www.instagram.com/ford)

Action shots.
> Don't just post perfectly lit "studio shots" of your products. Show people using them effectively. Show people having fun using them. These should be candid photos, not composed ones—or at least, they should appear as though they are candid.

Behind-the-scenes photos.
> Show some of the personality behind your brand. Introduce fans to your staff and to your family, or snap photos of "a day in the life of Sue's Shoes' CEO." You can even create a special hashtag to highlight the production of your products, from factory to floor—for instance, #MakingSuesShoes.

Contests.
> Contests are a great way to connect with customers and to spread the word about your products. Solicit photos from your customers, and give them a contest-specific hashtag to use. For instance, for Sue's Shoes you can ask participants to post a picture of their favorite shoes with the hashtag #WinSuesShoes. Better yet, have them post a picture of their favorite pair of Sue's Shoes.

Something crazy.
> This is not for everyone, but if your brand supports it, try posting something bizarre yet related to your products. It just may attract the attention of people who have previously ignored your images.

There are three good ways to find people to connect with:

Use Instagram's "Find and Invite Friends" feature.
> If you didn't already do this when you went through the registration process, simply open the Instagram app, click on the gear icon at the top right of your profile, and select "Find and Invite Friends."

Search for users and hashtags on Instagram.
> Look for people and hashtags who are related to your industry. There may be other businesses you can follow that are related to your industry but aren't direct competitors.

Comment on other people's pictures.
> This gets your name out there in front of a lot of other people who can potentially follow you. Commenting on photos is far more effective than simply clicking Like. If nothing else, definitely comment on photos that mention your brand.

You may also want to set up a dedicated page on your ecommerce site for Instagram photos. Not all of your customers (or potential customers) are going to be on Instagram; why should they miss out on the fun? Create a separate page on your site just for your Instagram photos. There are a few third-party sites that allow you to easily do this. The ones we're aware of are:

- Websta (*http://web.stagram.com*)
- Followgram (*http://followgram.me*)
- IconoSquare (*http://iconosquare.com*)

Hashtags are extremely important on Instagram. They enable your image to be indexed on each tag's page, which makes it easy for people to search for and find your images. For example, if your ecommerce business (Sue's Shoes) sells designer shoes, you may want to use hashtags like #designershoes, #shoes, and #suesshoes. You can also use hashtags that describe specific products or product lines.

A word of warning: use popular hashtags sparingly. While they do receive lots of searches and uses, this also means your image won't stay at the top of the list for long. #shoes, for instance, is too popular to get much exposure from, as you can see in Figure 3-2.

Figure 3-2. Searching for hashtags

Instead, use less popular, more specific hashtags so that you can have more than a few seconds in the spotlight. Also, when you first start out—and periodically thereafter—check to see what hashtags others are using for photos that are similar to yours, and try them out.

Instagram allows you to add a brief description called a *caption* beside your photos. Use captions to add a bit of personality to your photos, emphasize your message, or add alternate perspectives to your images.

You can also tag photos of your favorite followers and they can do the same for you. To do this, tap a spot on a photo and select a user's name.

Be sure to let your other social media followers and contacts know that you're on Instagram so that they can begin following you. Even users without a smartphone or tablet can view and follow your photos by accessing your web profile or the dedicated Instagram page on your website.

Pinterest

Much of what we've said about Instagram applies to Pinterest. Social photo-sharing strategy doesn't change much among different sites. Pinterest has a few fundamental differences from Instagram, though: it's a real website (not reliant on mobile devices), you can pin videos as well as photos, you can put prices on images (which will add them to the Gifts section), hashtags aren't very useful, and boards make it much easier to organize photos by subject.

Pinterest is widely known as a source of recipes. So if you've got a food-related business, photos of the recipe, the process of making it, and the finished product are all excellent Pinterest content. Pinterest also does well with apparel retailers; you can pin several different views of an article of clothing, show it on different models with different colors and sizes, or perhaps show a celebrity wearing it.

If you can, include text on the actual image; it will increase the photo's chances of being shared. Also include prices with all of your product images. According to ecommerce software and service provider Shopify, pins with prices get *36% more likes* than those without. Unlike social networks like Facebook or Twitter, which are focused much more on social interaction than products, you don't need to be worried about scaring people off by including prices on Pinterest. In fact, including a dollar sign with your pin will make it appear in the Gifts section of the site (see Figure 3-3).

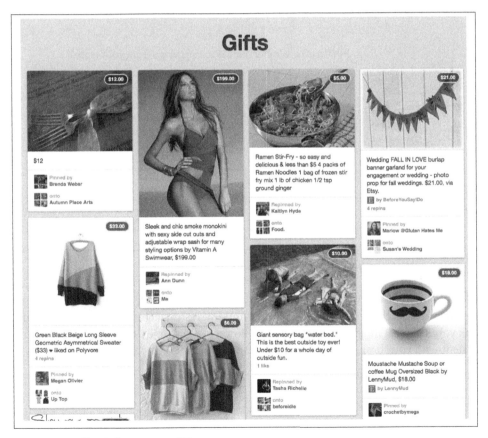

Figure 3-3. The Gifts section of Pinterest

Pinterest may be product-based, but it is completely fueled by user interaction. Show some appreciation for your loyal and active pinners by making sure you follow them, repinning their content, and engaging with them by commenting on their pins. You can even create a *repin* board specifically for posting their pins.

Don't count on your ecommerce site visitors having a Pin It bookmarklet or browser plug-in. Although avid users will likely have one of these, many users will not. To accommodate them, include a Pin It button where appropriate on your site so that your photos are easy to share, but don't overdo it. You can also use the Button and Widget Builder to install board widgets on your site to enable you to invite people to follow your pins or use the cool mouseover widget that shows the Pinterest logo when you hover your mouse over a picture (Figure 3-4).

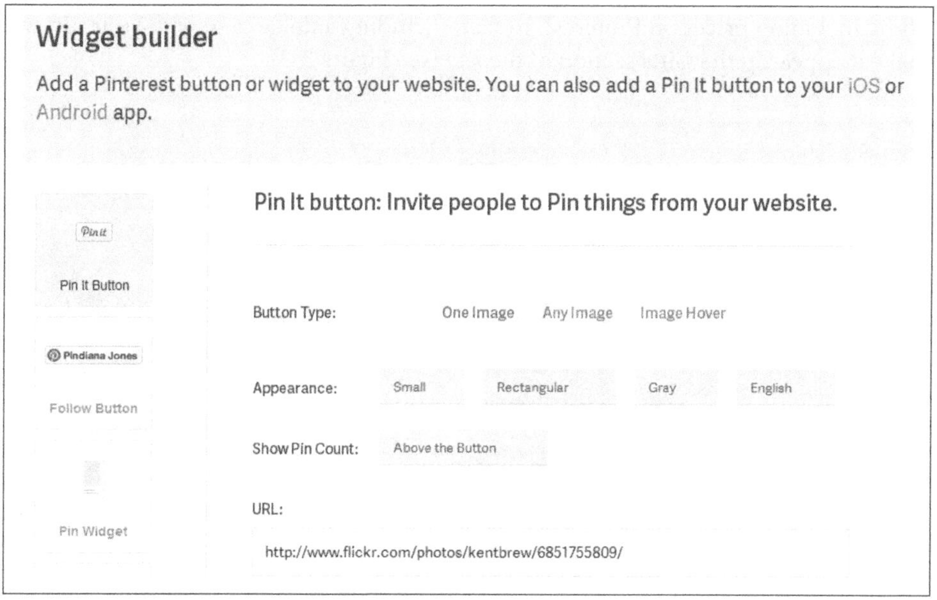

Figure 3-4. Pinterest Button and Widget Builder

Don't just pin products; pin other types of images as well, such as quotes, memes, and creative images that your audience would find interesting. Think outside the box and ask yourself what images or quotes your followers would enjoy that would also be consistent with your brand. 3-5 and 3-6 show some examples of such content.

Figure 3-5. An example of a pinnable ad graphic that doesn't directly advertise a product

Include good keywords in your image description. This will increase the chances of someone finding your pin, both through Pinterest's internal search and through external search engines. Hashtags are not effective on Pinterest, and won't increase a keyword's searchability. However, if you include hashtags in your description, and you link your Pinterest account to your Twitter account, the hashtags will transfer to Twitter posts. On Pinterest, however, a hashtag is not distinguishable from a normal word or phrase in the description.

Figure 3-6. Another example of an interesting ad graphic that will help you build a following without being too "salesy"

Also put a call to action in your description. It's OK to admit that you're a retailer on Pinterest, so go ahead and include a good call to action in your pin's description (see Figure 3-7). Use phrases like "Click image to buy," or "Visit our site for more info." Links in descriptions don't work, but interested users can copy and paste the URL.

Figure 3-7. An example of a good call to action that shows the product in a creative way

Leverage other social networks to increase Pinterest followers; promote your pins to your Facebook fans and Twitter followers. A great way to do this is to hold a "pin it to win it" contest, and promoting it via other social networks.

Case Study: Pinterest versus Facebook

In early 2012, online fashion and jewelry retailer Boticca (*http://boticca.com*) compared how Pinterest fared against Facebook in terms of engagement levels, conversions, and sales on its primary website.

Based on a sample of 50,000 Facebook users and 50,000 Pinterest users, Boticca found that Pinterest users are typically not as engaged as Facebook users, and don't convert as well. However, overall:

- Pinterest users spend more than twice as much as Facebook users ($180 average spend compared to $85 spend).

- Pinterest influenced 10% of Boticca's overall transactions, compared to 7% from Facebook.

- Pinterest helped Boticca acquire 86% more new users, as compared to 57% from Facebook.

As with all social networks, the more active you are on Pinterest, the greater the benefits to your business. And when used properly, Pinterest holds ever-increasing potential for ecommerce businesses to increase engagement, visibility, and sales.

Tumblr

The multimedia-rich nature of the platform makes Tumblr an obvious choice for businesses with high-quality photos or videos that need some traction. If you're not able to get high-quality photos of your products, then Tumblr probably isn't for you.

Tumblr is also largely about *curating* content (collecting and sorting through images and videos on a particular theme), and presenting and commenting on the most valuable pieces. Content curation certainly can involve sharing your own content, but it also means sharing excellent content by others. Only interested in posting photos of your product? Then Tumblr may not work as well for you as you'd hope.

To this point, one of the industries that is using Tumblr most effectively is the fashion industry. This probably comes as no surprise, given the highly graphic nature of the industry. In fact, the very first ecommerce business to jump on the Tumblr wagon was Of a Kind (*http://www.ofakind.com*), a company that commissions limited-run pieces and promotes them until they're sold out. (See Figure 3-8.)

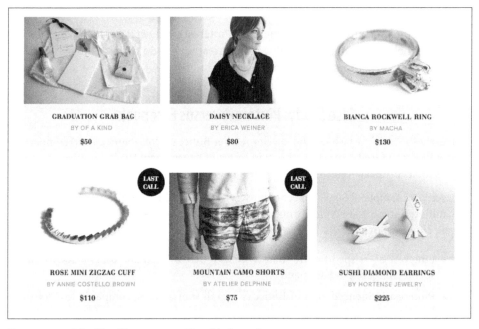

Figure 3-8. Of a Kind has a great Tumblr-based store

Claire Mazure, one of the company's founders, said at the time of its launch, "We're bringing our product to a place where our customers are already sharing things they love. I think Tumblr lends itself really well to the distribution of visual content. There's a rabid fashion following on Tumblr. And it targets early adopters."

Case Study: Purveying Curiously Awesome Products

Vat19.com (*http://vat19.com*) bills itself as a "purveyor of curiously awesome products." We have to admit that in researching for this case study, we were struck by just how awesome a lot of those products really are (see Figure 3-9).

Figure 3-9. A sampling of Vat19.com (http://vat19.com)'s "curiously awesome products"

The site's owner, Jamie Salvatori, didn't jump right into social media:

> I was slow to believe in social media. Frankly, I'm not a huge fan of it from a personal perspective. I remember staring at the status update box on Twitter and wondering to myself, "What the hell do I have to say that would be of any interest to anybody?" It was very intimidating, so I didn't bother.

> Essentially, it wasn't until I started seeing Facebook URLs on TV commercials that I thought it was necessary for my business. I didn't think it would drive sales and I wasn't sure how we would use it. I thought that we wouldn't have much to say other than to announce new products or videos, which I thought would be redundant to our website.

Despite being experienced in ecommerce, Jamie admits that there were some early flaws in his social media marketing plan:

> The two biggest mistakes were being so late to the party, and thinking that direct response advertising would work on social media.

> We were one of the first to try Facebook Ads. We did it all wrong. We tried to get people to leave Facebook, come to our website, and buy something. It was a nightmare. It just doesn't work that way.

> In my experience, we could only use social ads to drive people to become fans of our page. But even that wasn't cost-effective because the value of a "purchased" fan appears to be quite low. We track the conversions from every imaginable source. Social platforms have the lowest conversion rates and the lowest number of conversions. It just doesn't drive new sales in the way that the search engines drive sales.

> That being said, there is other value in social networks for businesses. The beauty of the social network is to leverage a person's existing personal connections to promote your company. So, while you can create opportunities for existing customers to introduce your brand to their network of friends, I don't think it always works well for the company to be the one to make that initial introduction.

> Essentially, we see Facebook as the ultimate platform for running a fan club for your business. We assume that the people who have liked us on Facebook are superfans and we try to give them the tools to promote us to their friends. We try to provide more personal, behind-the-scenes engagement on social media.

No matter how you start out, your social media strategy has to evolve. Here's how Jamie stays current:

> I read a few technology blogs to keep track of the bleeding edge. I also watch where my friends are engaged. It isn't that difficult to find out "what's hot" if you keep your eyes open.

> Our strategy has evolved from at first trying to use it as a direct sales channel to treating it more as a fan club platform. Once you view it in that light, it gives you a lot of great ideas for what to post.

> Additionally, social media has become an ad hoc customer support mechanism. However, that's simply a function of it being easier for a customer to fire off a tweet to @Vat19 than to load up our website, find the customer support form, and fill it out. There is also some marketing advantage in other users seeing how quickly we handle the situation.

Lastly, we asked Jamie to estimate how much it would cost to try to get these kinds of results without social media (using traditional advertising, marketing, and customer support methods):

> All advertising works. It's just a matter of effectiveness. I don't think that social media is an effective method for achieving direct sales. Or perhaps it's simply difficult to measure because the cycle can be complicated. Seriously, where did that order originate? That's a very difficult problem to solve as it could be a combination of many sources.

> Again, I see social media as a fairly personalized medium, which is why I think that businesses should view their connections as superfans. These are your best customers. They are the ones who buy from you on a consistent basis. Your goal is to keep them

happy, keep them engaged, and keep them talking about you to their friends. This may happen via their network or it may happen via word of mouth.

I think it would be impossible to create a social "fan club" without social networks. They provide a lot of value, but it can be easy to overstate its effectiveness. Basically, don't put all your eggs in one basket. Stay engaged with social networks, but don't lose sight of your goal as a business: sell stuff. Amassing fans is not the end goal. You can't pay the bank with likes. Rather, use it as a barometer. If you're getting more fans, you're probably doing a lot of other things correctly in your business.

It would be criminal to mention Vat19's social strategy without also mentioning its YouTube channel. Its introduction video hits all the high notes: "Our killer philosophy is to present killer products with killer photography, killer video, and killer descriptions." The channel has just under 700,000 subscribers, and they have over 440 million views across all their videos. The company's success comes from its remarkability. It of course shows advertisements featuring a product, but adds an extra flashy and shareable element to each. For instance, the video for its product "The Beardo" (*http://bit.ly/ 1jxTNsj*), shown in Figure 3-10, features funny graphics.

Figure 3-10. Vat19's "Beardo" hat

The Vat19 YouTube channel has also created quite the reputation with its product music videos. The videos use over-the-top flashiness paired with a mock-serious attitude that perfectly fits the products being sold. The result is a super-shareable, hilarious promotional video. Figure 3-11 shows a screenshot from a music video (*http://bit.ly/ 1nl2JRa*) the company made to promote its 26-pound gummy bear.

Figure 3-11. Vat19's promotional video for its 26-pound gummy bear

Real-Life Q&A: Expanding Your Reach

Q: I built up a decent audience with ads and on-site promotion, and I am sticking to my content plan, but very few people are interacting with me. I've got 500 likes on Facebook, but no one is commenting on my posts. Where am I going wrong?

A: The number of likes or friends doesn't represent your actual reach. Posting something on Facebook puts it only on a small fraction of those 500 News Feeds. If there is some initial engagement, the reach expands to a larger percentage. Those first few likes and comments determine whether more people are exposed to your content.

That's pretty frustrating, isn't it? It's a catch-22.

You may not be posting content that is interesting enough. It may not be engage-worthy. Ask questions that people will want to answer. Let them speak out about something. If you're selling cellphone accessories, post a photo of an old rolodex and ask people what they did to stay in touch with friends before they had a cellphone. If you're selling beauty products, ask your fans what makeup items they carry with them at all times.

Always include an eye-catching image. They'll be seeing your post in their newsfeed and you need to catch their attention and pique their interest. Another way you can increase engagement is to ask folks to play fun games like "Name a city in California that doesn't have an *i* in it." Theme your posts, like Hangman Wednesday. Those are the types of posts that are engaging and will get comments.

You may not have done anything wrong in setting up the ad. The problem may lie in your headline, image, ad copy, or call-to-action. You should get in the habit of split-testing your ads to discover the best performing variants.

Content must be more than just interesting. Many people are content to sit back and read interesting content, but unless it inspires engagement, they aren't going to interact with you.

Q: I tried to make Google+ work for me by cross-posting all of my Facebook posts, and then by writing posts with unique content, but there's just no interaction. I'm in 11 circles after months of posting. My girlfriend, somehow, is in more than 1,000 circles, and all she does is post pictures of puppies and romantic movie quotes. Is that the secret— puppies?

A: Maybe. Google+ interaction is heavily skewed in favor of picture posts and other things that people can admire at a glance and click +1 on. There's a good opportunity to reuse content that you post to Instagram here. You can also host all of your pictures in Picasa (the picture app built into Google+) and pin them or link out to them elsewhere (as opposed to hosting them on Flickr or Facebook).

Maybe pictures of puppies aren't such a bad idea. Borrow someone's puppy and pose it with your product. Make LOLcat memes about your brand.

Or you could have your girlfriend run your Google+ campaign for you. Clearly she has some natural talent!

Summary

As an ecommerce entrepreneur selling physical things on the Web, you should now have a realistic impression of how social media can benefit you. Social media is not a miracle cure for anything, but it is a necessary component of a business that is at or near the top of its potential.

You now also know what will and won't work in terms of content posted to social media. If you've already begun a social media marketing effort and are reading this book to get some tips on how to achieve more success, we're certain you've run into at least one forehead-slapping moment in this chapter. It's not too late to reform your social media strategy.

The next two chapters deal with selling digital goods and services, and marketing a local storefront. There is some overlap in content among these three chapters, but there are many key differences in how a strategy is formed and refined, and some of the tactics are dramatically different. Read on if you're curious, but try not to let the wrong wisdom influence what you've learned in this chapter. It makes more sense to go directly to Chapter 6 to learn more about how to design good social media ads and run successful advertising campaigns.

Head over to the *Social eCommerce* site (*http://www.socialcommercebook.com*) for more Q&A and to post your own burning questions! You'll also have access to exclusive offers, discounts, and coupon codes on various social media tools and services.

To get exclusive access to instructional videos related to the concepts in the chapter, simply send a text with your email address to *+1(213)947-9990* and we'll send you some awesome links!

CHAPTER 4

Marketing Strategy: Digital Goods and Services

If you just read Chapter 3, there probably isn't going to be much in this chapter that is useful to you. In fact, some of the information here could be harmful, if applied, because it is geared toward a completely different market than the advice in Chapter 3. If your ecommerce business is not selling digital goods and services (such as webinars, ebooks, software licenses, online media streaming, etc.), then skip this chapter and head to Chapter 6 to get a comprehensive education on ad design and testing.

In the beginning of this book, we said that a successful strategy has three components: intention, context, and tactics. This is why we have separated the sale of digital goods and services—things that are delivered and consumed digitally—from the sale of other sorts of things. There is a low barrier to entry for this kind of sale compared with other categories. This is where impulse buys thrive, and viral marketing can bring a tidal wave of sales.

The key to successful ecommerce sales is driving prospects to opt in, partake in free samples, and make impulse purchases. You can use these separately or combine them. We'll get into the details for both of these approaches in this chapter.

Let's start with Figure 4-1, which shows a sales funnel as a visualization and planning guide for your business.

Leads come into the top of the funnel through advertising and marketing channels such as Facebook ads, Google ads, SEO, radio ads, billboards, etc. At the top of the funnel is a lead magnet. This has to be an irresistible offer, basically an ethical bribe. In exchange for someone's name and email, you're offering this great piece of information. It can be a report, video, or downloadable tool—ideally something that is consumed in 5–10 minutes maximum. If it is longer than that, the person will feel obligated to wait until she has time to consume the whole thing, which can slow the sales process.

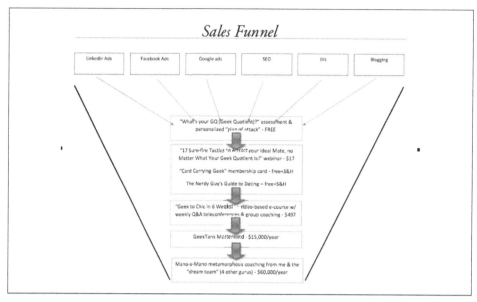

Figure 4-1. Sales funnel of Stephan Spencer's self-help products/services, offering personal transformation assistance for geeks

Next in the funnel is the *tripwire*. A tripwire is a low-cost physical or virtual product that is offered to clients. It can be a book that is free (other than shipping and handling), or an online lesson or webinar for a low amount of money. As an example, say you sell guitar lessons. A great tripwire would be a low-cost lesson on how to play the F chord, since it is difficult for learners. Once people are pleased with the result they got from the tripwire, they are more likely to buy the core product. Frank Kern calls this "results in advance." This "trains" people to get used to spending money with you. Essentially, you are creating a list of buyers. Consider making your tripwire a physical product that you ship. Nobody wants to go all the way to the post office to return an item just to get a few dollars back.

Automation is so important in this step. Although this is the lowest amount of profit, this step is critical in warming up a list of buyers for your core product and for profit maximizers. But you don't want to waste talent on the low tiers of profit, you want to use it on the narrower end of the funnel. This is where automation comes in. If your tripwire is something like a webinar, using automated emails or texts as reminders can dramatically increase the show rate for webinars (which is usually less than half of the sign-up rate).

The core product is the next thing in the funnel. This could be a $97 ebook, a $200 video-based course, or something else in that higher price range.

Profit maximizers are at the small end of the funnel. They could be a live event, a group coaching program, or a yearlong mastermind program. If you don't sell profit maximizers, only your core product, you're leaving on the table easily half the amount of money that you could potentially make.

Change one-on-one consulting into a group coaching model. This means moving from addressing individuals by one person at a time through your product, to addressing an entire group simultaneously. Because you are addressing all of your clients at once, this is the most fiscally smart and time wise option. It allows you to achieve scale.

Digital Goods and Services That Do Well on Social Media

No matter what you're selling, a good social media presence will help you in some way —direct sales, customer service, or brand awareness. In our combined experience, though, companies in these industries see a much more significant sales increase through social media:

- Books (links to Amazon/Audible; this is a grey area in terms of strategy because you probably aren't doing the fulfillment yourself)
- "Daily deals" sites, such as Groupon, AppSumo, LivingSocial, and Restaurant.com (*http://restaurant.com*)
- Apps—for mobile, Facebook, or browsers
- Bands and music promotion
- Games
- Software
- Video services (such as music lessons)
- Online coaching
- Webinars

The Right Intent

Being successful on social media means engaging people with interesting content. You must start with this mindset; if you don't, you'll default to "sales mode," and be ignored by the people you're spending time and money to reach. Social media is where people go to hang out and have fun with their friends. That makes it a bad environment for selling stuff—everyone is focused on the content, not the sales pitches—so work with that instead of against it. Here are some guidelines for staying in the right frame of mind:

Bigger isn't better.

You don't need tons of fans to make sales. Social media engagement is definitely a "quality over quantity" situation. Overlook the vanity metrics: likes, fans, friends, and followers. Instead, focus on the actions that drive sales.

Incorporate ratings and reviews on your sales pages.

Make them prominent. This is an excellent way to get simple, introductory engagement.

Reward people for referrals and recommendations.

Figure out why your current customers recommend you, and start using this information to assist with your sales follow-ups.

Engage.

Look for a problem you can solve and a question you can answer, and send a relevant, helpful response.

Listen.

Look for buying signals: questions, concerns, and complaints.

Be authentic.

Show the real you with photos of yourself, your staff, and your office. Show that you're a real business by posting videos of your office or studio.

Hopefully, you didn't expect to just sign up on Facebook, post a few marketing messages, and kick back to watch the orders pour in. If so, if our advice up to this point hasn't sunk in then now's the time to sober up.

You have to do more than post messages on social media. That serves a purpose and it is important, but it's not the whole plan. To turn more friends and fans into customers, you've got to create plenty of content to support the sales process. That means product tutorials and demos, case studies of success stories, newsletters, updates, niche landing pages, in-person events, conference attendance coverage and reports, blog posts, and podcasts—in other words, education-based marketing.

Since "digital fulfillment" goods are pretty much exclusively marketed online, you should already be familiar with the fundamentals of online sales and marketing. Think of Facebook as an extension of your other online advertising efforts, to a certain extent. Beyond that, social media is more about awareness and promotion. If you have a new product and want to get maximum exposure for it, a contest or giveaway on social media will work marvelously—better and more cheaply than any traditional AdSense or DoubleClick campaign.

You should have an idea of whether your products are "impulse buy" material or not. If they are inexpensive and either very cool or very necessary, then they're impulse buys. If that's the case, before you start your social media campaign, you must streamline your sales process to make it as effortless as possible. If you can complete the sale in one click (via PayPal or Google Wallet or Amazon Payments), then do it. Every extra step in the sales process loses sales for you.

If you're not in the "impulse buy" category, then you need to give away free stuff. Excerpts, free trials, free videos (if there is a series you're selling), and limited-use licenses are all examples. This helps establish the quality of the paid products. Use that free trial to show how "worth it" the rest of the product is.

If you have multiple products, you can heavily promote one of them for free and use it to advertise the others. There are many different tactics for this, depending on your industry.

Last but not least is *freemium*—free for most functionality, but costs for the really good stuff. *Words With Friends*, for instance, is free to play, but to remove the ads and get the extra "pay to win" features, players have to pay. Since the game is connected through the app stores of the platforms it's on, it's a low-barrier sale that is quick and easy to complete. It's a perfect example of freemium in action.

If you are above the impulse buy threshold, fall back to the opt-in. You can combine this with the free-stuff approach by offering the free stuff only after a very simple opt-in form. Just a name and an email address and one more click to the free stuff. A great example here is ArtistWorks (*http://artistworks.com*) (shown in Figure 4-2), which offers interactive video lessons for a variety of musical instruments. Each product page shows the pricing plans up front, with an introductory video and a quick opt-in form to access some free lessons. The real value isn't so much the lessons as it is the video interaction and feedback from the teacher, so there's quite a lot of free content on the site after the opt-in, while the true value of the paid service is made quite clear. The first opt-in email ArtistWorks sends comes from the VP of Marketing's own email address, and he encourages you to reply to him directly with the answer to the prompt: "I would love to know WHY you want to improve your playing NOW." If you reply, he responds. Not only is this a friendly interaction with the company, but it also gives the company direct feedback on how to improve future marketing efforts. The entire operation is brilliantly combined with giveaways and other promotions through magazine ads and social media posts.

James Schramko is also a genius at using the free stuff approach to draw more attention to his paid services. He has many different products that all complement one another. In his podcasts for one of those products, he'll casually mention the others without explaining them so that you're forced to look them up on your own. Curiosity is a fantastic way to drive traffic.

Figure 4-2. ArtistWorks is a great example of free stuff plus opt-in—perfect for social media campaigns

Forming a Superior Strategy

Now that you've established proper context and intention for the sale of digital products and services on social media, it's time to commit to a plan. Use this list as a framework for your strategy:

Define your sales funnel.

That includes your lead magnets, tripwires, core product, and profit maximizers.

Prepare your landing pages.

Don't start marketing until your sales infrastructure is ready. Make sure all of your ducks are in a row on your online store. Remember to calibrate your landing pages to do either a low-friction impulse buy or an opt-in with free stuff. Optimize your landing pages for maximum conversion. LeadPages (*http://www.leadpages.net*) is a great service that can make high-converting landing pages for acquiring opt-ins and registrations for newsletters, Google Hangouts, webinars, and all sorts of other cool stuff you might be offering. One thing that sets LeadPages apart is its unique "lead box" feature. Basically it's a sign-up button with instant access. There are no name or email form fields to fill out until you click the button, then a pop-up/overlay appears with a small form to fill out. This increases signup by changing the landing page from a "taking" page (a demand for data from the prospect) to a "giving" page. Visitors are promised information, resources, and answers. Once they click the button and get the pop-up asking for their name and email, they are already mentally committed.

Set goals and checkpoints.

How many sales and/or referrals is it reasonable to expect from your social media work? This is a hard question to answer accurately. Try to choose a conservative estimate so that you aren't discouraged with sluggish results. Some markets can be slow to reach, and will take more effort over a longer period of time. It might be more useful to set a goal to get more social media traffic to your landing pages; the conversion work happens outside of social media.

Make a content plan.

We published a good content plan in Chapter 2 that you can easily adapt for your market. You must have some kind of plan for how things are going to play out. For instance, it does no good to offer an amazing deal if you just set up your Facebook page 10 minutes ago. You need an audience first, and then you need some engagement, and *then* you can push it over the edge with a special offer or giveaway.

Establish a presence.

Identify the social networks that you're prepared to maintain a presence on, and set up your pages there. Make sure each page is fully customized and has a good account name that represents you properly.

Build a "starter" audience.

Advertise and promote your social media pages to build an audience. Only you can determine how much is a good minimum target. It may be 500 Twitter followers, or 1,000 Facebook likes. This is just the beginning—what you jumpstart your social media marketing effort with. This number is not the endgame goal. You should have some good starter content to post as well; this might be a good time to release some of your supporting material—the how-to guides and other ancillary marketing materials that you will offer on a permanent or long-term basis—or begin promoting your free stuff.

Execute your content plan.

Start posting on the schedule that you've laid out for yourself. Your content plan might allow for a minimal audience at first, so you don't necessarily have to wait until you have your target "starter" audience in order to start posting.

Increase engagement.

Now that you're up and running, the stats and feedback should have some hints as to what kind of content is and is not working. Streamline your efforts, adjust your content plan, and advertise and promote to gain maximum engagement (not maximum likes/fans—you only want good leads at this point).

Site-Specific Tactics

Now that you have a plan, you must identify tactics to help you achieve it. We've already covered the basics in Chapter 2, but now we're going to get more specific for your industry segment.

When it comes to selling digital goods and services, you want to put effort only into the networks that are going to give you the highest level of engagement. Niche networks are probably not going to help you achieve your goals, though there may be some exceptions in outside cases. For the most part, you're going to want to stick to the big social networks.

Facebook

Facebook works really well for impulse buy products (low-cost, high-need). It's also a good way to advertise specials and deals. You can maximize the effectiveness of a "deal" announcement on Facebook by clearly showing the benefit, discount, and urgency of the deal. For instance, a webinar service that is usually $150 per month is available today only for $75 for a lifetime membership.

Bands and musicians can do well on Facebook through promo clips on YouTube, pre-release tracks, contests, ticket sales, events as concerts, and show announcements through highly targeted local advertising.

Pinterest

Pinterest has quickly become essential for business owners, because it is great for posting wares, developing a brand, and establishing a following. Pinterest isn't necessarily the place for deals, but it still touts impressive stats. According to a 2012 study done by BloomReach, Pinterest converted to sales 22% more than Facebook did. Also, Pinterest traffic spent 60% more than Facebook traffic did. Keep those numbers in mind.

Twitter

Twitter is useful for customer service, brand/product awareness, and deal announcements, but only if you have a decent number of followers. It's more time-consuming to build a Twitter following than it is a Facebook following, but you have a much greater opportunity to reach a lot of people with impulse buy deals. Twitter is ephemeral; it's here one minute, gone the next. People who see a limited-time–deal announcement on Twitter may be more inclined to jump on it right now than any other social network.

MySpace

Whoa, MySpace?! Blast from the past, eh? Yes, MySpace still exists, and is either on its comeback tour or playing for "pass the hat" tips at rundown clubs. No way to tell where it's going at this point. However, the only thing MySpace has consistently been good at is promoting music, and Justin Timberlake's guidance behind this network may eventually make it the Web's social hub for new music. If you are serious about promoting your band or album, MySpace is worth a look. It doesn't take much effort to establish a basic presence by setting up a page and uploading the songs that you're willing to give away for free on a promotional basis. The same rules apply here as everywhere else: post interesting things (not just promotional material), and engage with people constantly. (See Figure 4-3.)

Figure 4-3. MySpace is making a comeback as a music discovery and promotion social network

YouTube

How-to videos are great for tutorials for software and games. If you're selling a video series or an album, it might make sense to put your freebie content on YouTube and heavily promote it there rather than on your main site. First of all, you'll save on bandwidth, which could otherwise be a substantial cost if your video goes viral. Secondly, you'll be able to leverage YouTube's social features—such as commenting, favoriting, liking, subscribing—boosting these engagement metrics will help your YouTube search rankings.

Music and concert videos for bands are also great YouTube material.

Professional blogger and business guru John Chow is one of the kings of educational marketing to Internet entrepreneurs. Figure 4-4 shows a screenshot of one of his YouTube videos.

Figure 4-4. John Chow uses educational freebie content to establish his credibility

Case Study: Group Coaching, Systematized

Best-selling author Robert Allen teamed up with business expert Ted Miller III to create "The Fortune in You," an online coaching system for aspiring authors. Miller describes the situation:

> Robert Allen, my partner, is 65 now. He's been known in the industry since the 80s. But the way he stays relevant is through social media. He's an author and has six *New York Times* bestsellers. He loves printed books. But he used this early stage of social media to recognize that people wanted that digital capability. Did you know that Robert Allen, through his partnership of licensing agreement of Ethan Wilson's company, had sold 1 million ebooks before Amazon sold a single one? It just shows you how we're utilizing social media to keep our finger on the pulse of capitalism and how to stay advanced. Because he stayed on the cutting edge, he eventually sold over $100 million of his training materials and coaching through that licensing agreement. That's the most important thing: not responding, but anticipating where the marketplace is going, simply by looking at the past, the current trajectory, and the future pace. That's what social media is to us; the ability to anticipate where the market wants to be at and how to best serve it.

Allen and Miller realized that people responded far better when they weren't being sold at. Instead, *The Fortune in You* chose to immediately prove to potential clients why it was a worthwhile investment. The two started doing a revolutionary strategy: giving the public their best stuff even before the sale. They found that the prospect becomes more responsive to higher ticket sales. Miller elaborates:

> We looked at how can we better use technology throughout our entire sales cycle. One of the things that I use is "Stop selling, start adding value first," meaning in a new relationship, the one we have with our prospects, someone has to go first. That's the way it is in every relationship. In a love relationship, someone had to say "I love you" first. If you're looking to be an expert, you'll have that credibility. You'll have way more commerce because you cared enough to give first. The way I give first is through education. How can you do so in a way that they are dying to hear more of what you have to offer? I found that if you educate them on the topics that you have to discuss, they'll be exponentially more likely to want to hear what you have to offer and learn more than hear you sell them anything. So I use education as a way to go through my sales cycle.

> You may be trying to automate your sales cycle to improve the conversions. Think of not trying to do the next thing to make them spend money. You may be thinking to yourself, *I want them to get from this circle to this circle.* Maybe you should stop thinking like that, [and change] to *How can I add value?* so it will be logical for them to take the next step on their own. I'll give it to you right up front. You don't hold the best you have to offer until later. They're learning; you're constantly giving them tremendous value. And what's really strategic is, you can educate them in a way that it is logical for them to do business with you. Maybe they are a chiropractor, and this chiropractor's office does not just heal you biomechanically and provide structural correction; maybe they also offer emotional technique. Maybe they also help you with toxicity. What they'll do is they'll educate the prospective client. These are the reasons you'd want to adjust your body. But then they'd also say "but if you just get it adjusted, you'll never address the emotion that triggers the need for adjustment. You'd get adjusted for the rest of your life and not ever address the emotional problems manifesting themselves as pain." That's a very classy way of educating someone. But they'd do it in a way that they want to go to that chiropractor instead of any chiropractor in town.

> I've got a book in the works called *Webinars That Sell*. Before we started selling these manuscripts, we went online and said, "Hey, we want to you to have access to this before the rest of the world gets it because you're following us online or you're in our database or engaging with us in some way on social media." We say, "We'll get you the book; all you have to do is pay for shipping and handling." And that's our quid pro quo for giving us their name and email address. Now they've opted in, we deliver them that book, and they listen. We say, "Hey, I bet you'd love to talk to the author of this book. Well, we do these trainings that are online and interactive, compared to our live events that have a thousand people in the room and you're lucky if you ever get your question answered. Here, we'll do it online so you don't have to travel; [it's] convenience from the comfort of home or office chair; it's a small group so you can keep it interactive and ask questions, and the author will guide you through that process." So we do a couple hundred bucks for that training. Think of all the automation we have in there. We don't throw a human being in the mix until they've spent money. If they choose that $4.95 to get our books, once they've spent money with us or done one of our webinars, we've got human beings engaging with them. We're able to use our best talent with our clients, not our prospects. Automation empowered us to keep our best talent on our greatest impact areas. Take

the best talent you have and put them on the single most important initiative you have in your company and watch your company grow exponentially. And take the mundane stuff they are doing and automate it. That's the power of technology today.

Real-Life Q&A

Q: I'm getting a lot of traffic, but no conversions.

A: I haven't seen your landing page, but I'm betting it's got some kind of problem. Have you tested it on mobile devices and multiple desktop browsers? How's the load time?

Beyond the obvious technical stuff, you're going to have to look at your web visitor stats to see if there are more clues. A high bounce rate, for instance, can suggest a number of things (slow load time, poor design, content that's not interesting enough).

If you're sure that your server and content are in top shape, then look next to your sales process. It's got to be a one-click, low-impact buy. Simplify and shorten this process any way you can. If it's longer than one click, then make your landing page into an opt-in page with as few fields as possible. Lots of opt-in fields will chase people away. We suggest a name and email address only, and possibly a password if you're creating a personalized on-site account for each visitor.

Q: I have a five-part product strategy that involves an entry-level ebook, a physical product, a video course, a seminar that I do at certain conferences, and personal coaching. I'm not getting how to incorporate social media into this complex (and profitable!) process.

A: Well, start with a Facebook page. Get Twitter going as well; follow people you want to get the word out to and start interacting with them. Facebook and Twitter should always form the foundation of a bare bones social framework. Once you're in motion, start promoting your ebook through social media. Choose days to give it away for free. Make the first video in your video course free on certain days, and make sure everyone knows how much it would have cost otherwise. Offer some of your clients a free personal coaching engagement, with the condition that you be allowed to film parts of it for a promotional YouTube video. Start a free monthly podcast where you talk about client successes with your product. Do product demos on YouTube. Get product endorsements from clients; take photos of them with your product and put them on Instagram, or create a Pinterest board for client successes.

Q: I'm a self-published fiction author with an ebook. What can I do through social media to increase sales?

A: This is a tough one because fiction is, and has always been, very expensive and/or time-consuming to promote, and the results are never guaranteed. If there were a perfect formula for this, every major book publisher would be using it to make everything a bestseller. Instead, only a tiny percentage of fiction books go beyond their advance.

We've actually dedicated an entire chapter to this subject later in the book. Here's some quick advice before you skip ahead to it, though. First, don't openly promote your novel; people don't seem to respond well to that. Instead, talk about the themes indirectly. For instance, let's say the movie *The Matrix* never existed, and you just wrote it as a science fiction novel. Put up a web page that shows the synopsis, the first chapter, any art that is associated with it, and links to all of the major sites that sell it (e.g., Amazon, Barnes & Noble (*http://bn.com*), or Kobo). Create a Facebook page for the book and a Twitter account for you as an author, and link out to your book page prominently there. Get some good Facebook ads going on a budget of $10–$20 per day to gain more page likes. Every day on your Facebook page, you would offer a paragraph or so on the nature of reality, Turing test theories, artificial intelligence, Buddhist philosophy as it relates to the plot, computer hacking, the semantics of hacker handles, news stories that deal with any of these subjects, and so on. On Twitter, you would post questions to your followers about these same subjects. You'd follow actors from science fiction shows and engage with them. You'd try to find people who talk a lot about science fiction and have a lot of followers, and try to get them to notice you (refer to Chapter 13 for more information on influencer outreach).

Summary

We hope this chapter has helped you to think holistically about social media. Of all the reader segments we wrote this book for, yours is the one that probably has the most experience in online marketing. That's a blessing and a curse; you're familiar with the game, but you have probably been playing at least some part of it in an inefficient way until now, and it's going to be tough to change some of the initiatives that are already in motion and modify habits that you didn't know were bad.

At this point, you might want to stop and reflect on what you're doing, why you're doing it, and what you should change in order to achieve your goals. Don't make any big changes just yet—start with small but important adjustments.

In our experience, defining an effective sales funnel can be an epiphany for struggling digital entrepreneurs. Even those who are aware of it aren't always optimizing all stages in the funnel for maximum effect. This might be a good place to start if you're redesigning your online marketing strategy.

Chapter 6, which covers social media advertising, should be your next stop. Chapter 5 is customized solely for entrepreneurs who have a local storefront.

You can also head over to the *Social eCommerce* site (*http://www.socialecommerce book.com*) for more Q&A and to post your own burning questions! You'll have access to exclusive offers, discounts, and coupon codes on various social media tools and services.

To get exclusive access to instructional videos related to the concepts in the chapter, simply send a text with your email address to *+1(213)947-9990* and we'll send you some great links.

CHAPTER 5

Local Services and Storefronts

If your ecommerce business is not selling something to a local market (such as a club, restaurant, storefront, kiosk, or local service), then you should probably skip this chapter and head to Chapter 6 to get a comprehensive education on ad design and testing. Having said that, there's a lot of interesting content in this chapter regardless of what industry you're in.

In the beginning of this book, we said that a successful strategy has three components: intention, context, and tactics. This is why we have separated local services and storefronts from the sale of things exclusively to remote customers. Online stores have a potential customer base of billions of people, but you are limited to the people in your city or region. That means you're going to have to work much harder at customer service, atmosphere, and a sense of safety. To actually go out to a specific location requires a higher level of trust. To come back after the first visit requires a high level of satisfaction.

More than ever, ratings count for local businesses. A single negative online review or rating can cost you thousands of dollars in lost revenue. Recurring business is extremely important, and your online presence must match the experience you provide in person. If your site looks cheap, that sends a message about what it's like to be at your store or restaurant. You must be consistent in appearance and message.

The Right Intent

Being successful on social media means engaging people and posting interesting content. You must start with this mindset; if you don't, you'll default to "sales mode," and be ignored by the people you're spending time and money to reach. Social media is where people go to hang out and have fun with their friends. If you have the sort of business that also has this atmosphere, by all means show that with your photos, videos, and other content. If you're running a storefront, make it look like this is a place where people's friends would go. Get them engaged, and make them a part of your public business culture. Here are some guidelines for staying in the right frame of mind:

Bigger isn't better.

You don't need tons of fans to get customers, and it's probably not realistic to aim for tens of thousands of fans or followers if you live in a small metropolitan area. Social media engagement is definitely a "quality over quantity" situation. Overlook the vanity metrics: likes, fans, friends, and followers. Instead, focus on trust and quality of atmosphere.

Incorporate ratings and reviews on your sales pages.

Make them prominent. This is an excellent way to get simple, introductory engagement. Positive reviews build trust very quickly. You're going to have to monitor the reviews constantly, though. One negative review can cost you many customers.

Reward people for referrals and recommendations.

Figure out why your current customers recommend you, and start using this information to assist with your sales follow-ups.

Engage.

Look for a problem you can solve and a question you can answer, and send a relevant, helpful response.

Listen.

Look for buying signals: questions, concerns, and complaints.

Be authentic.

Show the real you with photos of yourself, your staff, your customers (with their permission), and your store.

Hopefully, you didn't expect to just sign up on Facebook, post a few marketing messages, and kick back to watch customers flock to your store. If so, if our advice up to this point hasn't sunk in then now's the time to sober up.

You have to do more than post messages on social media. That serves a purpose and it is important, but it's not the whole plan. To turn more friends and fans into customers, you've got to create plenty of content to show that you're trustworthy and friendly. That means product tutorials and demos, case studies of success stories, newsletters, updates, niche landing pages, in-person events, blog posts, and podcasts. Essentially, we are talking about educated-based marketing again.

So far, most of what we've said shouldn't be a new concept to you; these are the fundamentals of local business marketing. Twenty years ago, you would have used this same marketing theory to create print ads, local TV and radio commercials, mailers, and sponsorships. Very little of that kind of traditional marketing is cost-effective anymore, especially when compared to a solid online presence. To most people who grew up in the Internet era, if you don't have a website or a well-curated Facebook page, then you don't exist or your business is probably shady and unprofessional, or at least old-fashioned and uncool. Even if you're running a retirement home and trying to appeal to older people who aren't as Internet-savvy as their kids or grandkids, a good online presence is still the most important positive thing you can do for your business. Someone in the decision-making process is going to go to the Web to look you up, and if she finds nothing, there is no way that she will trust you.

Beyond establishing trust and atmosphere, social media is about awareness and promotion. If you have a new product, menu item, or service and want to get maximum exposure for it, a contest or giveaway on social media will work marvelously—better and more cheaply than any traditional media campaign.

Is there something you can promote at a discount or for free? A good tactic along these lines is to offer a discount for your slowest business day of the week, or a coupon to help sell a certain product that you want to turn over. If you have something you can't seem to get rid of, give it away as part of a contest.

Forming a Superior Strategy

Now that you've established proper context and intention for promoting your storefront or service on social media, it's time to commit to a plan. Use this list as a framework for your strategy:

Prepare your website.
> The central piece in your marketing strategy should be your website, and it should look good and provide all of the information that potential customers are looking for. You can set up some social media pages right away, but don't start marketing until your website is ready.

Set goals and checkpoints.
> How many sales, new customers, and/or referrals is it reasonable to expect from your social media work? This is a hard question to answer accurately. Try to choose a conservative estimate so that you aren't discouraged with sluggish results.

Make a content plan.
> We published a good content plan in Chapter 2 that you can easily adapt for your business. You must have some kind of plan for how things are going to play out. For instance, it does no good to offer an amazing deal if you just set up your Facebook page 10 minutes ago. You need an audience first, and then you need some engagement, and *then* you can push it over the edge with a special offer or giveaway.

Establish a presence.
> Identify the social networks that you're prepared to maintain a presence on, and set up your pages there. Make sure each page is fully customized and has a good account name that represents you properly.

Build a "starter" audience.

Advertise and promote your social media pages to build an audience. Only you can determine how much is a good minimum target. It may be 500 Twitter followers, or 1,000 Facebook likes. This is just the beginning—what you jumpstart your social media marketing effort with. This number is not the endgame goal. You should have some good starter content to post as well; this might be a good time to release some of your supporting material—the how-to guides and other ancillary marketing materials that you will offer on a permanent or long-term basis—or begin promoting your coupons and discounts.

Execute your content plan.

Start posting on the schedule that you've laid out for yourself. Your content plan might allow for a minimal audience at first, so you don't necessarily have to wait until you have your target "starter" audience in order to start posting.

Increase engagement.

Now that you're up and running, the stats and feedback should have some hints as to what kind of content is and is not working. Streamline your efforts, adjust your content plan, and advertise and promote to gain maximum engagement (not maximum likes/fans—you only want good leads at this point).

Provide incentives.

Offer some check-in deals on Foursquare, Facebook, Twitter, and/or Google+. For instance, you can offer $5 off the purchase price for those who check in at the given location. You can also offer discounts for reviews (on social media, Yelp, or your product page).

Site-Specific Tactics

Now that you have a plan, you must identify tactics to help you achieve it. We've already covered the basics in Chapter 2, but now we're going to get more specific for your industry segment.

When it comes to promoting local stores and services, you want to put effort only into the networks that are going to give you the highest level of engagement. Niche networks can help here, if they are specific to your industry (food blogs for your restaurant, for instance) or are specific to your geographic area. For the most part, though, you're going to want to stick to the big social networks.

Your content, no matter what it is or where you post it, needs to stand out from the crowd. No matter what kind of business you have, show positive personality and make your location look like a nice, safe place to go. Have fun and build loyalty. Find ways to get people to come back. Create a frequent-customer program, such as a stampcard or punchcard, or set up a perks program for people who have spent a certain amount or ordered a certain number of things. Then, on your site or on a social media page, feature the most prestigious members in that program for the month. Offer recommendations for frequent/loyal customers. Reward people for loyalty. Make people feel like they're a part of something; inspire a neighborhood feeling. Make your business feel like something unique, like a specialty boutique for celebrities, and not a sterile big box chain-store experience.

Facebook

Aside from setting up your page and engaging with fans, you can do quite a lot of effective advertising through Facebook Ads if you patiently work through the details of targeting and ad design. We've dedicated an entire chapter to this subject later in this book, but the basics are:

- Very specific targeting
- An absolutely killer image
- A specific headline
- A price in the ad text

Google+

Signing up in Google+ will give you local search visibility. This isn't a should, this is a must. Your first stop will be Google My Business (*http://google.com/business*), the central portal for updating your business information across Google search, Google Maps, and Google+.

YouTube

If you're promoting a restaurant, create a seasonal menu and do a video of it, or do a cooking segment with the chef in which he shows how to prepare one of your signature dishes.

If you're promoting a storefront, do a slideshow video with photos of your store, staff, and happy customers.

Any TV commercial that you would have made for traditional television can work on YouTube. Kitschy, stylized, silly TV commercial-like videos may have some viral potential as well. If you can make a funny video that isn't offensive or negative and in some way involves your store or restaurant, go for it!

Pinterest and Instagram

Pinterest is widely known as a repository of recipes, so if you're promoting a restaurant, consider putting up some of your recipes here with photos of the process and the perfectly presented dish at the end. If you have a willing and photogenic chef, you might even offer a weekly cooking demonstration that involves a limited-time menu item.

Anything that you would have put into a YouTube slideshow should go on whichever photo sharing site you're participating in.

Post promotional photos of people who have won your contests or defeated your challenges (restaurant eating challenges, for example). Instagram is great for taking photos throughout the day of happy customers at your location. You can do a "mystery customer of the day" promotion where you take someone's photo and if she sees it on Instagram, she gets a $50 gift card.

Work photos of a mascot or logo into your photos. CreditDonkey created the infographic in Figure 5-1, and slyly incorporated its own mascot, the donkey, in the background.

Figure 5-1. The CreditDonkey is depicted as a teacher giving tips for social media in this clever infographic

Craigslist

Craigslist is a free "want ad" site for major metropolitan areas. If you have a store with irregular, unpredictable, and sometimes rare stock (for instance, a pawn shop, vintage clothing store, used car dealership, or specialty food market), Craigslist is a great free method of posting ads for individual items. Just make sure you post in the right category, and update your ad on a regular basis until it sells—and then remove it.

Foursquare

Foursquare is a mobile app that enables users to broadcast where they are and find out who else is there. It isn't the same big deal that it used to be, mostly because other social networks started offering check-in functions. However, it's still pretty popular as a way of connecting with the people who are wherever you're shopping or hanging out.

Offer check-in deals on Foursquare, such as $5 off an entrée or a free dessert, or 10% off any item under $100. Each check-in is a low-level personal recommendation to someone's friends, and puts your store on the map for those who didn't know it existed.

Local Blogging

Blogs qualify as social media insofar as they are interactive with readers and offer readers the ability to comment and rate or vote. Many cities and regions have local blogs that have usurped the position of the now-dead or dying local daily newspaper. If you have an interesting story to share about your business or your life, see if you can arrange an interview with a local blogger.

If the blog sells ads, buy one and see how it goes. It might get you some new business, and it might be a complete waste of money, so don't commit too much to it right away.

If you have the time and enthusiasm for it—or if someone you know, or someone who works for you, does—then start your own local blog. Write about local events and people, and put up ads for your business.

Yelp

Yelp is a site that enables people to rate and review local businesses, and it can have a huge impact if you are reviewed well or poorly there. If you maintain a storefront, encourage positive reviews by posting a "People Love Us on Yelp" sticker on your storefront window, having a sign near the register asking people to post a Yelp review, and asking customers personally to go to Yelp and post positive feedback.

Go to Yelp and register your business there. Put up a photo and contact information, and then watch that page like a hawk. If anyone posts a negative review (anything under 4 stars), reply to him publicly in a sympathetic manner (don't get angry!), and if possible, contact him directly off-site through email or by phone. Do everything you can to get him to be your ally, even if it seems like he's in the wrong for complaining.

Do not ignore filtered reviews. The review filter is Yelp's way of trying to weed out the spam, but it is notoriously overzealous, and mostly just isolates very negative and very positive reviews, and any review that mentions a competitor. Serious Yelp users know that the filtered reviews are often where the good stuff is. At the very least, it is typically a repository of honest negative reviews. If anything, you should pay more attention to the filtered reviews than the normal ones. Smart Yelp users know not to trust glowing 5-star reviews from reviewers with few friends and few other reviews.

This isn't related to Yelp specifically, but if you're in a business that sees frequent abuse or fraud, consider turning the tables on your customers by participating in a customer review program. If you encounter a scammer or abusive person, report it. The mobile car-hiring app Uber, for instance, offers customers the chance to rate their drivers, and the drivers also rate the riders. If you're a 2-star passenger, you might not be able to find a driver who wants to bother with you. This is proprietary technology for Uber, but it isn't difficult to use standard rating applications internally in your business to rate and review customers. This would be especially helpful in businesses that buy or trade things, such as pawn shops or antique stores.

Twitter

Twitter is useful for customer service, brand/product awareness, and deal announcements, but only if you have a decent number of followers. It's more time-consuming to build a Twitter following than it is a Facebook following, but you have a much greater opportunity to reach a lot of people with impulse-buy deals. Twitter is ephemeral; it's here one minute, gone the next. People who see a limited-time deal announcement on Twitter may be more inclined to jump on it right now than any other social network.

Verifying Driving Directions

What a disaster it would be if your potential customers couldn't get to your location because their GPS or mapping app doesn't know how to guide people to the correct building! There are many ways automated directions can go wrong:

Closed roads/temporary construction.
 Most navigation apps are not aware of road construction. For very large road construction projects, the entire street may be diverted for a few hours, or a few days. The detours may change depending on which half of the street is being worked on. There may be vehicle restrictions for rough patches of road. It's your responsibility to make sure that your customers are informed of road construction and blockages near your storefront.

New road not yet on the map.

Most GPS owners probably don't realize that their device has hardcoded maps that have to be manually updated for an extra cost. It's not like Google Maps; a GPS is not a service, it is a device. Updating the maps costs extra and isn't done automatically. Some taxi drivers purposefully use old GPSes with very old maps so that they can run up their fare by searching for the right street.

New building not yet on the map.

If your building was constructed within the past five years, it's not going to show up on a lot of GPSes; it may not even show up in Google Maps.

"Trap streets" that don't exist.

Since the early days of professional cartography, mapmakers have been adding tiny falsehoods to their work so that anyone who copies it will be easily identified. This is to protect against copyright infringement, but it has the added side effect of misleading people who follow maps literally. Sometimes a street will be purposefully misnamed, and sometimes (especially on the edge of a settled area where streets come to a dead end) they will appear to connect even though they don't.

Similar road names.

Adjacent cities or counties can have different rules that cause street names and numbers to change after a certain intersection. There can be a huge difference between "Main Street S" and "Main Street N." Do not be ambiguous on important parts of your address. If it's an American address, it helps to specify the four-digit postal zip code extension.

Incomplete road names (not including Street or Avenue).

To add to the previous point, while Main St. N and Main St. S may have identical street numbers, they won't have the same zip code. However, Raeford Road and Raeford Court can be in the same zip code and have the same numbered addresses. So if you don't specify the St., Rd., or Ct., it can throw people off. The moral of the story is: print the full address and don't leave anything out.

Every map service has a correction procedure. As previously mentioned, though, if GPS owners never update their maps, they won't get the corrections. If you know that some customers have been led astray in the past, make sure you print a notice about erroneous GPS directions prominently on your site, and provide directions yourself. Encourage customers to call if they get lost, and make sure you know the area well enough that you can guide them to your location.

Sometimes the directions are technically accurate, but nonpractical. For instance, a newer road may have been constructed that cuts the route in half, or avoids a rough unmaintained road, but is not on the map. Correcting inconvenient routes can involve several actions, such as adding a road, adding a building, and altering the route. While this may seem like a hassle, keep in mind that you are losing money every time someone can't find your location. How much money will you lose from a single customer?

Google Maps

Google provides a Report Errors feature in the Directions view in Google Maps, as Figure 5-2 shows.

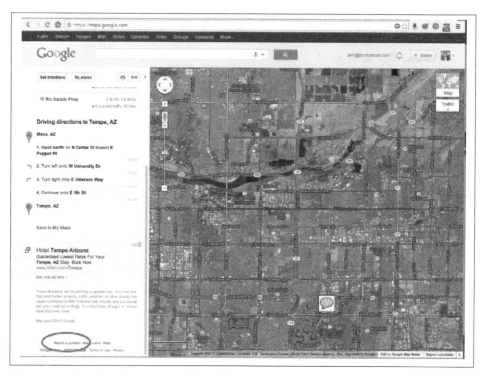

Figure 5-2. Google's "Report a problem" function in Google Maps

Click that link in the lower left, below the step-by-step directions, and you can submit corrections and other feedback about the directions.

Mapquest, Yahoo, Bing, and Garmin GPS Devices

Mapquest, Yahoo, Bing, and Garmin GPS devices get their maps through Navteq, which has a Map Reporter correction page: *https://mapreporter.navteq.com*.

If the misdirection came from a Garmin device or app, you can alternatively report it through the Garmin site, if you know the model number of the device (*https://my.garmin.com/mapErrors/*).

Garmin customers can also update their maps through the Garmin site.

TomTom

TomTom makes GPSes, including specialty GPSes, and also provides its maps to the Apple Maps mobile apps. You can report inaccuracies through the TomTom Map Share Reporter tool: *http://www.tomtom.com/mapshare/tools/*.

Case Study: The Celebrity Next Door

Celebrity chef Robert Irvine is famous for his food, his personality, and his high level of engagement with fans. It's the perfect recipe for a social media strategy. His Hilton Head Island, South Carolina, restaurant, Robert Irvine's Eat!, competes with about 200 other restaurants on an island with a lot of tourism and a small local population. It's tough competition, especially when Chef Irvine is on the road doing shows and other events about 300 days per year. Robert Irvine's Nosh restaurant is eight miles away on the mainland, in Bluffton, South Carolina, and appeals to the same demographic.

Chef Irvine entrusts the everyday operation of these two signature restaurants to executive chef Lee Lucier, who has also participated in popular Food Network television shows with Irvine. In addition to running both restaurants according to Chef Irvine's famously high standards, Chef Lucier also participates in the social media strategy that helps them stay successful:

> We're on a very small island, but there are so many ways to advertise here, and they cost a ton, but there is little return for restaurants. The best way we've found to give people value is to do in-house specials and features, and tell people about them on social media. That gives people a lot of value. We've done tie-ins with other businesses to get some exposure, and Facebook ads of all kinds, and that's been working for us, so we keep going with it. Financially, social media ads offer a much better return than print. TV is great if you're in the right market. Here on Hilton Head Island, we're in a vacation market, so television is not as effective as it would be in bigger local markets.

Robert Irvine's Eat! launched before Robert Irvine's Nosh. By the time the second restaurant was open for business, according to Chef Lucier, the social media strategy was already solidified:

> We followed what we were already doing. We track things pretty closely—what the responses are, the analytics of certain campaigns and how they're doing. Both restaurants go hand-in-hand since success for one means success for the other. The demographics and customer base are the same, so we can combine the marketing efforts. These places are within eight miles of each other. However, when we do a *Restaurant: Impossible* show, we often encounter situations where people think that they can do the same thing for every location. Many people make this mistake—they use the same marketing for each location, and they fail because the customers can be different in each market. Take Phoenix and Sedona, for instance. They're both in Arizona, and not too far from each other, but they have a completely different clientèle. You can't use the same tactics for the same restaurant in both locations.

Even if you have a celebrity chef's name attached to a restaurant, there is no guarantee of success. All of the same things that make Robert Irvine's restaurants successful will apply to any chef's restaurant if he's willing to work for it, says Chef Lucier:

> On Tuesday nights we do all our tapas at half price. This is incredibly popular, and guests love it; they make reservations months in advance. The cost of that discount comes out of our advertising budget. It covers a huge portion of our weekly bills—and on a Tuesday night, which is usually a bad night in the industry.

The websites for both restaurants have three, small, unobtrusive but easily seen buttons for Twitter, Facebook, and Yelp (see Figure 5-3). The Yelp link is different for each, but because they're in the same market, they share a Facebook and Twitter page (under the Robert Irvine's Eat! name):

- *https://www.facebook.com/RobertIrvinesEat*
- *https://twitter.com/RobertIrvineEat*
- *http://chefirvineseat.com/about-eat/*

Figure 5-3. Excellent social media integration on his site

There is also integration with Google Maps for directions, and a Facebook social plug-in showing recent posts and people who like the page. On the Event Calendar page, there is seamless integration with Google Calendar; click on any event listing, and it can easily be added to your calendar in your Google profile.

Despite his passion for his brand and his dedication to quality, there are occasional negative reviews on Yelp. Chef Lucier prefers not to respond to them:

Responding to reviews is something you either do or don't do. We like to think that people are qualified enough to comment on their own experience, so I think it's a failed tactic to try to change reviews after the fact. It's intrusive. We keep track of bad reviews and talk to our staff about them, but we've recently implemented a system to try to avoid them before they happen. We get instant analytics on about 65% of our tables through a special feedback tool that we're using. And that is available to me no matter where I am. I could be out on my boat, and still be able to see what guests are saying while they're in the restaurant. We'd much rather correct a situation in real time. If someone complains while in the restaurant, our in-house system allows us to address that immediately. Someone in the back of the house is always watching for complaints, and addresses them so that people don't have to leave the restaurant with a negative experience.

Social media can be the prize or death of your restaurant. When bad reviews happen, you need to attack the problems that people are talking about, and get those situations corrected. So many people spend money based on what they see on social media, so you have to be aware of it and limit mistakes.

Despite his busy television and tour schedule, the man at the top doesn't lose touch with what's happening on the ground—or on the Web. According to Chef Lucier:

Robert makes decisions on all paths that we take. He has a full-time social media director on staff, but Chef is the one who posts messages to Twitter, and he makes all decisions as to what goes into his restaurants. Robert responds to everyone who tweets him. Not many people take his kind of interest in their fans, whether it's at his restaurant going around to every single table to make sure everyone's having a good experience, or on one of his shows, or even out on the street. He wants everyone to have a great time, so he chose partners for social media who share that passion for quality and a superior brand.

Chef Irvine's marketing and PR representative, Dan McLean, handles the analytics side of the restaurants' online presence, and notes:

It's all about engagement, and the numbers we look at have to do with quality, not quantity. If 100,000 people follow us but only two of them are talking about us, then there is little value in the other 99,998. You want to get the right people to the page. People enjoy engaging with Robert, and the rest of the team helps build on that experience. We always take it a step further than the surface metrics to see who's talking about what, and we use that information to help make a lot of decisions.

Case Study: Destination Marketing with Flair

GoVisitCostaRica (*http://govisitcostarica.com*), an ecotravel advising site, delegates its social media to a third party, and that third party is its tiny imaginary tree frog mascot named Javi the Frog. The site, created by Costa Rica enthusiast Todd Sarouhan, began using the avatar frog a few years ago, and the success has been notable.

"Javi is famous in Costa Rica; hotels love it when we take pictures with him there, because they know people will look," says Javier Navajas, content editor and social media strategist for the site.

It's almost like people think that they are talking to an actual tree frog. People will go on the Facebook page and post, "Hey, Javi! I'm looking for recommendations," or "Thanks, Javi!" And if you check out the GoVisitCostaRica (*http://govisitcostarica.com*) web page, it certainly seems like he's real. On the About page, Javi is listed in the Bio page right alongside the owners (see Figure 5-4). If that isn't enough information about him, you can check out the "About Javi the Frog" page on the website, which describes the entire past they created for him: "I was born in the rainforest of Gandoca-Manzanillo National Wildlife Refuge, where I grew up with my mom, dad, and 24 brothers and sisters." There is then a series of pictures of Javi visiting hotels and doing dozens of recommended activities, from ziplining to boogie boarding (Figure 5-5). Javi often takes advantage of the popular Instagram and Twitter tradition #selfieSunday, where users post pictures of themselves.

Figure 5-4. Javi's bio

Figure 5-5. Javi boogie boarding

"The customers love it because it proves that we've been there; we aren't just going off of a review or a picture. We've been to the hotel, and here's a recent photo of it," Todd adds. Because GoVisitCostaRica does not need to worry about selling its own product, it simply connects travelers to destinations, meaning Javi the Frog does not need to constantly be selling. Instead, he is free to answer questions, create authentic dialogue, and make his own recommendations. Through this type of direct interaction with both hotel owners and clients (virtually), Javi has been branded as a trustworthy, eco-friendly, and approachable guide to travel.

According to Todd, "The red-eyed tree frog has always been one of the symbols of Costa Rican wildlife. I actually asked Javier if I could use his name even before he worked for me...I remember calling him up and asking, 'Hey, is it all right if I use your name?'" Now Javier is the voice of the tree frog that bears his name over Twitter, Pinterest, Facebook, and Google+.

GoVisitCostaRica also has TV commercials advertising local sweepstakes for hotel stays on a Costa Rican government channel. "The sweepstakes run every few months, and since it is a government channel, everyone sees it," Todd explains.

The result of GoVisitCostaRica's efforts and advertisement is just over 27,000 Facebook likes and a featured spot on Pinterest's home page; Javi and Todd have created an excellent forum for questions, recommendations, and interaction.

Mobile Marketing

Mobile advertising is critically important to local businesses because people often use their mobile devices to find local goods, services, and events. The key points to consider are:

- Your site must be mobile-friendly.
- If possible, create a mobile app for your customers.
- You must be able to be found on mobile mapping apps.
- You must have a presence on Foursquare, and on popular local deals sites like Groupon and Restaurant.com (*http://restaurant.com*).
- If you are advertising on Facebook, you must create mobile-specific ads (these ads will show up only in mobile app feeds).

If you find yourself dragging your feet when it comes to building a mobile commerce strategy, here are a few interesting statistics for you:

- According to comScore, four out of five smartphone users in the U.S. access retail content on their mobile device.
- According to Prosper Mobile Insights, 25% of consumers shop online only on mobile.
- Compuware claims that 40% of users would go to a competitor's site after a bad mobile experience, and 57% wouldn't recommend a company with a poorly designed mobile site.

- Consumers spent six times more in December 2012 using retailer's apps than they did in 2011, according to Flurry.

In case it's not clear: mobile is a big deal for local markets. Next we'll cover three areas of concentration that will ensure maximum mobile conversion.

Optimize Your Website

Your site should be designed to be responsive; it must adapt to users who are viewing it from a big screen desktop monitor view, to a smaller laptop display, to a tablet, to a mobile phone screen. No matter how a customer accesses your site, he should be able to easily access and view all of your content. See Figures 5-6 and 5-7 for examples of sites that fail and succeed, respectively, at responsiveness.

Figure 5-6. An example of a site that does not cater to mobile users; this site would be much better off if it were mobile optimized

Figure 5-7. A good example of responsive design on a mobile device

There are three different ways to serve users a mobile website experience. The first is to have a mobile-specific website on a subdomain. For this, you'll want to set up bidirectional links to the two sites (the desktop site and the mobile site). On the desktop site, you'll want to have a rel="alternate" tag that points back to the mobile site. On the mobile site, you'll want to link back to the desktop by having a rel="canonical" tag. This will aggregate the PageRank and collapse the two together on search engines. It is essentially a redirect. Google is able to keep this straight due to the bidirectional redirects.

Another is dynamic serving, where the HTML varies according to user agent. For this, you'll need to use the "vary" HTTP header that alerts Googlebot to the fact that you are varying the HTML based on the user agent.

The third kind is a responsive design where the HTML is the same but the CSS renders the page differently depending on screen size or user agent. This is the approach Google recommends.

Web design is best left to the experts; in itself, it is the subject of entire books, so we're not going to go into detail on the finer points of what makes a good mobile site and how to accomplish it. Hopefully you're working with a design firm that can test your site for mobile friendliness, or you have an in-house web designer who can develop a mobile site, or you're using a modern content management system (CMS) that can detect and adjust for tablets and smartphones.

Of course, you can test out your site yourself just by visiting it with your phone or tablet, or by using developer tools such as the mobile device testing features built into Google Chrome. Is your site usable on your device? Do you have to zoom in and tab carefully, or does the site adjust to the screen? If there is a mobile version, does it offer all of the required functionality to complete a sale? If you're not satisfied with the responsiveness of your site on a mobile device, enlist the help of an experienced web designer who can develop a good mobile version.

Mobile Retail Apps

Another way to offer a mobile-friendly experience for customers is to create a mobile app. We can't ignore the fact that this can be extremely expensive and/or time-consuming, and it may not be appropriate for every market and budget. Also, mobile apps are not suitable replacements for mobile-friendly websites. If you have a limited budget to spend on web design or development, put all of that money into your website, not a mobile app.

If you do have developers or the budget to develop an app, then aim to produce something elegant, robust, useful, and multiplatform (Android, iOS, Windows RT). Here are some potential ideas for app functionality for local businesses:

- A catalogue app with a wish list feature
- A touch-to-pay system
- Barcode scanners
- Store location finder (if you have multiple locations)
- Coupons and promotions

Integrated Product Reviews

According to eMarketer, 36% of smartphone owners use their mobile devices to read product reviews. Why not make it easier for them (and help guide them to positive reviews) by incorporating reviews into your mobile-friendly site or app?

If you don't have the resources to incorporate reviews from other sites, at a minimum you should offer personal testimonials from past customers. There are also inexpensive review solutions that can be added without heavy-duty customization, such as Bazaar-Voice (*http://www.bazaarvoice.com*), Power Reviews (*http://www.powerreviews.com*), Testimonial Director (*http://www.testimonialdirector.com*), and the WP Customer Reviews plug-in for WordPress (*https://wordpress.org/plugins/wp-customer-reviews*).

Mobile Advertising

In Bizreport's 2012 Mobile Advertising Survey, 64% of respondents who had smartphones made a purchase after viewing a mobile ad. You can easily take advantage of that with Facebook mobile ads. Most Facebook users, after all, access the service through a mobile device. There are three options to choose from, all of which appear in users' News Feeds: page post engagement, clicks to website, and app installs (for retailers who have an app).

You can also promote tweets and Twitter accounts. Twitter ads (*https://ads.twitter.com*), which are not really ads in the traditional sense, can be targeted by keywords, interests, or similar accounts.

There are several advertising networks specializing in mobile marketing that you may want to consider:

- AdMob (*http://www.google.com/ads/admob*) by Google
- Millennial Media (*http://www.millenialmedia.com*)
- MdotM (*http://www.mdotm.com*)
- InMobi (*http://www.inmobi.com*)

Real-Life Q&A: Think Locally

Q: I've got a Facebook page and a Twitter account going, and I'm excited to build an audience. How much should I spend on ads?

A: That's a complicated question, and we're going to address it as best we can in the next chapter. There's a ton of experimentation and testing that has to happen before you can start thinking about an ad budget. If you've already got some ads going, then our basic suggestion is to start at $10 or $15 per day and see how that goes. If it's successful, try doubling it for a day and see what happens.

Q: My competitors have a huge, well-designed online presence, and here I am starting from scratch. How can I possibly keep up?

A: Compete! Surely you have some advantage over your competitors; otherwise, you wouldn't be in business. Follow the advice in this chapter, make your social media pages look clean and professional, and move forward. Post, engage, and persevere.

Q: I have a local costume and makeup shop that is doing very well. Should I expand into online sales? How would I even do that?

A: You can certainly give it a shot. Keep in mind, though, that a large part of the reason why you may be doing well locally is that you're selling something that your customers want to be there in person for. On the Web, you're competing against hundreds or thousands of businesses that are selling most of the same things, and they've probably managed to do it at a lower price. If you feel you can compete in that space—if your costumes are so good that you can compete on quality alone—then it's worth exploring an expansion to ecommerce. This is a big task that involves payment processing (your existing credit card processor will probably work), web design (you'll probably have to hire that out), web hosting, and product fulfillment (you'll probably need at least one new employee to help with that). That's a bit beyond the scope of this book. However, if you're already set on all of those aspects of ecommerce, just follow the directions in Chapter 4, and keep your online marketing strategy separate from your local strategy.

Summary

Local businesses and storefronts are usually the least Internet-savvy and least prepared to adopt a social media marketing strategy. That's why we swung for the fences on the case studies: we wanted to show how two different businesses, both in highly competitive tourist spots, used social media to distinguish themselves from hundreds of high-quality competitors. Even with celebrity status or deep relationships with tourism boards, you can't rely on foot traffic and word of mouth to put enough "butts in seats" or "heads in beds" in competitive markets. In this era of smartphones and cars with built-in voice navigation, people are doing a lot of research online before choosing an establishment. This is exponentially more important if you hope to attract tourist traffic. Giving cash kickbacks to the hotel concierges (where they still exist) for referrals isn't going to cut it anymore—not in the digital age.

You must project a digital beacon that guides people to your location from a variety of online sources. We hope we've given you a treasure trove of options to consider to help broadcast and amplify your signal.

You can also head over to the *Social eCommerce* site (*http://www.socialcommerce book.com*) for more Q&A and to post your own burning questions! You'll have access to exclusive offers, discounts, and coupon codes on various social media tools and services.

To get exclusive access to instructional videos related to the concepts in the chapter, simply send a text with your email address to *+1(213)947-9990* and we'll send you some awesome links!

CHAPTER 6

Designing and Testing Ads on Facebook

You can send traffic from Facebook ads, pages, or posts to anywhere. To make that redirection profitable, though, you need a well-defined strategy. There must be a reasonable expectation of what's going to happen to that traffic once it reaches its destination. Hopefully, by this point in the book, you've got that worked out, and now you're looking for ways to amplify your efforts. Facebook ads are an excellent way to do that, but you must proceed with caution. Take a slow and steady approach to this, and don't lose sight of your core metrics. It's very easy to waste hundreds of dollars by getting lost in the wrong numbers. Proceed with caution: do not jump into the deep end without a proper flotation device.

Start with a low budget—anywhere between $5 and $15 per day, depending on your overall marketing budget—and use your initial results to prove the effectiveness and value of your ads before making a big investment. If it doesn't work at $50, it's not going to work at $500, so don't scale it up until you've found the right formula.

Once you have a set purpose, know what your objectives are. No matter what you're doing, you're going to want more fans or followers, but what kind? Location-based, interest-based, or relationship-based? Perhaps you just want to encourage current fans to buy something—converting from fans to customers. Or you need to test a new offer or program by sending traffic to your site to test a demographic, price, product, or conversion tactic (ad, layout, design, options). Or you need more opt-ins in the form of viewers, listeners, or subscribers. When you're designing ads, it's too easy to make the wrong choices, so, again, knowing what your objectives are will save you time, cash, and disappointment.

This chapter is about Facebook ads. At this time, no other major social networks offer direct advertising. Although Twitter offers sponsored posts and accounts, it offers no direct advertising opportunities.

Campaign Types

On Facebook, an ad must belong to a campaign. In some situations, you are better off driving engagement; in others, you need more fans in order to hit the sweet spot; and in still others, you need to drive traffic off-site to a landing page or sales site.

In the broader sense (not just on Facebook, but in advertising in general), a campaign represents a marketing effort. There is a plan, a budget, an execution, and a measurement of results. The following subsections describe some potential campaign models for you to consider.

Traditional Sales

In this model, you put up an ad on Facebook to drive traffic to a landing page on your website. This is no different than advertising on any other online platform. Depending on what you're selling and where you're trying to sell it, this may be an excellent option for you.

Branding

Traditional branding involves associating a certain message with your brand, rather than selling a product. Branding, as a standalone function, is typically the province of very large corporations. As a standalone effort, it is often an expensive proposition for smaller businesses and doesn't usually provide an ROI (return on investment). However, when combined with traditional direct response marketing, branding is a smart and savvy way to increase your presence and to communicate your unique values, characteristics, and attributes to your customers and prospects.

In the branding campaign model, you put up ads that drive traffic back to your Facebook page. You could also drive traffic to a Twitter account, or to any other page on a social network (for instance, if you're promoting a band and focusing on MySpace, you would drive traffic there). Although nothing is sold in branding, you should always build the groundwork for a value proposition (such as offering a coupon, an educational piece, or a valuable newsletter) to get your audience to take the first step in the buying process.

On Facebook—more so than most other online advertising platforms—branding is essential. You can offer the best features, the highest quality, or the lowest price on any product or service, but if your brand isn't trustworthy, many of your prospects simply won't bite. Even if you're trying to drive sales above all else, you should still reserve some effort for branding. This should always be a part of your campaign.

It's important to make sure that you are strategically implementing the fundamentals into your ad campaigns. Defining what sets your business apart from the crowd is foundational to your marketing plans. As you are advertising a specific product, service, or event, it is increasingly important to show potential customers why someone should pick you over your competition. Just think of branding as telling everyone what is different and valuable about you—a unique value proposition.

Think about something as simple as a hamburger. Different restaurants that sell hamburgers define themselves in specific ways: McDonald's defines its offering by volume, touting that billions of hamburgers have been sold; Burger King offers a fire-grilled burger; and the trendy West Coast chain In-N-Out Burger offers a simple menu, but also a (well-known) secret menu. While each restaurant has a similar product, its branding is dramatically different. This marketing concept has been around for ages, but it has never been more important than in our online age. The sea of competition is fierce, and solid branding is often the difference between future success and failure.

Here are some popular examples of other brands and companies defining themselves against the market:

- *Pandora Internet Radio:* Play only the music you love
- *eBay:* Shop victoriously
- *Starbucks VIA:* Never be without good coffee
- *Zappos:* Free shipping, free returns
- *Hyundai:* 100,000-mile warranty
- *The Four-Hour Work Week:* Escape the 9–5, and join the new rich (Tim Ferriss)
- *FedEx:* When it absolutely, positively has to be there overnight

What makes your product, service, or event different from the rest? Why should customers pick you over another similar competitor? If you haven't answered these questions or given the answers any thought, your business might be due for a little soul searching.

Traditionally, companies have distinguished themselves by price, availability (or lack thereof), location, expertise, quality, value, customer service, and product guarantees, to name a few. Today, many new online businesses attempt to establish themselves by offering extremely low prices, but this isn't always possible and doesn't always work. Sometimes, it's a path to bankruptcy. As a business owner, you may not need to compete heavily on price if you can clearly show what makes you different. Understanding *why* your customers buy your product will help you to understand exactly *what benefit* you are providing. If you understand what benefit you are providing, you are one step closer to finding your brand identity.

Another way to understand your brand identity is to ask: what pain is my product or service alleviating? In the preceding list of brands and companies defining themselves against the market, every tagline addresses (and alleviates) an ideal customer's pain. Tim Ferriss's message of "Escape the 9–5, and join the new rich," touches on the pain that book-buying people feel going to a job they don't like. Pandora offers Internet radio that aims to "play only the music you love," saving listeners the agony of bad music.

Whatever your findings are, they represent your brand, and should be the focus of your ads.

Special Events and Holidays

Holiday ad campaigns are a great way to get started with Facebook advertising. The audience is receptive, and people have money to spend on things that they don't ordinarily buy. At other times during the year, people are not actively looking to buy something, so many ads attempt to catch buyers off guard. However, during the holiday season and amid the excitement of holiday sales, people often search for gift ideas, so good-quality ads are much more effective and profitable.

When people are in the holiday spirit, let your ads match their feeling. You can add a little holiday bling to your ad or incorporate the holiday tone into your ad copy. People are busy preparing for the holidays, going to parties, and generally preparing for a little break. So get into the mindset of your target audience and figure out what they would be interested in doing/buying this year.

Selling a "better you" in the new year

The new year is famous for being the time when gym memberships and diet commitments skyrocket. It's a time when people tend to reflect on where they are and how they can improve. Appeal to your audience's desire to look better, feel better, or become smarter, richer, and more efficient this year. Think about this as you are picking your image and writing ads. Before the end of the year is generally a good time to focus on building up your email list. By January, advertising a "better you"-type product is the logical next step.

A whole new round of testing

During the winter holiday season, the things that don't usually work might magically start working. The holiday shopping season presents an unusual, highly profitable special-case situation in terms of ad design, marketing campaigns, and even Facebook ad approvals. Content that was consistently rejected in the past, like multilevel marketing (MLM) and network marketing opportunities, could suddenly start working. We have also seen a lot of positive results from straight CPM campaigns (directing Facebook ad traffic directly to your website landing page rather than your Facebook page), so it could be worth a try to see if it pays off for your business.

The rules of this game are always changing, and this applies even more so to holiday campaigns.

Matching the reason to the season

Ad campaigns can be created to match any season or holiday celebrated or observed by your target audience. We are surrounded by pitches that use the change of season or holiday to sell a product or a service. Springtime? Buy spring-cleaning services! Fourth of July? Time for a new grill! Take advantage of the established patterns and expectations of your audience, and adjust your message accordingly. You may not have spring-cleaning services to sell in April, but perhaps you have a service or product that offers your prospective customer a fresh new start. Perhaps you have no grill to sell in July, but your product can promise some type of independence, or its use and application can evoke some feeling of summertime fun. f600.431

Market Research

Now you need to know what keywords and key phrases you should target. You know your audience, you know your brand, you know your product, and now you need to know the exact terms that apply to it. This will help you with identifying the most popular interests for your target audience. Knowing which keywords are the most popular will also come in handy when you are writing copy for your business description, ad copy, and so forth. To do your keyword research, you're going to start with search engines.

Let's say that you've got a stationery store. Think about the products that you're targeting, and then go to Google and Facebook Graph Search and look for the subjects related to that term. Try to think about the subject broadly and come up with as many terms and short phrases as you can. For instance, if you sell supplies to make party invitations, you might search for:

- Party invitations
- Mother's day cards
- Wedding invitations
- Wedding stationery
- Cards for party invitations
- RSVP cards
- Card designs
- Custom stationery

Basically, you're taking the fundamental words associated with this product, which are *stationery* and *cards*, and attaching related terms to them that will help you figure out how to market them effectively. It doesn't do much good to advertise Christmas cards in July, for instance. Take advantage of holiday seasons, traditional habits, and regional cultures.

In addition to search engines, you can also use the ad systems built into Facebook. You'll have to go through the process of setting up your advertising account first; then, create an ad and use the keyword tools to see what the range of audiences and prices is for each of your terms.

Beyond these elementary resources, there are some other keyword research tools out there that you can use for Facebook ads:

- Google AdWords Keyword Planner (*https://adwords.google.com/KeywordPlanner*)
- Google Trends (*http://google.com/trends*) (Figure 6-1)

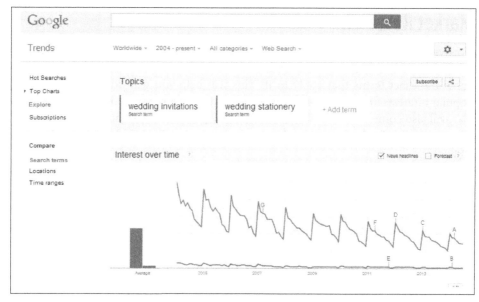

Figure 6-1. Google Trends

Beyond keyword research is audience research. You want to know who is using these keywords to find things to buy. To learn that, you have to look at publicly available analytics for sites that rank highly for the keywords you're targeting.

If you have an established website with a decent amount of traffic, just look at your own stats. You can also look at competitors' stats and demographics through these tools:

- Quantcast (*https://www.quantcast.com*) (see Figure 6-2)

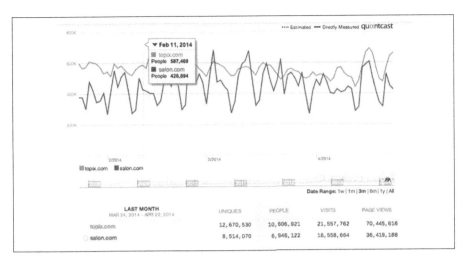

Figure 6-2. Quantcast

- Alexa (*http://www.alexa.com*)
- Compete.com (*http://compete.com*)

However, if you want to peek at your competitor's ranking keywords, we recommend these tools:

- SEMrush (*http://www.semrush.com*) (see Figure 6-3)

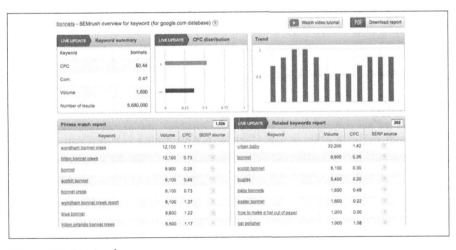

Figure 6-3. SEMrush

- Searchmetrics (*http://suite.searchmetrics.com*) (see Figure 6-4)

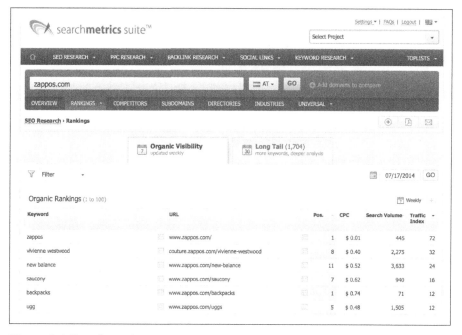

Figure 6-4. Searchmetrics

- Spyfu

Any website associated with your target keywords (the sites that turned up when you were using Google to search for your keywords) can offer valuable insight into the demography of your customer base.

The more you understand your market, the more effective you'll be. The more specific you can be, the better off you are.

Targeting

Target exclusively. In other words, if you've got multiple ads in one campaign and you intend to target them to different demographics, make sure there is little or no overlap. Otherwise, you're just showing the same ads to the same people and paying twice for them.

Along these lines, one big mistake people make is to create too many campaigns with similar targeting. They'll create a whole campaign aimed at women age 30–45 in the U.S. who like yoga, and another campaign for women 30–50 in the U.S. who like Oprah Winfrey, and then put the same ads in both campaigns. There's a lot of crossover there, and that shows double (or triple, or more) ads. Not only is this costing you a fortune, it's also reducing your *click-through rate* (CTR), which increases the cost of your ad and annoys the people viewing it.

At the very least, use different ads in campaigns that have some overlap.

Creating Audiences for Facebook Ads

We've established that the more focused your campaigns are, the better. Every member of your audience who doesn't find your product or service enticing is a waste of your time and money. One way to improve focus is by targeting an ad. Another way to do it is to define the audience, and then assign that audience to a campaign—working backward, essentially. This is especially useful when you have an opt-in email list from which to work.

The Facebook Ads Power Editor has an Audiences section that lets you create an audience based on a number of selective criteria such as interests and demographics, and a Custom Audience built on an external list. Custom audiences can be created from lists of email addresses or phone numbers. Facebook user IDs are not an acceptable datapoint to create a custom audience on unless you have each user's permission to advertise them.

One thing you'll definitely want to start with is a Fans Only audience. Facebook used to have this as a default audience option, but at the time of this book's publication, the only option available is "Fans and Friends of Fans." Frankly, this is a horrible option that will almost certainly not benefit you. Your fans are definitely interested; their friends are probably not. To create an audience of your fans, click Create Audience, and then select Saved Target Group. In the configuration window that appears, type your page name into the "Target users who are connected to" field, and save this as "Fans Only."

You can create other audiences in a similar way by using different options. You can even create an audience that targets the pages of your competitors.

To create a custom audience, first make sure that you have your opt-in list in a text file with one entry per line. You may have to export it from your mailing list software, if it's an email address list. Then go to the Power Editor in Facebook Ads, and click Create Audience, then select Custom Audience. Select the option that corresponds to the type of information that is in your list, and give it an appropriate name.

If you can, definitely take advantage of the Custom Audience feature. The results are impressive, with ads generating CTRs of 4% in a landscape where 0.04% is considered the norm. However, one major issue business owners should know of before using Custom Audiences is that you have to read, fully understand, and agree to its terms and conditions. While Facebook has come under fire for issues about privacy, it requires businesses to inform their subscribers about using their information for purposes like Custom Audiences.

Once you have your Custom Audience based on your email list, you can have Facebook create a Lookalike Audience of users who have similar tastes, interests, and demographics to your email list. That list will probably be huge (as in millions of users), so cross-section that list further with additional filtering criteria.

A more recent feature of Facebook's that is quite valuable in understanding your target market in Facebook is Audience Insights. Found within the Ads Manager, it allows you to drill down into specific target audiences (who are not already fans) and examine those segments' demographic and behavioral data. Definitely check that feature out.

Unpublished Post Ads for Facebook

When certain published posts that appear on your page are irrelevant to the fans you've targeted, you risk losing your audience. To work around this, you can promote *dark* posts, also known as *unpublished posts*, to a subset of your target audience. In a sense, it's filtering the already filtered audience.

These unpublished post ads may come in the form of a status update, a photo, a video, or a link share. The "dark" post will not appear on your brand's page but rather on a targeted customer's News Feed. For example, if your restaurant has a new organic vegan menu, you could promote it to a receptive audience by sending a post to vegan and vegetarian fans.

The results will be better engagement, a retained customer base, improved branding, and perhaps even increased fans from niche markets.

In addition to delivering relevant content, unpublished posts also allow you to perform *A/B testing* of ads: you can create two different campaigns and determine which one works best for which market.

Budgeting

Don't pour a lot of money into social media advertising right away. Start slow, start low, observe results, and then ramp it up once you're profitable. Once you get going, it's worth it to take a risk on increasing your budget. You can raise it by a certain amount —say, $50—and see if your *KPIs* (*key performance indicators*) scale linearly with it. It might be easier, though, to double your ad spend and see if that results in a doubling of your profit. If it does, then double it again and again until you find the point of diminishing returns, and then scale it back to the sweet spot.

The tricky part here is that things can change quickly, and you probably won't know why. Something can work one day and flop the next. It's impossible to predict what will happen with ads, so you must be quickly reactive; keep an eye on the graphs and reports. If your clicks or impressions go down and/or the bids go up, then pause the campaign. Your CTR should be high (0.03% or higher) from the first day onward. If you're above that and profitable, then you're OK. If you're below that, pause the campaign and start a new one with new ads.

The Basics of Ad Design

A great social media ad follows this formula:

Great offer + interesting image + compelling headline.

This is a simple formula, but its individual pieces are going to take some effort to achieve.

If you have successful campaigns in other mediums, then you can start by using the same text and graphics on Facebook. Beyond that, the following tips will help you create great ads.

Give a Reason for Clicking Like

If you are trying to increase fans and engagement with your ads, then a great offer should involve something unique for social media participants. Provide an incentive for viewers to click Like and become part of your community. For instance, Tim Ferriss, author of *The 4-Hour Body*, offers a fan-only chapter.

Think of some "Facebook exclusive" promotions you could offer. Also think of announcements that you could submit to your Facebook fans first. What are the incentives that your ideal customer would appreciate?

Godiva does a nice job of offering a "rewards" chocolate club that you can join for free from its Facebook landing page. Free chocolate is definitely a nice incentive! Godiva collects email addresses and complete contact information when viewers opt in to the Reward Club.

 In the past, on Facebook, good strategy included getting many likes for your business in order to build your audience and your reach. The people who liked your page were the people most likely to see your posts in their News Feeds. Although this is still a very good strategy, at the time of this book's writing, the organic reach of business page posts has significantly decreased. We suspect, though we cannot definitively say, that this is the reason Facebook has added the new feature Boost Post (formerly Promote) as a way of encouraging business-page owners to advertise their posts.

Interesting Photos

This is hard to qualify. If you're using models, make sure they look like they're having fun. If you're using product photos, make sure they're high quality and that they make the product look amazing. On a more basic level, an interesting photo has bright and vivid colors that differ from the Facebook color scheme (blue and silver).

Great Headlines

Profitable headlines sum up the message you wish to communicate. The normal rules of copywriting are: headline, ad copy, ad image. On Facebook, however, the order of importance is: image, headline, ad copy. The image must be relevant to the ad and the destination, and also draw attention. This is to break through the clutter of all the other images on Facebook. When writing headlines for Facebook ads, be sure to make them short and punchy—questions work great. For example:

"Love Science?" "Need More Clients?" "Love Tony Robbins?"

Next, you need ad copy to go with the headline. It is important that the ad copy be a call to action. In the following examples, the headlines from the previous example are followed by ad copy that demands a call to action. For example:

"Love Science? Then *LIKE* this page" "Need More Clients? Get Frank Kern's Free Book" "Love Tony Robbins? Click here to get 4 hours of FREE training"

If you're all out of ideas, try asking these questions:

- Who is your customer?
- What is his current pain?
- How can you solve it?

Focus on the benefit and outcome for your customer, and try to make your headline show that with as few words as possible. You can also try focusing just on relieving the pain.

Humor is also a good bet; it gets attention and catches people off guard, lightens the mood, and helps you connect.

Here are some common headlines you can use as a template for your own pages:

- Discover the Secret to…
- How to…
- 3 Tips That Help You…
- 5 Quick Steps to…
- Get A Free…
- How I…

Images That Sell

There are a lot of old articles that talk about how your Facebook ads need to have a photo that involves cleavage in order to be successful. Whether or not this is true, it certainly is no longer valid for many markets. You might get more clicks, but you're not necessarily going to get more conversions—unless it is a good fit and relevant to the ad.

Women feature everywhere in advertising: in men's magazines, women's magazines, tool ads, makeup ads, and virtually anything else that could reasonably involve a model. Women are selling everything. Therefore, it's wise to at least test ads with pretty women, as long as you own the images. If you're going to try this, then concentrate on an ideal image of a close-up of a pretty girl's face looking directly at the camera and smiling—but don't do a three-quarters shot that shows cleavage, unless the image is relevant to the headline and ad copy. Use a green background, and put your logo in the corner. This composition will work with just about any product or service on the market.

Another image that sells well? One with eyes that are staring or appearing to look straight at you. And, expanding on this model, a good seller is also a picture of your product with a model's eyes looking at or toward the product. Have an attention-grabbing image and a call-to-action button like "Click here" or "Click here to get this XYZ." Images for ads can have a maximum of 20% text. Finally, the best images are almost always custom built. Begin with your basic image and add the elements as needed. In Figure 6-5, most of these elements have been added, such as the eyes looking at the user and the call-to-action button.

Figure 6-5. An effective Facebook ad

Understanding the Metrics

Facebook has a number of metrics that can tell you how a post or an ad is performing. On your page, there are two measurements that show how many people have viewed each of your posts: one for organic reach, and one for paid reach. The latter is only for *boosted* posts. At this time, we don't recommend using the Boost Post option because it costs a lot and its targeting options aren't as good. Facebook has recently made some changes adding some targeting options to Boost Post that may make testing it a more feasible option in the near future. Instead, promote an individual post with an ad inside your Ads Manager.

In the Ads Manager, there is much more data on the performance of each ad and campaign, as you can see in Figure 6-6.

Figure 6-6. Ad metrics in Facebook Ads Manager

Each column in the Advertising Performance screen has a tool tip that explains exactly what it represents. Some of these aren't going to be important to your campaign, but that depends entirely on what you're advertising and how the ad is targeted. However, CTR and Actions are applicable to all ads; that's the basic measure of how many people interacted with your ad. The average CTR for Facebook Ads is 0.02%, but a well-performing ad is anything above 0.09%. The rest of the numbers in this view need to be individually interpreted; only you can define success for your business.

Multivariate Testing

There are only three main variables in an ad: the image, the text, and the targeting (the audience). How do you know that you've got any of them right, let alone the perfect combination? The answer is *multivariate testing*.

Multivariate testing is a more advanced version of A/B testing (also known as *split testing*). In the latter, you are merely testing between two single changes—for instance, testing an ad by using different graphics, but the same text and targeting. If you run two ads that are identical except for one change, you're doing an A/B test between the two.

Multivariate testing is advanced A/B testing. Once you find the best graphic, you then vary the text until you improve results. The idea is to come up with the perfect ad—one that gets as many clicks or conversions as can be reasonably expected, given your resources and audience.

This can make the difference between success and failure. The most famous instance of the power of multivariate testing is from Barack Obama's 2008 presidential campaign. Obama's director of analytics, Dan Siroker, tested a variety of options for graphics, videos, colors, and text for the Obama campaign website. He discovered that the options that the campaign staff liked the most were, in some cases, the least effective in terms of actual conversions. Due to his multivariate testing success, Siroker's testing resulted in a 40% increase in conversion rate, which in turn raised an estimated $60 million more for the campaign. He's now the CEO of Optimizely (*http://www.optimizely.com*), which makes software that supports the multivariate testing process.

The key to successful multivariate testing (or split testing, for that matter) is simply to get in the habit of doing it constantly. Don't just go with your gut most of the time. The best performing ad copy, images, landing pages, and so forth may be counterintuitive. You won't know unless you test it.

Testing Headlines with Bit.ly

You can use a tracking link through a service such as Bit.ly to test out each headline in isolation. This will enable you to find the best headline without spending any money on ads.

First, you're going to need something to link to. You can try to use your landing page, but that might be too spammy for your Twitter followers. It might be more appropriate to write a blog post on whatever subject applies to the headlines you're testing. It doesn't have to be long; 500 words would work pretty well.

Next, go to Bit.ly and set up tracking links to that page or blog post. You'll need as many links as you have headlines to test.

Then go to Twitter and post your headline as a tweet, and link to the blog post using the corresponding Bit.ly link. You can use Hootsuite to post each tweet at a reasonable interval, and then check back at Bit.ly in a few days to see which one got the most attention. And that's your ad headline!

Good Landing Page Design

A good landing page is vital for our sales efforts. We want to have a landing page to send our traffic to. In direct response marketing, we want to give our prospect only one option on our landing page—inaction will result in a default choice. A Subscribe button will not be accompanied by a Don't Subscribe button. That is why we use a landing page instead of a home page. If a prospect is given more than one choice, she will usually make no choice. For instance, if I want to sell something, then the only option on my landing page is to Buy. Similarly, if I want my prospect to sign up for my newsletter or get a coupon code, it is the only option on my landing page. See these Facebook examples (*http://on.fb.me/1n1Swdw*), or, outside Facebook ads, check out *http://ndstuff.com/joeball-3/* or *http://ndstuff.com/helmet/*.

Interestingly, the plain and unbranded direct response landing page (the one without the background image of football players and fans) got a 22% higher opt-in rate. We split-tested using Visual Website Optimizer (*http://visualwebsiteoptimizer.com*), though Optimizely (*http://optimizely.com*) would have worked equally well. Time after time, the unbranded landing pages convert higher. Why is this important? You have already spent money on advertising to get potential customers to your page in order to get more sales or subscribers. Spending no additional advertising dollars, you convert your page visitors to subscribers.

Remove Clutter and Improve Navigation

Again, it must be immediately obvious what a visitor should do on your landing page. Make your call to action clear. Specify exactly how you want the viewer to interact with your page. Just focus on one action—for example, clicking Like, buying something, or subscribing.

The Approval Process

Once you've created an ad, it will be submitted for approval. Someone in Facebook's vast organization will look at your ad and determine if it meets the company's terms of service. This is an unpredictable process that can take anywhere from 10 minutes to 3 days. There are no discernible triggers that make the process take longer.

If you are wondering what's going on, go in and create one more ad in the campaign and submit it to see what happens. Link this test ad to a blog post or something totally harmless and completely different from the first ad. Facebook may have put you into a holding pattern to review further.

Facebook changes the rules all the time, so you may want to read the terms of service and make sure that you are in full compliance. For instance, if your ad leads to an off-site landing page, you must have a privacy policy on that site. There must also be a Contact Us or About Us link clearly visible. Facebook wants to know that you're a legitimate, trustworthy business.

Real-Life Q&A

Q: I see ads in my Facebook sidebar, but I also get larger ads in my News Feed (it usually says Suggested Post at the top and then says Sponsored below it). Are the News Feed ads different somehow? Is one more expensive than the other? What's the difference?

A: There are three different placements for ads: Mobile News Feed, Desktop News Feed, and Right Column of Facebook. The key distinction is that Right Column ads do not show up on mobile devices; therefore, you lose 50% of your prospects. According to Facebook, as reported by SocialMediaToday (*http://bit.ly/1zBnbCy*), 48% of daily active users and 49% of ad revenue come from mobile. However, we've been involved in campaigns where 60% of our daily active users and our ad revenue came from users on mobile devices.

News Feed ads are in your prospective customer's News Feed. In general, they are more social and more effective than the other ad placements. Plus, you can populate the News Feed with great images—it is much easier to grab attention in a News Feed. The reason you see Suggested Post on some of the posts in your News Feed is because the owner of the advertisement has targeted you—either you have an interest in the subject matter and/or you fit its target demographic. The reason you see Sponsored at the bottom of an ad just means that it is a paid advertisement. And, no, one is not more expensive than the other.

Q: I am split-testing (A/B) my ads by showing more than one ad to the exact same audience. Some of the ads get thousands of views and some get almost none, within the same campaign. One is showing to 15,000 people and one is showing to 156 people, with the exact same audience selected. Am I doing something wrong?

A: This is because as soon as one ad gets a click, Facebook floods that ad with impressions, and the other ads are ignored. The best way to handle this is to pause all other ads in the campaign, and let the first one run for a day or so. Then pause the first ad and reactivate all the others until one of them pulls ahead. Repeat this process until you have at least three ads with decent CTRs. Then pause everything and let those three run simultaneously. You'll find that all three will get equal impressions, and you can run a proper split test.

Q: What's the longest you've had to wait to see if an ad was approved or not? Typically, it's a few hours until approval for me, but two ads have been in review for more than 12 hours now. These ads send traffic to my website, which I've never done before; I always used my Facebook business page as my landing page. Could that have anything to do with it?

A: Three days is the longest I've ever waited, but that was a rare case. It is possible that your landing page is holding things up. You might want to check to see if your page conforms to Facebook's guidelines. If the Facebook Ads rep who reviewed your ad saw anything questionable there, he might have placed you in a "holding pattern" for a supervisor to review.

Q: I just saw a huge tower ad in Facebook today. I've never seen that before. It looks like a Google AdSense tower ad. Is this something new?

A: These big banner ads are a form of malware and are not hosted through Facebook. If you see these, your operating system or browser has been infected with adware. You should run a virus scan and/or clear all cookies from your browser right away.

Q: I'd like to use President Obama's image in my ad. Can I do that?

A: No. Don't even try it. Never use anyone's image, name, or likeness in an ad without that person's written consent.

Q: I have ads that lead to an opt-in tab on my Facebook page. They're getting me about 12 new opt-ins and 30 likes per week. Or at least they were. Then I changed the content and layout of the opt-in page, and opt-ins dropped to two per week. Bad idea, right? So

I changed it back to the original format, but it's stayed at two per week even though I'm still getting the same number of new likes. What could be wrong?

A: Potentially a lot of things. Are you targeting the same people? Are there more than 200,000 people in your target group? What is the reach of your campaign? Has most of your target group already seen your ad at least three times? Can you set up two landing pages for opt-in content, and split-test them? Have you tried setting up a new campaign with new images, headlines, and ad copy, but with the same landing page? Conversion is a complex process with many factors. It's important to dissect as much as possible to understand what is going wrong. New campaigns can cure many ills. On the other hand, maybe the whole thing was a coincidence, and you've already reached all of the people who are willing to participate in your target audience.

Q: What's a good Facebook Ads CTR?

A: It depends on your market. Some demographics have CTRs hovering around 0.4%, while others are lucky to get above average (0.02%). If you have good competition, it's going to be tough. In untapped markets, Facebook ads have a great CTR. Personally, we wouldn't run an ad with a click-through-rate below 0.9%—we find that the ads are no longer profitable when CTRs fall below 0.9%.

Q: How long should it take before I see more impressions from a new campaign? I haven't had any impressions at all, and I'm wondering why.

A: If you're not getting any impressions, you will need to either increase your spend or check your targeting. Maybe you are bidding too low to be clickable. After a certain amount of time, if the impressions aren't coming, it's time to test some new ads.

Q: What is *bidding* for a Facebook campaign, and why would I want to do this?

A: There are two ways you can bid on traffic in a Facebook campaign. One is CPM (cost per mille—your ad gets shown 1,000 times) where you pay for impressions, and the other is CPC (cost per click) where you pay per click, or each time someone clicks on your ad. You can also let Facebook automatically bid for you, or you can manually bid CPM or CPC. Facebook gives you a suggested range and you just put in an amount that is the maximum you are willing to pay for the click. According to Facebook, the suggested bid range is there to help you pick a maximum bid so your ad will be successful. It's based on how many other advertisers are competing to show their ad to the same audience as you are. You don't have to pick a bid in this range, but you can use it to help you pick a bid that will result in a decent-sized amount of impressions and clicks. According to Facebook, you will never pay more for an impression or click than necessary, so entering your true maximum is the best way to make sure you don't miss out on impressions and clicks you could have received. That being said, we always bid manually, because that is how we find our ROI in advertising. However, when you're doing a "LIKE" campaign (a campaign for "Like Us" clicks only), this is automatically set up as optimized CPM by Facebook.

Q: How do I get my ads to show to more people? For example, I have one ad with a reach of only 635, but the ad targets 155,000 people. My bid is 45 cents, and the actual cost is 30 cents, so I'm already above the bid I need. What can I do to get the ad to show to more of the 155,000?

A: What type of ad are you running? It's generally harder to get impressions on a socially recommended ad (so a page post ad or page ad that includes stories about their friends liking it); if you have it socially recommended, try removing that and see if you get more impressions.

Try this: start a new campaign with an identical ad. Facebook Ads doesn't show an ad to all 155,000 users at once. Your targeted users have to log into Facebook to view the ad. So it will take time to reach all users. You can try raising your bid even higher for a few days; that might get you more impression share. Put it at $1.25 and let it run on a $30 per day budget. A higher bid, even beyond the actual cost, can increase impressions by quite a bit. Facebook Ads wants to see how high of a CTR your ad is going to get, so it will deliver a high amount of impressions until it has an estimate. If your ad doesn't get a high CTR, Facebook drops your impressions in favor of an ad that does. The higher the CTR of an ad, the more Facebook makes per impression.

Q: I launched an ad, and the low-end bid recommendation was $1.95, but I went ahead and bid $1.00 anyway. Two days later, when I check its stats, it says the bid recommendation is $0.35–$0.83. What's going on?

A: This can change drastically from moment to moment. Facebook is guessing the CTR of your ads and weighing it against the average ad CTR. This is no different from other popular ad systems on other networks. It starts at the average CTR in the marketplace, then gives a CPC estimate and uses that to establish a ballpark CPM. The CPC price adjusts as your ad history gathers more data. No data (on a new ad) means an almost certainly inaccurate estimate, so plan on running the ad for a day or so, then adjusting your bid at regular intervals.

Q: Of the clicks that you get from an ad, how many will actually make a purchase? My ad goes to an external site and so far I have 62 clicks from a campaign reach of 21,000. Of those 62 clicks, statistically, how many would actually make a purchase? Is there a formula that would determine this? I'll know if anyone purchased in a day or two, but I'm curious to know the numbers that are involved.

A: You'll know this only from testing. It's different for every product, market, service, and offer. It depends on how much your product costs and how much you spend on your ads. Spend a few bucks, and then pause and assess the results. It's impossible to give accurate figures for CTR and purchases unless you compare against someone in the same vertical.

Expect to see lower CTR and purchases from Facebook than from a search engine ad campaign. When people surf Facebook, they are not intending to buy something, even if they click on your ad. Mostly they want to see what is new with their friends.

If someone searches for a term related to your product or service on Google or Bing, then she has intent and is more likely to click on the ad and then purchase the product. So rather than focus on expected purchase rate, just focus on return on investment. As long as you have a positive ROI, keep running your ads and landing page, and ramp up your spending while continuously testing variations to attempt to improve CTR and purchases. If you have a negative ROI, make changes quickly or abandon the campaign and move on to another product or media venue.

Q: I see some industries/services really just having a hard time targeting enough people to make their ad campaigns both scalable and profitable for lead generation. If you had to pick the top five industries/services for being able to leverage Facebook Ads with a positive ROI, what would they be?

A: All markets can benefit from having a solid Facebook presence, even ones you wouldn't expect. Search engines are giving more weight than ever to social cues. Having said that, the best markets for Facebook ads are: entertainment, gossip/tabloids, employment, fitness, health, travel, personal and household services, self-improvement, ecommerce for physical goods, webinars, and live events.

With today's advanced targeting and the gigantic Facebook user base, any vertical has potential to benefit from Facebook Ads. Any product or service that can be marketed via traditional media can be marketed via Facebook.

Q: What is the range of people I should try to target? The first ad I made a long time ago initially focused on 3,000 people, but someone recently told me that I should shoot for 200,000. Is that true?

A: It depends on your target audience. Is this a local business, nationwide, worldwide? Ideally you should find 200,000 people to target. This keeps Facebook sending enough impressions for a while, so your ad stays alive longer without going beyond your targeted audience. However, if you are a local business with a very specific niche demographic, then don't try to go beyond that targeted audience, and compensate for that limitation by refreshing your ads more often.

Q: How often should I increase my bid before Facebook starts displaying my ads? I started low, $0.25, and increase $0.05 every half hour. Is that the way to go, or should I do something different?

A: Bidding can be tricky because it changes based on day, time, niche, demographic, location, account age, and other factors. Some people have a policy to start low (which you've done) and increase the bid until you get a decent number of impressions. In our businesses, we start high. We normally double the low end of the suggested range. We never pay that much, but it helps to ensure that our ads get shown quickly.

Q: I've reached 15,000 views and have gotten 28 clicks. Are those statistics good or not? It's been a while since I've created an ad and I'm not sure what's good and what isn't. My CTR is 0.077%.

A: If your CTR is above 0.020%, then you are above the stated average. That doesn't mean that this is as good as it gets or that you should be satisfied. As we've mentioned before, in our businesses, we pull any ad that has a CTR below 0.09%—it just doesn't produce enough of a return. Certainly, keep an eye on your CTR and start creating new ads with different (but similar) photos. Test a few ads at a time, with the goal of getting a higher CTR and conversion rate. Try different photos first, then different headlines.

Q: Today I was following a Google Shopping link to an ecommerce site. I didn't click on anything in the page, not even a Like button. Now I'm on Facebook and the company's ad for the exact product I clicked on is following me around Facebook. How am I being targeted from Google to the company website to Facebook? It's not just a company ad; it's the exact product I looked at.

A: This is called *retargeting*, and it can have a huge positive impact. Google definitely does retargeting on Facebook. You just have to put a Google AdWords retargeting cookie on your Facebook landing page; then your ads can follow those people around the Web. This is excellent for product launches and affiliate offers. It helps create social proof—many images of your product increase your authority and credibility. This helps to ensure that customers buy from you instead of your competitors.

Summary

Our goal in this chapter was to help you determine your advertising objectives and design the appropriate campaign to achieve them. At the very least, any do-it-yourselfer can begin a Like campaign to build an audience for her business and design some ads with the necessary elements to start a basic advertising campaign. You should now be conversant with campaign types, market research, targeting, budgeting, the basics of ad design, the metrics of how your Facebook ad or post is performing, and multivariate testing. You should be able to spot good landing page design (and why it's essential), and know what to expect in the Facebook ad approval process.

We also hope, by the end of this chapter, that any other questions you had have now been answered and any misconceptions cleared by the lengthy Q&A provided.

Head over to the *Social eCommerce* site (*http://www.socialecommercebook.com*) for more Q&A and to post your own burning questions! You'll also have access to exclusive offers, discounts, and coupon codes on various social media tools and services.

To get exclusive access to instructional videos related to the concepts in the chapter, simply send a text with your email address to *+1(213)947-9990* and we'll send you some awesome links!

CHAPTER 7

Guerrilla Marketing

Guerrilla marketing means using low-cost, unexpected, and/or unorthodox promotional strategies to market a product or service. Guerrilla marketing isn't usually something you can pay for, so it typically substitutes an ad budget for an investment of time, energy, and creativity. It requires a high level of engagement, excitement, and innovation.

This may be your best shot at success in ecommerce through social media if you're not prepared to invest a ton of money and a ton of risk. There's an ethical line, though, and you don't want to cross it. Creating a bizarre ad that attracts a lot of clicks is one thing, but creating a knowingly misleading ad in order to trick people into buying from you is never a good idea.

You have to be careful here, because it's easy to upset people and cross the line into black hat territory. If you stay on the straight and narrow, it's boring; if you go too far off the road, it's offensive.

The main concept to remember here is: be original and creative and address the trends, but don't use things for unintended purposes. Don't exploit any bugs or loopholes, and don't game the system. If you do, you'll be discovered and punished eventually, and that can erase all of the gains you've made—maybe more. With that in mind, let's take a look at some unique, niche tactics that you can add to your marketing strategy.

Honor Competitor Coupons

The majority of people who like a brand on Facebook clicked the button only to receive special offers and discounts. Rather than just offering your fans coupons or deals, why not advertise that you'll honor any of your competitor's coupons as well? That way you can piggyback on your competitors' ads.

This is a great way not only to increase your sales, but also to increase customer loyalty *and* keep an eye on your competition.

Offer Giveaways, Prizes, and Challenges

Because you're saving some money with low-cost, innovative social media campaigns, invest some of your marketing budget into giving away products for free. Free stuff can attract a ton of attention.

Set aside a certain number of products to give away in social media campaigns. This is a fantastic way to generate some buzz around your brand, and to gain new followers and fans.

You don't have to give away your own products. In fact, giving away something that is somewhat expensive and heavily in demand or hard to find may be a much more cost-effective method of attracting both opt-ins and sales traffic. For instance, if you are an orthodontist, you might purchase five of the latest Apple iPads and offer to give one away to the first five people who come in for a free consultation and end up getting braces. Or you could give away the latest, hottest gaming entertainment system to the 1,000th customer on Black Friday. Just make sure that you either already physically have what you're promising to give away, or specify that you're giving away only a voucher that enables the reward to be purchased by the winning customer.

If you're an author promoting a new book, you could offer a prize (a signed copy of your new book, a private in-home reading, or an invitation to an event; if you aren't quite famous enough for those things, you could buy a signed copy of a famous author's book and offer to give that away instead) to the first person to defeat you at *Words With Friends* or *Scrabble*.

Local businesses can set up scavenger hunts, either in your store, or out in the local community (with the final clue being in your store somewhere).

There are many interesting and creative possibilities for challenges and giveaways. All you have to do is identify your goal or target, think of a fun challenge or valuable prize, and develop a compelling process to connect them. If your ideas are good, you won't have to do more than a basic level of promotion in order for them to go viral. Be careful, though, that the people you are attracting with your giveaway or challenge are part of your target demographics.

Be Controversial

Writing a controversial blog post related to your industry can do wonders for driving traffic to your site and getting attention on social media. For instance, if you run an ecommerce site that sells nursery accessories, try writing a post on "why you should let your baby cry it out," or some other controversial topic. Just be careful not to alienate your readers.

Use Facebook Offers to Generate Leads

Offers are shown directly in the News Feeds of those you target, just as ads are. This means optimal placement within Facebook, not to mention that Facebook sends an actual email (not just a notification) to those who click on the offer. However, when someone claims an offer, it can't go to an external page. That's the difference between an offer and an ad. Because it is limited in scope, you can't take it to a landing page.

Post an Infographic

An infographic that shows interesting statistics and facts can attract a lot of attention, if well designed and properly promoted. Many bloggers like to do *infographic round-ups* periodically, or center entire blog posts around meaningful demographics in their niche. To see some examples, go to Google Images and search for "infographic." You can spend an entire afternoon engrossed in clever representations of interesting data points.

If you don't have access to original data or statistics, grab data from reliable sources on the Web and have a designer create a graphical representation of them.

Airbnb wanted to release a data intense economic impact study highlighting the positive effects on local economies when would-be travelers choose to stay at someone's apartment or home versus a hotel room to time as a counterargument to claims made in New York City that tax revenue was being deprived of the city due to occupancy loopholes. Partnering with CopyPress, Airbnb developed out an HTML interactive infographic (*http://www.airbnb.com/economic-impact*) to not only express the information in a visual manner, but used it as an opportunity to expand into deep sections of the website it wished to rank for. Following the creation of the digital asset, Airbnb's PR team and CopyPress's native ads team were able to perform outreach and place advertisements on a variety of publications such as *Time.com* and *Washington Post*, highlighting one of the key attributes of interactive infographics (they're difficult for another publisher to steal!). The result was both a moral victory for Airbnb users in NYC as well as the SEO team of Airbnb; the stunt netted over 130 higher quality links.

Create a LinkedIn Group

Creating a LinkedIn group for your niche or industry is a great way to get known in your field without overtly advertising yourself or your business.

Keep in mind your LinkedIn group should be centered on an industry or topic, *not* on your business. So if you're in the online marketing field, you could create a group for Online Marketing Professionals," but not Jim's Online Marketing Service.

Creating a LinkedIn group not only drives traffic to your website, it also establishes you as a leader in your industry, and is fantastic for making new connections and generating leads for your business.

Create Awards Programs

Creating an industry-specific awards program can be another inexpensive way to get other business owners to spread the word about your business.

Here's how it typically works: design an awards program where entrants encourage their customers, newsletter subscribers, and social media followers to vote for them. The contestant with the most number of votes wins. Along with a small cash prize, winners (and often nominees) are given badges they can put on their sites to recognize their achievement.

For a relatively small cost, you've just gained new social media followers, buzz for your brand, and inbound links from all the badges you've awarded.

If you don't have the resources to set up your own awards program, you might be able to connect with an existing program that can help you bring in new customers (Figure 7-1).

Cross-Promote with Complementary Businesses

Social media is the perfect platform for working together with complementary businesses in your industry. For instance, if you sell culinary tools, you might cross-promote with a grocery store or a cookbook author. By cross-promoting one another's blog posts, tweets, pins, and Facebook posts, you can generate buzz in a totally nonthreatening, non-self-promoting way.

Use Photography with Branding

If you're into photography, get serious about photo-sharing sites—Pinterest, in particular. Make sure all of your photos have watermarks with your URL or brand name. Include prices in the description of your product photos so that they're included in the Gifts section. Where appropriate, you can also put text on the image, but take care not to be too spammy. See Figure 7-2 for an example.

Figure 7-1. If you don't have the resources to set up your own awards program, you might be able to connect with an existing program that can bring in new customers, such as American Express Membership Rewards

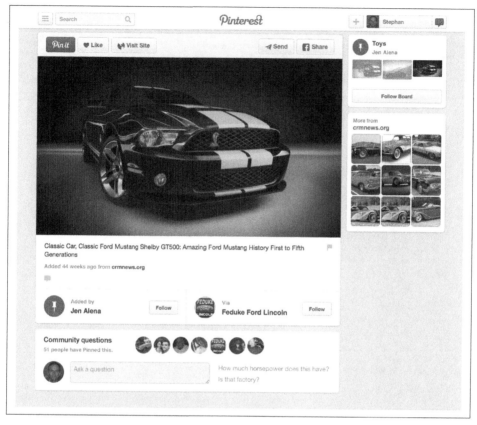

Figure 7-2. A good photo of a hot brand-name item can showcase a brand, a model, a reseller, a fan club, or all of the above

Arrange Meetups for SEO, Networking, and Marketing

Meetup (*http://meetup.com*) is a great way to network if you live in a decent size metropolitan area and are somewhat extroverted.

Start a meetup group related to your industry and promote it. Host interesting events and be sure to hand out your business cards to attendees. Completely fill out your Meetup (*http://meetup.com*) profile, include a link to your site on it, and make it public.

Make and Post Memes

Take a look at the most popular memes on quickmeme (*http://quickmeme.com*) and memebase (*http://memebase.com*), and think of ways you can use them to fit your branding messages. Make memes and post them to your social media accounts.

The possible exception is Facebook, where meme content is less likely to be seen than it used to be. You can still generate great traffic from meme-type content, just less than before the recent updates. Travel membership club Worldventures took advantage of the popular meme template Philosoraptor to make its own travel-related meme, and then posted it to its blog (Figure 7-3).

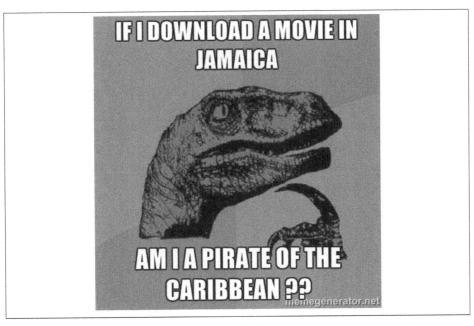

Figure 7-3. Memes are great, highly shareable, humorous ways to communicate a message about your brand, store, or product. Be careful not to violate copyrights, though!

Leverage Viral Videos

If viral videos were easy to do, everyone would have one. This is just something you're going to have to experiment with on your own, if you're able. One tip we can offer is that humorous videos work very well. Even if you're a local business, it can work for you. You could do a spoof or parody—even if it is only tangentially related to your business. This can generate a lot of traffic. It's not so much product related, though it can involve products. You're just trying to generate attention and incoming links. Figure 7-4 shows Dollar Shave Club's excellent take on creating a viral video (*https:// www.youtube.com/watch?v=ZUG9qYTJMsI*) that is still centered on its product.

Figure 7-4. Dollar Shave Club capitalized on a very successful commercial by also sharing it on YouTube

If the news media reports on your topic, make your own video about it in response or as a commentary on the news item.

Unboxing videos—videos that show a product being unpackaged, assembled, and used for the first time—are typically very popular. Do you have products you could use for an unboxing video?

Get onto Wikipedia

A Wikipedia entry for your company or organization lends credibility to your brand and gets a Wikipedia link onto the first page of Google search results for your company. Unfortunately, it's against the rules to write an entry for yourself (conflict of interest), and the Wikipedia editors have an uncanny ability to detect rule breakers.

You might be tempted to work around the rules by creating a new Wikipedia account on a network that is not associated with your business—for example, your home computer, a coffee shop, or a friend's house—and then, over time, becoming a trusted contributor by making virtuous edits and correcting typos. This, too, is dangerous and not recommended.

The first step is to make sure your organization is notable. In other words, worthy of a mention in an encyclopedia. You'll need feature articles about you in mainstream media, not just passing mentions or soundbytes.

Next, you'll need to befriend a Wikipedian who will create the article for you. Make sure the article is sufficiently cited. Wikipedia relies on verifiable facts in the form of studies, papers, and news reports. If you cannot cite anything, then your article is likely to be deleted.

Case Study: Giving Pays Off

Kurt Shuster is cofounder and CEO of *Noomii.com*, a directory of life coaches and business coaches. In 2011, Kurt's marketing team had been trying for a few months to hit the gas on their content marketing plan. They had tried blogging and a few contests, but such is the case sometimes, the payoff was yet to come. Kurt then hired co-author Stephan Spencer to assist them with SEO and buzz marketing.

Figure 7-5. Noomii's advent calendar from 2011, 2012, and 2013

Under Stephan's guidance, Noomii started thinking differently about building buzz and links. In their brainstorming, they thought it would be beneficial to focus on the upcoming holiday season, and a fun new idea came just a day before December 1st. The team sensed that this one might be the big idea they were looking for, and the whole team decided to work through the night. By morning, the site was ready to go. Noomii's Advent Calendar (*http://www.noomii.com/advent-calendar-2011*) was a WordPress-based microsite that Noomii put up annually for the Christmas season starting in 2011.

Unlike most Advent calendars where you *get* something each day, Noomii's Advent calendar instead prompted you to *give* something every day. Users would put in their email address, and Noomii would send a daily idea for a random act of kindness for users to do. Or you could simply go to the website to check. The design was quite simple, just a basic WordPress homepage with icons for each day of Advent. Users then click on the icon to view the post, that then tells them about the day's activity.

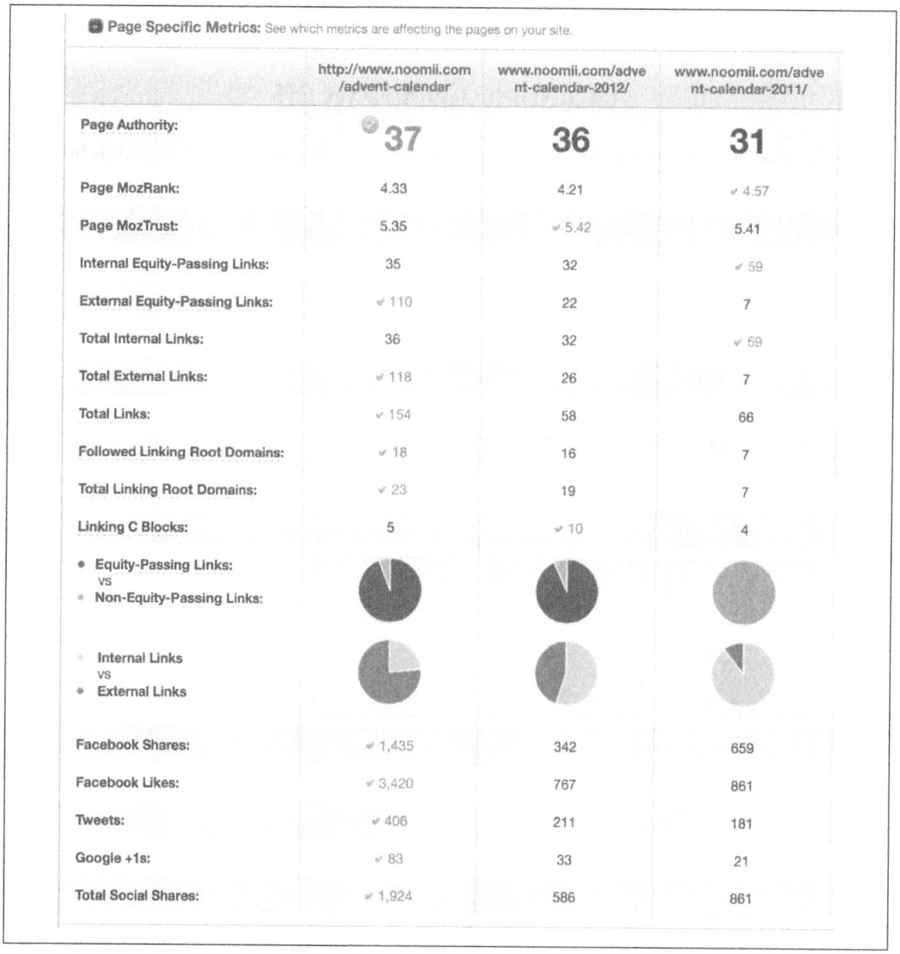

Page Specific Metrics: See which metrics are affecting the pages on your site.			
	http://www.noomii.com /advent-calendar	www.noomii.com/adve nt-calendar-2012/	www.noomii.com/adve nt-calendar-2011/
Page Authority:	37	36	31
Page MozRank:	4.33	4.21	4.57
Page MozTrust:	5.35	5.42	5.41
Internal Equity-Passing Links:	35	32	59
External Equity-Passing Links:	110	22	7
Total Internal Links:	36	32	59
Total External Links:	118	26	7
Total Links:	154	58	66
Followed Linking Root Domains:	18	16	7
Total Linking Root Domains:	23	19	7
Linking C Blocks:	5	10	4
● Equity-Passing Links: vs ● Non-Equity-Passing Links:			
● Internal Links vs ● External Links			
Facebook Shares:	1,435	342	659
Facebook Likes:	3,420	767	861
Tweets:	406	211	181
Google +1s:	83	33	21
Total Social Shares:	1,924	586	861

Figure 7-6. Noomii saw growth in equity-passing links and valuable social shares with each passing year

For promotion, Noomii asked Stephan to engage a power user on social media to share it. That power user got a lot of traction for Noomii for particular on StumbleUpon—over 15,000 stumbles. And of course, Noomii mentioned it in their newsletter and social channels; but, a lot of social spread happened organically because of its shareability.

Noomii encouraged the liking and sharing in the email by featuring a like and share Facebook and Twitter widget at the bottom of the email, and partnered up with a few "acts of kindness" groups on the Internet that shared it with their fanbase. Their first year Advent calendar saw around 700 subscribers. The second year (*http:// www.noomii.com/advent-calendar-2012*), the number of subscribers was around 2,000, and in 2013 (*http://www.noomii.com/advent-calendar*), it was around 9,000. Noomii saw a large increase in site views and subscriptions over these three years. Noomii has significant reason to believe this content marketing initiative has a significant role in its SEO success. They moved the yearly Advent calendar to a stable, permanent URL now, instead of a new URL each year, which will further help with SEO, since the previous years' link authority will pass to the current calendar.

Real-Life Q&A: I Love It When a Plan Comes Together

Q: I've made some advice animal memes related to my business. Should I post them to reddit?

A: No. Everyone will know that they are marketing material, you'll be downvoted and ridiculed, and your reddit account may be banned for spamming. Don't try to game reddit in any way. If you want to post something there related to your business, make it a news story on a reputable news media site. The possible exception is if you have a genuinely funny or intriguing viral video. Think along the lines of "Will It Blend?" Are your videos that interesting? If not, then don't try to post them.

In general it's a better strategy to get lots of fans, friends, and followers on social media, and then post your video there and let other people submit it to reddit.

Q: Can't I just make anonymous edits to my Wikipedia article? They can't track me, right?

A: Wikipedia logs IP addresses of users who are not logged in. If your new article or edit traces back to an IP block associated with your company, you will be found out. It's not worth the risk.

Q: My company already has an article on Wikipedia. If I want to make changes, but I don't want to break Wikipedia's Conflict of Interest rules, what other options do I have?

A: Post a note to the "Talk" page for your article explaining the situation: who you are, what you need changed, and why (back up your facts with sources). Factual inaccuracies are easily addressed this way. Other changes/additions may prove much harder. If you aren't getting any response/action after a month or two, post a note about your needs on the Conflict of Interest notice board in Wikipedia.

Summary

Posting ordinary content and appealing to traditional demographics isn't the only way to reach people. When you start getting into creating and posting viral content, you're wandering into the realm of guerrilla marketing, whether you realize it or not. There's a lot of opportunity here, and it's usually inexpensive, but there is also the potential to cross the line and get yourself in trouble—with a customer, a competitor, a major service provider, or even a national government.

So be careful. Research the boundaries before you push them. Successful marketing always involves a certain level of unorthodox thinking and a high amount of creative thinking. Just be careful that you don't throw it all away in your pursuit of success.

Head over to the *Social eCommerce* website (*http://www.socialcommercebook.com*) for more Q&A and to post your own burning questions! You'll also have access to exclusive offers, discounts, and coupon codes on various social media tools and services.

To get exclusive access to instructional videos related to the concepts in the chapter, simply send a text with your email address to *+1(213)947-9990* and we'll send you some awesome links.

CHAPTER 8

Professional Presence and Damage Control

This chapter is about *reputation management*—the art of looking good online. In the pre–social media era, all you needed to do was worry about search engine results based on a relatively small number of sites. Now, though, there are many social media sites that offer upset customers or competitors the ability to post negative reviews or rants, as Figure 8-1 points out.

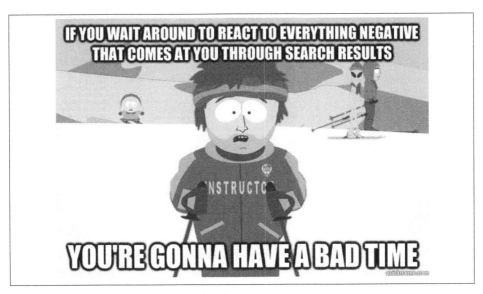

Figure 8-1. A clever meme that illustrates the point of this chapter

So let's be proactive. First, we'll identify all of the user-controlled social networks that play a major part in online reputation. Then we'll explain how to enhance your strategy to include responding to negative feedback in a positive way before it can drive people away from your business.

Throughout this chapter, keep one fundamental principle in mind: reputation management is not just about avoiding looking evil; it's about being good and doing the right thing always, not just when people are looking.

Finding Problems

If you're starting from scratch, you've got to survey the virtual landscape and identify your biggest reputation problems. You could run around to every site that you can think of and search for names associated with your business, product, and brand, but that would take a lot of time and you can't necessarily guess which sites are going to have the most damaging content.

Instead, use Soovle (*http://www.soovle.com*), illustrated in Figure 8-2.

Figure 8-2. Soovle can show you popular search queries from multiple sites on one screen

We've mentioned this site in previous chapters as a keyword research tool, but it's also useful for finding negative content. Using Soovle for reputation management is a two-step process: first you must try to identify any popular keywords that have a negative slant by seeing whether those show up as keyword suggestions. Soovle is convenient as a one-stop shop for checking Google Suggest, Yahoo Search Assist, YouTube Suggest, and more. Second, look at what is ranking for those keywords as well as just your brand keywords by themselves. You'll want to displace the damaging results with good ones —or at least innocuous ones.

When you're searching, you're going to have to get creative with your queries. You can't just search for your brand name and sort through the pile of results. What sorts of complaints have your customers called or emailed about? What would you say about your brand if you were an upset customer? Think about those subjects, and the questions and statements that they evoke, and use those as search terms. For instance, if your brand were Acme and you sold anti-roadrunner products:

- Acme anvils suck
- Acme ripoff
- Acme scam
- Acme products don't stop roadrunners
- Are Acme products worth it
- Do acme traps actually work

Put yourself in the angry customer's shoes. Ask the questions that he would ask; make the statements that he would make.

Perhaps you won't find anything. If so, that's good! But you'll want to check back on a regular basis—say, once every quarter—to make sure nothing new has come up.

Another recommendation is to set up ongoing monitoring for the terms readers use to search for negative sentiment about your company. A simple option for this is to set up Google Alerts with daily emails for those terms.

Case Study: Celebrity Damage Control

Few companies are willing to admit their failures; it was difficult to find a good case study for this chapter. Instead of the usual story of zero-to-hero, we've decided to draw attention to something you've probably already taken notice of: celebrity reputation management.

Remember Pee-Wee Herman, lesser known as the actor Paul Reubens? Well, the Internet does. His mugshot and an article on TheSmokingGun (which specializes in celebrity arrests) are still in the Google top 10 results for arrests in 1991 and 2002 (see Figure 8-3). These events were so long ago and there have been so many other potentially newsworthy events since then that you'd figure it shouldn't be a problem for Reubens to force the old and embarrassing ones off of the first page—that is, if he were taking his reputation management seriously.

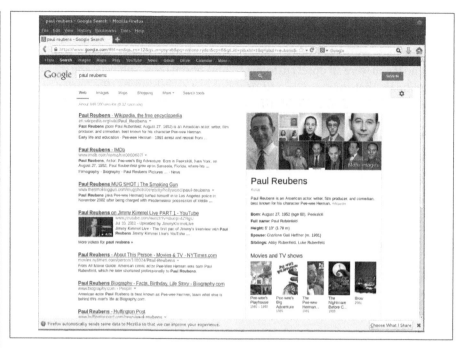

Figure 8-3. Miss Yvonne would not approve of Pee-Wee's mugshot being in the #3 slot in Google

By contrast, search for Charlie Sheen (Figure 8-4). Not only was he named in one of the most high-profile prostitution cases of all time, but he also famously had a public meltdown in 2011 when he was fired from his hit television show and made a series of bizarre statements on talk shows and social media. For a while, it seemed that it couldn't get worse for Charlie Sheen in terms of reputation. Search for him today, though, and you'll see that he has a vast, well-curated social media presence, and in the Google search results it's nothing but good news, even from the celebrity gossip sites that attacked him during his scandals. Again, enter online reputation management firms. It's possible (though, of course, not proved) that Charlie Sheen's reputation was cleaned up by a celebrity (or online) reputation management company. The basic theory behind much of the cleanup is to put out lots of online good content to nullify the bad.

Figure 8-4. #Winning

Quixtar was the ecommerce arm of Amway, a household goods multilevel marketing (MLM) company. While Amway enjoys a decent web reputation despite being an MLM (Figure 8-5), Quixtar was horrible (Figure 8-6). Eventually Quixtar was rebranded as Amway Global, though the core business remains largely the same. Even today, some time after Quixtar was reorganized into a more trusted brand, it still has a bad reputation on the Web.

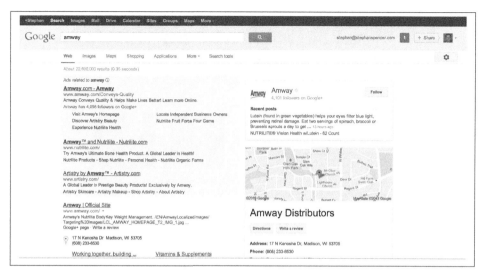

Figure 8-5. Amway appears to be very image-conscious on the Web

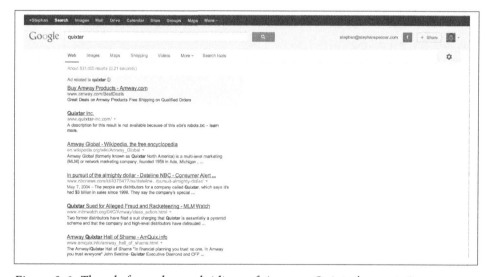

Figure 8-6. Though formerly a subsidiary of Amway, Quixtar's reputation management was and still is abysmal—could that have something to do with Amway's decision to rebrand Quixtar as Amway Global?

Separating Business from Personal

If you haven't done so already, siphon off all of your business-related content to social media accounts that are dedicated to your business. Don't use your personal accounts to host business content, and don't spam your friends with business stuff. Basically, use social media like your customers use it—for friendly and useful interaction, not for dictating a marketing message.

This is especially important on Facebook and Twitter. The only people who should be your friends on your personal page are those you'd invite to your home for dinner. Maintain an arm's-length distance from everyone else.

Even if you don't post crazy photos or political messages, it's not a good idea to use even the most benign personal social network accounts to market your products. You don't have control over who tags you in photos or videos, and your friends and family certainly are not going to ensure that they are in line with your marketing strategy before they post comments on content associated with you. Just the same, make sure your party photos are private, and lock down your private account so that it doesn't sabotage your business effort.

Never let an employee of your company keep the company's social media account logins a secret. You must set up the accounts for your company yourself, with your email address, and provide the login only to trusted employees. All employees should sign an NDA (nondisclosure agreement) that prevents them from speaking for your company publicly without express written permission. When an employee who has access to any of your social media accounts leaves the company, change the password immediately to ensure that she is not able to continue participating.

Or, you can consider an application like Hootsuite (the enterprise version) that allows site owners to assign permissions to social media team members or contractors without having to give away the official logins for the accounts. It also makes it easy to revoke access to social media accounts quickly—should that become necessary.

Maintaining Consistency

Whenever possible, use the same username and account details across all of your social media sites. If there is any inconsistency there, you'll look suspicious. Also, the more certain data is repeated, the more it is trusted in search engines.

At this point in history, most of the vanity URLs and usernames are taken. Hopefully your brand name is unique enough to be available across all sites and top-level domains, though. You can check quickly across dozens of social networks by using NameChk (*http://namechk.com*) (shown in Figure 8-7).

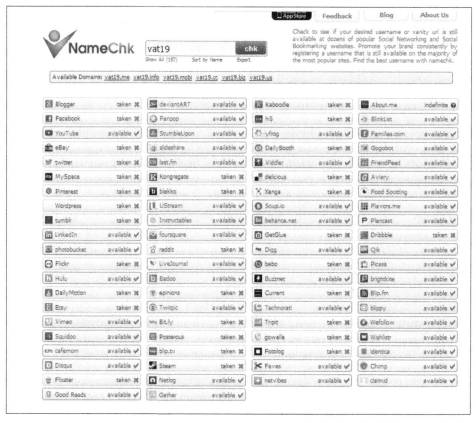

Figure 8-7. NameChk can help you search for potential user account names, which usu-ally are part of the URL on social networks

Being Deleted or Delisted

One of the worst things that can happen to your online business is to get blackballed from search engines or social media sites. It's not the end of the world, though; there is hope if this happens to you.

Facebook

You can have a great Facebook page humming along, getting you all kinds of sales, and then suddenly your page has been removed or your account has been disabled, and all you've got as an explanation is a vague form letter.

There may not appear to be rhyme or reason to Facebook's decision to suspend your business account, but you must have been pushing into some gray areas, even if it may have been inadvertent. Facebook changes its policies frequently, so something that was acceptable in the past may no longer be so. It's important to keep up with Facebook's current Terms of Service. Generally you'll get a warning that you're not complying with the Terms of Service. Then if you keep up with the bad behaviors, you'll likely get your account suspended.

There are two types of suspensions: you can get your ads account suspended, or your entire Facebook user account. Probably you'll get your ads account suspended. If that happens, you'll want to respond to Facebook with an explanation and request for reinstatement. The notice of suspension will include a link ("If you think you received this in error…") and from there you can fill out a form to get help and to contest Facebook's decision.

Google

Being blacklisted from search engines is even worse. Unlike Facebook, Google rarely makes mistakes in this area. So if you've been banned from Google, the first thing you need to do is clean up the dodgy black hat things you did (buying links is a popular black-hat tactic that will get you penalized, for instance), document the whole cleanup process, and go to Google with a mea culpa, detailing what you did wrong and what you did to clean up the mess. You do this through a "reconsideration request" that you file in Google Webmaster Tools (*http://www.google.com/webmasters*). This is only for when you've been manually penalized. If you have an algorithmic penalty, you still have to clean up the mess, then you have to wait for an algorithmic update.

LinkedIn: Your Online Business Card

As mentioned earlier in this book, LinkedIn is a great place to show your job history and make business connections. It's also a great place to get a new job, or to find a new employee.

When you're managing your reputation online, it's more important than ever to be proactive. Your customers are talking about you. If you're not part of that conversation, you can't help direct it.

While it's impossible to control what people say about you, it's a lot easier to get on the front foot and be proactive about the kind of information you want people to find about you.

You should, of course, complete your personal profile on LinkedIn, populating it with a good professional photograph, accurate professional information, and contact details. LinkedIn is an online résumé, with tons of extra benefits, so include your relevant past positions, awards, honors, clubs, associations, and so on.

Aside from your personal profile, you should also register and complete a profile for your company. This is a great way to ensure that all of the good stuff that people link to or say about your company or brand gets mentioned in proper context. When you're working on that content, remember to use relevant keywords and key phrases in your profile, and include plenty of links to your website, products, training programs, and other social media pages.

To increase your credibility on LinkedIn, answer questions in relevant industry groups, and in LinkedIn Answers. Be as helpful as possible. The more helpful your contributions are, the more valuable and trusted you become in your industry. You can enhance this effect by using SlideShare presentations to showcase your work, recent findings, and market updates. Don't overpromote, though. When you are helpful, people will actively seek out your services. If you have more time to post and manage content, then look into starting your own industry-, market-, or niche-themed group. As your company profile user, post news stories about your products, and keep the feed active with positive, relevant information. The spam threshold is a little lower on LinkedIn company profiles; this is where people go to learn more about your company, so it's perfectly relevant to show them as much information as you want to share.

Review Sites: The Harsh World of Direct Feedback

Seemingly everyone has a blog. Consequently, there could be countless potential sources for negative or inaccurate reviews. Oftentimes there is no easy way to contact the blogger —or even find out who he is.

While negative content on personal blogs is important, it's not the only thing to worry about. With the rise of social media, you also need to monitor key social media sites and respond quickly to anything negative that appears.

There are a few specialty social networks that focus solely on rating and reviewing businesses and products. The major players are explained in the following subsections.

Yelp

Yelp is mostly useful for local businesses, and by default, it detects your geographic area and limits search results to that region. If you are just starting out, or if you have no Yelp reviews at all, it's a good idea to establish a business presence on the site. Sign up, put in all of the relevant information about your company, and encourage satisfied customers to post reviews.

If you get a negative review, you can post a comment that explains the context. However, it's a better idea to try to contact that upset customer directly so that you can resolve the issue privately. If it works out to her satisfaction, then it's all right to ask her to amend the review. If she refuses to change the review, then explain on Yelp how you tried to help resolve the issue.

You can also actively encourage your customers to go to Yelp and post positive reviews. There is nothing unethical about this.

Glassdoor

Glassdoor is a site where employees and job interviewees rate and review companies. If your company has poor ratings on Glassdoor, it's going to be a major HR problem for you; you will have a difficult time attracting top talent, especially if you are trying to bring in people from other areas.

You can encourage current employees to write reviews on Glassdoor, if you feel that they are happy working there and you have the sort of work environment where employees can come to you with honest concerns.

If you have a high employee turnover rate, you can expect negative reviews on Glassdoor. The site allows you to sign up for an account and respond to reviews and comments. This might help you put certain reviews into the correct context for future employees.

Google (Search and Places)

The content that makes up good old-fashioned search engine result pages (SERPs) is still an important concern. If you have a negative review showing in the first 10 results on Google, it could cost you a lot of money. If the site it's on is an independent blog, you can try to contact the blogger to resolve the issue or sway his opinion. If it's one of the other sites mentioned in this section, then follow the guidance therein.

One thing you can do to push results off of the first page is to get positive or neutral content to outrank the negative. If you've got a negative review in the seventh result slot on Google, you will need to boost the ranking of four listings that are ranked below the detractor to be ranked above the detractor, or you can create some new, SEO-friendly content and promote it to try to get it to outrank the detractor. One way to do this is to have public pages on as many high-traffic, high-authority social networks as you can, all with good unique content. Link to them from your corporate site, your blog, all social media sites you have a presence on, and all sites that you have control over to give them some authority with Google.

You can monitor how many of the listings on page one in Google are positive or negative (or not relevant to you) by using BrandYourself (*http://www.brandyourself.com*) (Figure 8-8).

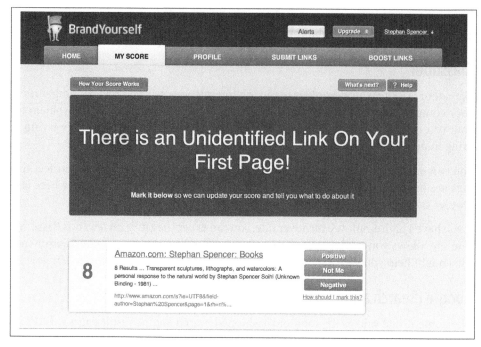

Figure 8-8. BrandYourself helps you keep track of top Google search results

Google attempts to connect all of its services whenever possible, and Google MyBusiness is an excellent example. It combines your Google+ profile, your Google Maps business information, and your location on Google Maps. If you do a normal Google search for, for instance, Costco, you'll see "X Google Reviews" in the search result listings (where X is the number of reviews). Click on that reviews link, and you'll be able to read people's reviews of local Costco stores in your current geographic area. You'll also see the map with an address and directions, relevant photos, and contact information.

As with all of the other review sites in this section, keep an eye on these reviews and try to contact anyone who writes a negative review so that you can try to address her concerns.

Wikipedia has a lot of influence on Google results. If you have a page on Wikipedia and it is mostly positive (at least in its initial summary), it is practically guaranteed to be near the top of the Google search results. If you do not have a Wikipedia page for your company, and you want to push some negative results out of the top 10, establishing a page with positive content is a great way to do that. However, you can't create the page yourself; neither can your employees. If you try, the Wikipedia editors will notice and delete the page, and you'll potentially have yet more negative content to deal with if someone exposes your Wikipedia promotional efforts.

If you're serious about a Wikipedia page, you need to seed the field a little by giving the editors something to use to establish encyclopedia notability. News stories are the best and most effective way to do this. Try to do some interviews and send out good press releases to potentially interested media outlets. News stories like these also have an influence on the top search results all on their own.

Having social media accounts that are reasonably active and popular is also a great way to push negative content out of the top 10 search results. Twitter, Facebook, and You-Tube, in particular, are highly trusted by Google, so if you have active, well-curated accounts on these services, you have a good chance of occupying some of the top 10 results with links directly to your company's social media pages.

If you're plagued by negative search terms in Google Suggest (the suggested search terms that Google drops down from the search bar while you are typing), you can try to push them out by providing links to search queries that are more positive. But be warned: This is a black hat tactic and you will run afoul of Google's guidelines. If you spam the world with Google search query links, Google will punish you. Some folks publish or provide these links, via social media. Google Suggest results are based on search query volume, so the more queries there are for positive terms, the less often the negative terms will appear.

Restaurant.com

This is like a combination of Yelp and Groupon, except it's specific to restaurants. You can get a ton of new people in the door by participating here, but keep an eye on the reviews and address any negative ones as they come in. If you're on this site, you've already got a business relationship with *Restaurant.com* (*http://restaurant.com*), so you already have an account and a line of communication with your customers.

Reviews should be easy to address on *Restaurant.com* (*http://restaurant.com*) because the site verifies that the reviewers have actually eaten at your restaurant, so there is less of a chance of a false review. It also connects a real person to the site account, so there is some accountability, and it will be easier to contact the upset customer and find a way to make amends.

Ripoff Report

Hopefully you'll never have to deal with Ripoff Report. It is a site dedicated entirely to negative reviews, all of which are written by anonymous site visitors. Unfortunately—for reasons unknown—Google gives it a high amount of trust and ranks its review pages very highly. If you have a negative review on Ripoff Report, it's almost certainly going to be in the first page of search results.

There is no editorial oversight on Ripoff Report. Anyone can post anything. A competitor of yours can post a dozen scathing reviews of your business; those reviews will be published and Ripoff Report will not remove them.

For a large fee, Ripoff Report will offer to bring in an arbitrator to analyze the truthfulness of each claim in the review. If any are found to be false, they are redacted from the review text, though the rest of the review will stay published.

You can also go to court and sue to have the review removed, or sue the person who posted it, if you can determine who it is.

It's free to post a rebuttal to any review on Ripoff Report, and that may be all you need to do. Even the Ripoff Report owners admit that it's not the complaint that hurts you, it's how you show that you've attempted to resolve it.

Another influential site of this same nature is Pissed Consumer (*http://pissedconsum er.com*).

Angie's List

This is one of the most powerful user-driven review sites on the Web. Like Yelp, it is mostly useful for rating and reviewing local businesses such as trades, services, physical stores, and restaurants. People trust it because it doesn't accept advertising from anyone —it is entirely monetized through subscriptions. That seems kind of backward in this day and age, doesn't it? Yet Angie's List is alive and well, and maintains a reputation as an unwavering source of customer honesty.

If you find yourself on the business end of a negative review on Angie's List, there is a documented complaint resolution process you can go through. According to site staff, there are only three ways to remove a review posted to Angie's List:

- The member who posted the feedback asks to have it removed.
- The complaint resolution process results in customer satisfaction.
- The review is shown to be fraudulently posted.

So if you get a negative review there, the only valid course of action is to address the issue with the customer who wrote it. This is the best policy anyway. You really don't want to fight a PR war on the Internet.

If you take Angie's List seriously and get good ratings there, the site will allow you to post discounts for members. This can be a great promotion for loyal customers, and can help bring new people in the door; they already know they can trust you, based on your Angie's List ratings.

Amazon

If you list your products on Amazon, and you get a negative review on your product page, you can contact the reviewer through the site and attempt to resolve it. Once you've done that, you can post your findings as a comment on the review, and click No next to "Was this review helpful?" at the bottom of the review.

If you're dealing with negative ratings or reviews on your seller account, Amazon has a more sophisticated process. If you are unable to resolve the issue with a buyer, you can contact Amazon and dispute the factual validity of the review. Amazon will not remove reviews unless they are posted under false pretenses, are for the wrong product or seller, or contain provably untrue information.

Taking Advantage of a Competitor's Blunder

Let's say that you've taken this chapter's lessons to heart and have an excellent online reputation. You monitor, you manage, you accentuate the positive, you avoid scandals and blunders—everything's perfect. Then one day you notice that one of your competitors has said something that you immediately recognize as a serious blunder. What do you do?

You take advantage of it. It sounds like a cutthroat Machiavellian maneuver (and it kind of is), but there is a lot of opportunity here not just to help your competitor make himself look bad, but to make your own company look better. You can do that by immediately and publicly speaking out against your competitor's gaffe.

There are plenty of examples of this to choose from. Examine any heated political campaign, for instance, and you'll find an almost daily gaffe-and-rebuke game being played between the politicians running for public office.

In the business world, consider the case of the Barilla Group, an Italian pasta manufacturer. In September 2013, Barilla's chairman said in a radio interview that his company's core values were in opposition to homosexuality. He further elaborated on his position with relatively mild but still quite offensive remarks about gay people, gay marriage, and adoption of children by gay families. In rapid reply, Barilla's competitors Buitoni and Bertolli immediately began campaigns to embrace those offended by the Barilla chairman's antigay statements. At a time when politicians, celebrities, and political groups were calling for a boycott of Barilla pasta, two other pasta manufacturers were enabled to gain influence with their disenfranchised customers.

A similar situation unfolded in March 2011, when a video surfaced of Bob Parson, CEO of web hosting company GoDaddy, kneeling with an illegally killed elephant, which he claimed to have hunted and killed himself. Animal rights group PETA started a campaign urging customers to close their GoDaddy accounts. Additionally, Namecheap, a web hosting competitor, ran a special offering to donate $1 to the nonprofit Save the

Elephants for every account opened with it after the Parson video went public. The response was overwhelming; the end donation totaled around $20,400. This is another instance of a company gaining an edge by both facilitating good press for itself and pointing out competitors' flaws.

Real-Life Q&A

Q: My ads are doing pretty well—or at least I thought they were. Over the past few days, I've gotten some really nasty comments about the ads people are seeing on Facebook. It's embarrassing, and exactly the kind of thing I was afraid was going to happen. Do I just delete them, or what?

A: First of all, let's make one thing clear: this is not about you. People who post hateful comments are usually angry at Facebook for interrupting their Facebook experience with an ad. They don't seem to understand that Facebook chooses where and how often to display ads.

You can respond politely and explain how Facebook makes money. You can ignore or delete the post. If you love inflaming the situation, and controversy is your *thing*, then absolutely follow your instinct and argue with the haters. Personally, we don't have time or interest in this. However, it can be a useful tactic because the more comments you have on the post, the better—Facebook will see your post as being very popular, and relevant, and will show it more often.

Let's assume that you want to be civil, though, because your question implies that. You can mitigate the problem by choosing different options for your ads. When advertising and promoting your content, select Current Fans Only instead of Friends of Fans. This way, only the people who already know your product or company will be able to comment. Sometimes Facebook will automatically promote your content to Current Fans *and* Friends of Fans. You have the option to delete the Friends of Fans ad units inside your Ads Manager.

Q: I understand where you're coming from regarding keeping my business and personal accounts separate. I'm concerned, though, that I'm not going to look *real* enough to my clients. It'll just look like a corporate façade with no one behind it. Shouldn't I do something to show that this is me?

A: Having a corporate social media presence is about relevance, not about showing or hiding things. Your clients don't need to see photos of your dog, or whatever else is on your personal Facebook page. They don't need to know which politicians you voted for —that's an easy way to lose clients!—or which football team you support. Bring people together instead of forcing them apart. Get people interested in your products, services, or events, not your personal life.

Corporate doesn't have to be boring. Show us your personality—your company culture is a big part of who you are. Give customers insight into how things run at your HQ. Show them the *backstage pass* type of experience: your office coffee machine getting a

---

good workout, a new delivery of iMacs, a photo of a new or long-term employee, an introduction to Bob in the warehouse, and so on.

Q: Someone left me an anonymous negative review on a review site, and then deleted his account. There is absolutely no way to contact him to resolve the issue, and the review site won't remove it. What are my options?

A: Virtually no review site will remove a negative review just because you asked it to. If it did, who would trust its reviews? However, most sites that post user reviews will correct, redact, or remove content that contains factual errors or lies. There may even be a legal obligation to do this, in some jurisdictions. You can't just point your finger and call someone a liar, though; you must provide a good reason for the site to go back to the reviewer to ask for more details. So dispute every fact in the review and ask for proof of the claims. Ask to see a copy of the receipt, or provide a tracking report from the shipping company that shows the product was delivered—ask for proof and provide proof. Since the reviewer deleted his account, he probably cannot be contacted to validate his claims, and you may be able to have the review deleted on these grounds. Amazon, for instance, has in the past removed negative reviews if the reviewer deletes his account or fails to respond to inquiries from a seller.

Make sure you do this under the pretense of good customer service. You want to resolve the issue with the customer, not just nuke every bad review you find. Even if your true focus is removing that review, keep in mind that if you are successful and the customer is still upset, he'll just go somewhere else and post his review plus a follow-up that paints you as a vindictive and predatory business. When it comes to online reviews, if you fight fire with fire, everybody gets burned.

Summary

In *Breakfast at Tiffany's*, Holly Golightly said that there are certain shades of limelight that wreck a girl's complexion. The same concept applies to online entrepreneurs. The Internet never forgets, but it's also obsessed with popularity and novelty. We hope that you never have to fix an online reputation problem, but even the best people with the noblest of intentions sometimes find themselves on the receiving end of an undeservedly negative comment, review, or rating.

You can't stop people from publishing things on the Internet. Sometimes you can get service providers to remove or modify something, but ultimately you have no control over what other people do. While we have given you many tactics in this chapter to establish and maintain vigilance, we want to remind you that being aware of your reputation is only half of the equation. The other half is responding in a positive, peaceful, and professional manner. A lot of people will excuse a negative review if they see that you've personally and publicly attempted to address it. We all know that life isn't perfect and no commercial interaction is always going to work out as planned, but we want to know that if something goes wrong, we as customers are not left out in the cold, and you as the business owner are going to do something to show that our professional relationship is more important than the details of a single sale.

Head over to the *Social eCommerce* website (*http://www.socialecommercebook.com*) for more Q&A and to post your own burning questions! You'll also have access to exclusive offers, discounts, and coupon codes on various social media tools and services.

To get exclusive access to instructional videos related to the concepts in the chapter, simply send a text with your email address to *+1(213)947-9990* and we'll send you some awesome links!

CHAPTER 9

Keeping Up with Changes

How do you stay up to date in a field that changes every day? That's the challenge of this business, and it can easily be a full-time job. In fact, you might need to make it someone's full-time job now that you've seen the dollar value of social media. Or if you don't have the resources to hire someone, there are a few good reputable firms that you can out-source it to.

Even the authors of this book, whose fulltime jobs *are* keeping up with trends and finding new ways to be successful in online marketing, don't stay on the cutting edge. Why? Because it isn't always relevant. Much of what passes for "cutting edge" in social media is hypothetical or a rumor, so while it is a good idea to stay informed of what may be coming soon, it's probably a bad idea to try to take advantage of it before it's actually an advantage.

Once you find something that works, don't sit back and let it run in the background. It's dangerous to assume it's going to continue delivering the same results. This may be possible with appliances, some kinds of machinery, and computer software, but it doesn't typically apply to social media marketing. You've got to keep your eye on the ball.

What that in mind, this chapter explains several ways to keep up with changes in the social media landscape.

Hire the Experts

If you're a marketer or business owner working solo, employing the aid of a social media agency could be a great idea. In addition to taking over your initial efforts, a social media agency can help you refine your process in the future.

There are a lot of so-called experts in this field. Unfortunately, there are no regulations that restrict claims of professionalism to only those who are truly qualified, so it's critical to do a few key things before making a final decision about a social media marketing firm or professional.

Ask the Hard Questions

Experience is the first thing to consider. Look for a specialist or company that's been operating for a while, one with a reputation for helping clients attain a satisfactory degree of success. If they can't provide examples that show the results they can deliver, then find someone who can.

Take into consideration your type of business, and ask specifically how this expert can help your company. If he can't offer you a straightforward answer and you aren't confident he can do the job right, don't hire him.

Take a Look at the Agency's Social Media Pages and Business Sites

The way a social media agency promotes its business can help demonstrate what it'll be able to do for you. Visit its site and take a good look around, and do the same with its social media pages. If its social media links aren't prominently displayed, then something's wrong.

You can't fake many years of dedicated participation on social media, so take a look at a potential vendor's public social media history and see how far back it goes and how it's progressed over time. Pinterest can be assembled to look full, organized, and well groomed in a matter of days. But a site with a time element like Twitter cannot be so quickly built. These are the true tests of a company's experience, commitment, and value.

There will, of course, be various differences in the methods each company will use to promote different businesses, but you can determine the quality of what it will deliver by its own presence in the social media world.

Determine What the Agency Is Planning for Your Business in the Long Term

As already mentioned, social media marketing isn't a system you can simply put on autopilot and expect it to work indefinitely without maintenance. It's an ongoing process just like any other type of successful advertising. You need to collaborate with your chosen social media agency in order to plan the best course of action for your business, as well as how it will continue in the long term. When this is done correctly, your company should be able to see measurable results in the form of a growing, loyal client or customer base that stays up to date with your organization's activities and progress.

Ask Trick Questions

By this point in the book, you know enough about social media to understand the major dos and don'ts. So take some of the "don'ts" and make questions out of them:

- How much will it cost me to buy 10,000 Facebook fans?
- How can I set up my social media to work on autopilot—set and forget?
- How many fans do I need to start seeing sales?
- How long will it take me to get to x number of fans?
- We want to grow our fan base as quickly as possible. Can you help us?

There should never be concrete answers to any of these questions. The correct response should instead be: "Why?" Why do you need more fans? The social media professional you're interviewing should ask you what the overall goal is. Do you want more customers, sales, website visitors, exposure, or something else?

Almost everyone who has read this book should reply: "Yes, we want more sales, visitors, and exposure." That being the case, the solution is not to "get more fans." Rather, it is to "get more of the *right kind* of fans." Targeting is the key to conversion on Facebook. Fifty thousand names on a Facebook page are useless to you if they never comment, click, watch, listen, read, ask, or buy from you.

A reputable agency will work with you to identify your objectives first, then design a campaign that will deliver qualified, targeted leads to your page.

Ask About Cost

Once you know more about what your goals are and how they can be accomplished, start asking questions about cost, but be prepared for a little bit of sticker shock here. A reputable social media marketing company should cost anywhere between $1,000 and $5,000 per month, depending on what services it is providing and what your stated goals are.

It can be difficult to calculate the total cost of service, and some vendors may be reluctant to give you a realistic figure up front. It may be useful for you to set a reasonable budget that you can spend each month, and use that as a retainer. Ask what that retainer will get you on a monthly basis.

Keep in mind that a good social media marketer cannot make amazing guarantees, especially for a fixed cost. If someone offers you a certain number of followers or fans for a set price, she's almost certainly going to use bots and other unethical, unsustainable means to reach that number as cheaply as possible.

Follow the Thought Leaders

The best way to find out what's new in the industry is to pay attention to the people whose job or hobby it is to follow the latest rumors and development initiatives. Let's start with the authors of this book:

- Stephan Spencer (*http://www.stephanspencer.com*), Science of SEO blog (*http://scienceofseo.com/blog*)
- Jimmy Harding (*http://www.jimmyharding.com*)
- Jennifer Sheahan (*http://FBadslab.com/blog*)

Here are some other reasonably well-established people who are worth listening to:

- Gary Vaynerchuk (*http://garyvaynerchuk.com*)
- Neil Patel (*http://neilpatel.com*), Quicksprout blog (*http://www.quicksprout.com/blog*)
- Charlene Li (*http://www.charleneli.com/blog*)
- Chris Brogan (*http://www.chrisbrogan.com*)
- Mari Smith (*http://www.marismith.com*)
- Amy Porterfield (*http://www.amyporterfield.com*)
- Marty Weintraub (*http://www.aimclearblog.com*)
- Heidi Cohen (*http://heidicohen.com*)
- Jeff Bullas (*http://www.jeffbullas.com*)
- Taki Moore (*http://www.coachmarketingmachine.com*)
- Stephen Renton (*http://stephenrenton.com*)
- Rob Woods (*http://robwoods.org/blog*)
- Jeremy Schoemaker (*http://www.shoemoney.com*)
- James Schramko (*http://www.superfastbusiness.com*)

Follow Industry Blogs

The aforementioned experts usually contribute to a large number of social media sites and blogs. Beyond these few, there are many more industry professionals worth reading. You'll probably find them on one of these blogs:

- Mashable (*http://mashable.com*)
- readwrite (*http://readwrite.com*)

- GetElastic (*http://getelastic.com*)
- copyblogger (*http://copyblogger.com*)
- CopyPressed (*http://www.copypress.com/blog*)
- social triggers (*http://socialtriggers.com*)
- Duct Tape Marketing (*http://ducttapemarketing.com*)
- Socialmouths (*http://socialmouths.com*)
- Social Media Examiner (*http://www.socialmediaexaminer.com*)
- ViralBlog (*http://www.viralblog.com*)
- TheSalesLion (*http://www.thesaleslion.com*)
- pushingsocial (*http://pushingsocial.com*)
- Marketing Tech Blog (*http://www.marketingtechblog.com*)
- likeable media blog (*http://www.likeable.com/blog*)
- wayvs (*http://splashmedia.com/blogs*)
- AllFacebook (*http://allfacebook.com*)
- Marketing Land (*http://marketingland.com*)

 We have a longer list of resources available from the book's website (*http://socialcommercebook.com*).

Attend Relevant Conferences

What do the authors of this book and all of the people covered in the previous list have in common? They attend industry conferences and conventions like these:

- Content Marketing World (*http://contentmarketingworld.com*)
- South by Southwest (SXSW) Interactive (*http://sxsw.com/interactive*)
- New Media Expo (*http://nmxlive.com*)
- SMX Social Media (*http://bit.ly/1nQKUoI*)
- BlogHer (*http://www.blogher.com*)
- Social Media Marketing World (*http://bit.ly/1wVtVXG*)
- Social Media Week (*http://socialmediaweek.org*)
- Social Media World Forum (*http://www.socialmedia-forum.com*)

- Inbound Marketing Summit (*http://www.inboundmarketingsummit.com*)
- BlogWell (*http://socialmedia.org/blogwell*)
- Social Fresh Conference (*http://socialfreshconference.com*)
- Northern Voice (*http://www.northernvoice.ca*)
- Wordcamp (*http://central.wordcamp.org*)

eCommerce conferences also sometimes have bootcamps or tracks dedicated to social media. Here are some of our favorites:

- Shop.org (*http://shop.org*) Annual Summit
- IRCE Focus (*http://focus.irce.com/*)
- eTail West (*http://etailwest.wbresearch.com*)
- NRF Annual Convention & Expo (*http://bigshow14.nrf.com*)
- Online Retailer (Australia) (*http://www.onlineretailer.com*)
- eCommerce Expo (Australia) (*http://www.ecomexpomelbourne.com.au*)

Conferences and conventions are exciting places filled with ideas, discussions, and a whole lot of people just like you. Some of them are expensive, though. Whether they're worth it or not depends on how far away they are (travel expenses and time), and the number of people who will attend. Sometimes you can spend $10,000 on a conference and have it pay off in multiples from the resulting sales or deals. Aside from that, you can't assign a monetary value to the knowledge and industry contacts you'll gain by attending one of these shows. Hopefully you'll also have a good time!

If you have a bit more money to spend, and find a convention that is applicable to your industry, you can advertise there by buying a booth or a sponsorship.

Before you go, update your business cards to include your social media info, then print up a lot of them. If you're setting up a booth, you'll need to provide some kind of takeaway material or promotional item for attendees as well. That's a topic for another book, though.

Join Professional Associations

Another good way to stay up to date is to join professional associations or groups that deal with social media, ecommerce, and online marketing, such as the Word of Mouth Marketing Association (WOMMA) (*http://www.womma.org*), Social Media Club (*http://socialmediaclub.org*), or Shop.org (*http://shop.org*).

It might help to join associations that are related to your business as well if they address online marketing or social media.

Don't React; Respond

There is a balance to staying current with social media: don't let the flavor of the day determine your social media strategy, but do stay in touch with the possible future of the industry. The key idea here is not to fall in love with an emerging trend. Don't acquire *shiny object syndrome* and try to stay ahead of the game by investing in every upcoming fad. Perhaps if you have a large marketing budget and a strong corporate tradition of taking risks, this might be an interesting strategy to adopt, but if that doesn't describe you, then avoid the hype, and stick to what's working and what fits into your system.

We advise our clients to wait about six months for a new site, technology, or idea to become mainstream. By all means, stay aware of the hype, speculation, and hypothesis of what may or may not happen. Observe it, let it catch on a little (or die quickly), and then test it and see if it can make money for you. If something new is making huge waves in the social media world, it may be worth experimenting with right away, but err on the side of caution—or rather, profitability.

At some point, situations that require your time and money become zero-sum. Don't try to be everywhere at the same time. Don't spread your efforts over many social media platforms unless you have the staff to give each one the proper attention. It's like investments; don't spend $5 across 10 mutual funds, put it all into 1 or 2 that you've researched.

It isn't all about money. Social media sites always start out free so that they can gain widespread adoption. The *business model* part comes later when there are tens of millions of active participants. You don't want *junk followers*, and in order to get anywhere on a new social network, you have to actively solicit connections. If the site does end up becoming popular, you'll have to do a lot of work to clean up your friends list. Don't waste your time; be slow, steady, and wise.

Remarket and Retarget

Sometimes your results can change without warning, and for no apparent reason. Social media sites don't always announce the changes that end up affecting you. For instance, if you've found the CPC sweet spot for a certain Facebook ad or campaign, and then your results suddenly take a nosedive, it may be because a wealthy competitor gobbled up all of the top ad spots. This works two ways; CPC can go up or down depending on the market. You could end up overpaying for your ads in the absence of previously strong competition.

If you get priced out of your market on a high-traffic social media site, then retarget the ad for a lower-priced audience—you'll still have plenty of clicks.

Maybe you didn't get priced out. Maybe people got bored with your ad. Think about how you feel when you've seen the same television commercial or heard the same radio ad a dozen times.

If you're at the top end of the bid, you may just end up paying more per click without any results.

Case Study: Always Evolving

Sharon Pearson is a dynamic leader at The Coaching Institute (TCI) in Australia, where she's at the forefront of all things social media. We work with her team to promote their regular coaching seminars, in-person training events, and online workshops. By using a variety of engaging images, eye-catching headlines, and strong calls to action, we've been able to make Facebook a key traffic generator and high source of conversions for TCI. Here's how it happened: In late 2010, an Australia-based training academy that runs accredited, in-person and online coaching courses identified the need to stay ahead of the crowd, and continue to find new customers for their training programs. They noticed their Google AdWords traffic had maxed out, and they were targeting all of their main keywords with an active SEO campaign.

In order to grow their business, they needed a steady flow of new customers entering their sales funnel. To find those new customers, they'd have to find a fresh lead source. Could Facebook be the answer?

They decided to start with a personalized Facebook page, filling it with related content to encourage their current customers, clients, and students to interact with them on the social network. This was a success with over 1,000 of their existing customers "Liking" the page in the first few weeks.

The next step was to design a Facebook ad campaign. They took advantage of Facebook's targeting features and targeted potential students by age, gender, and location. For this company, being able to target their ideal students using keywords in the Likes & Interests section of Facebook was particularly effective.

They conducted a survey of their existing students and discovered a large number of them have worked as teachers or nurses. Using this information, they were able to identify keywords that are related to things their students enjoy, and careers they have chosen. With that in hand, the company was able to reach their ideal target audience at a fraction of the cost of Google AdWords.

The campaigns have been running for several years now and require constant review. Keeping on top of the changes inside Facebook and remaining relevant to their target audience is essential to maintaining the effectiveness of each campaign. This means new images, new headlines, and ad copy changes on a regular basis.

Because of their commitment to keeping up with changes, the results have been fantastic. The company director told us: "These ads have more than paid for themselves. They've helped us reach new customers that we could never have reached any other way." They've acquired students from all over Australia using Facebook Ads, and continue to have success by continually refining and adjusting their process.

Real-Life Q&A: Change You Can Believe In

Q: Everything was going fine; I had some good ads in a successful Facebook campaign, and then suddenly I hit a wall. Clicks dropped, I stopped getting impressions, and now sales have dropped. What could be the problem?

A: This is one of the most common questions we hear, and it's a lot like asking, "How long is a piece of string?" A lot of things could be the problem. Maybe you got priced out of your market all of a sudden, or maybe your audience is tired of your ad, or perhaps your CTR was too low so Facebook decided to stop showing your ad. Maybe your ads had a red border that made them stand out, right up until everyone else saw your success and copied you. Maybe your target audience has seen your ads so many times that it just ignores them.

Who knows? Whatever the reason, you need to start over. The good news is, it's much easier now because you know that the results are possible, and you know that you have achieved them in the past. You'll want to show all new ads to all new people to bring life back into your advertising.

Begin a new campaign. Create brand-new ads with new images and headlines. Go back to your initial market research and see what likes/interests you might be able to target with your new campaign.

It's important to make sure that all of your pages and links actually work. Sometimes a server goes down or a redirect fails. Sometimes Facebook changes its code or policies and things stop working. So, you'll want to check that you are advertising according to its current Terms of Service.

Next, check your campaign bidding strategy and make sure you're not priced far above or below the suggested bid. If you've been outbid to the point where your ads are not relevant, then you can try to wait it out and see if the higher-priced competitors go away after a few days. But if not, try increasing your maximum bid until you begin seeing a steady flow of impressions.

Q: All right, so I'm going to one of the conferences you mentioned. I'm guessing I don't just show up and soak in new knowledge. What do I do at these things?

A: Prepare before attending a conference. Know exactly what your outcomes are going to be, so when it's over, you can know that it was worthwhile. Identify your key objectives before you attend the conference. Are you going in order to learn something in particular, meet key players in your market, find new customers for your business, or just to have a good time?

For a lot of people, a conference is a huge investment. You're taking time away from your business and family. You're forking over huge sums of cash for the event, hotel, food, drinks, flights, transportation, and more.

Most conferences are composed of a show floor with vendor booths, and various conference rooms where talks, keynote speeches, and presentations are given. The booths and hallways outside the conference rooms are great opportunities for networking. That's where you see what is new in your market, discover what your competitors are doing, and interact with potential clients and vendors. Some conventions are so large that you can't expect to cover the whole convention floor in a single day.

Each convention day starts off with a keynote speech, and then every available room is filled with speakers and presenters. You also can't expect to attend every presentation. It's important to choose the sessions that will help you reach your objectives. You'll just have to get a schedule and figure out which talks are going to be most valuable to you. Then, arrive early, have your notepad/iPad ready to go, and take great notes along the way. Stick around after the presentation, and you might be able to get some time with the speaker and get more in-depth or personalized information.

Some conferences offer paid seminars that are much more in depth. The authors of this book regularly teach seminars like this. Depending on the content, the size of the venue, and the expected audience, seminars can cost anywhere from a few hundred dollars to more than $10,000 per person. Usually you can expect A-list material delivered by the industry's foremost experts, but research the speaker before writing a check.

Q: I've found a good social media marketing company, but it's expensive. I've got to make a business case for this. What do I say?

A: Well, what's your time worth? How much do you make an hour, when you break down your salary and work hours? Is that time best spent on social media marketing, or on other things? This isn't meant to be a rhetorical question; perhaps it really isn't worth the money. Some firms prefer to have fewer, higher-profit clients so that they can spend more personal time and deliver better service. That's not a bad thing, but it might interfere with your budget and marketing goals. If you can hire a skilled social media person for less than half your hourly rate, you probably should.

If you're the CMO, then you should be able to make the case to the CEO that it's worth it to outsource this work. If you're the webmaster, IT manager, or UI developer, it may not be possible to make the financial case right now, but you may want to make a more practical case that your job involves mission-critical systems that need proper maintenance and attention that you can't focus on while you're messing with Twitter posts.

Summary

One of Stephen Covey's most famous and valuable tenets is a quote from noted British economic historian Arnold Toynbee: "Nothing fails like success." Indeed, a successful outcome is often misleading in terms of what is required to maintain it at that level. Very frequently, the same process will not lead to the same result without at least some adjustments to the details.

Once you've read this book and put our advice into action, the journey isn't over. Social media is constantly changing the rules and enhancing services and features, and social networks are rising and falling like the unstable markets of an emerging economy. As we wrote this book, Facebook and Twitter were the slowly fading kings, and Google+ and LinkedIn were expanding aggressively. But if we'd written it just a few years ago, we'd have been talking about MySpace, Friendster, and Second Life; we'd be poking fun at the decline of the once-mighty America Online. Believe it or not, a lot of companies put a huge amount of money into advertising on some of those networks, and at the height of their popularity, they probably got a decent return for their investment.

Ironically, those sites and services failed for the same reasons that successful online marketing plans fail: they were unable or unwilling to adapt to an Internet culture that changes in slow but powerful swells. Like a declining suburb in the American Rust Belt, the exodus from one social network to another starts with one friend. Then it spreads to a family, then one digital neighborhood, and then third-party companies stop updating apps, and there are huge layoffs, the founding CEO is sacked, and the trendy San Francisco home office is vacated for more affordable rental space in an unhip town with no corporate taxes.

In the Hemingway novel *The Sun Also Rises*, Bill Gorton asks Mike Campbell how he went bankrupt, and Mike replies: "Two ways. Gradually and then suddenly." That's also how a successful social media marketing campaign fails. Hopefully we've convinced you to keep the "gradually" part from ever happening, thus preventing the sudden collapse at the end.

Head over to the *Social eCommerce* website (*http://www.socialcommercebook.com*) for more Q&A and to post your own burning questions! You'll also have access to exclusive offers, discounts, and coupon codes on various social media tools and services.

To get exclusive access to instructional videos related to the concepts in the chapter, simply send a text with your email address to *+1(213)947-9990* and we'll send you some awesome links!

CHAPTER 10

Book Promotion

These days, a book can be a physical or digital good—or both. While many of the same rules from both of these ecommerce categories apply to selling books, there is enough book- and author-specific information that the subject warrants its own chapter.

Traditional book promotion tactics still apply in the modern era, for the most part. We are social media experts, though, so we'll go into detail only on the aspects that apply to that medium. We'll cover how to get your book out there into the big, wide world without spamming everyone and ruining your chances of promoting anything to your friends, family, or followers ever again.

Fiction Versus Nonfiction

Most of the advice you can find on the Web about book promotion has to do with nonfiction books. Compared to fiction, nonfiction is enormously easier to promote, since it deals with a specific subject. All you need to do is get the attention of people who are interested in that subject. The demography and geography are not difficult to figure out, if you don't know them beforehand.

Fiction is very difficult to promote because it typically appeals to a wide audience, and there are a lot of fiction authors competing for the attention of a few influential fiction reviewers. You may need to narrow down your audience to a single demographic that appears to be easy to target. This is difficult to do. Even traditional publishers fail to promote good fiction books most of the time.

People also seem more skeptical of self-published fiction than nonfiction, so there is a bigger initial barrier to overcome. Unless you have a massive marketing budget (more than $20,000), the quality of your writing and/or the appeal of your subject matter has to be good enough to drive sales with social media alone.

Pricing is also different between fiction and nonfiction. A 99-cent ebook novel is probably going to sell exponentially better than if it were priced at $3.99 because many fiction readers consume a lot of novels and can't afford to keep their hobby going for $3.99 per book. There are also promotional services that only advertise 99-cent ebooks—nothing more expensive. That price point is a huge portion of the fiction market. Nonfiction, on the other hand, is by definition a kind of reference and an educational tool, so it has more long-term value and serves a purpose other than pure entertainment, meaning you can typically charge more. Don't base your pricing on famous novelists or celebrity biographies in hardcover format; these are unrealistic for you. Instead, look at other authors who are in your genre or related genres and price your book competitively. Never assume that you are competing purely on quality of content.

One genre that rarely sells well is autobiographies and memoirs. Autobiographies and memoirs are often fun and therapeutic to write, but publishing them and attempting to promote them for profit is probably going to be a waste of time and money. Unless you're already famous, or you have a truly extraordinary tale to tell (e.g., you're the sole survivor of a major disaster; you were Richard Nixon's private secretary; you're the former CEO of IBM; you are the child of famous parents; you worked on the Apollo program at NASA), a stranger isn't going to be compelled to buy your book.

Sometimes you can openly promote nonfiction books. For instance, if you're selling a book on desert gardening, you can more or less be open about the book's content and offer snippets from it, provide related tips, and post links to related subjects. There's a ton of inherently shareable, interesting social media content there.

Fiction, on the other hand, can't usually be openly promoted without some backlash and a lot of failure. People don't seem to respond well to "buy my cool story" posts, even if you have a really good pitch. Instead, talk about the themes indirectly. For instance, let's return to a scenario from Chapter 4 and say the movie *The Matrix* never existed, and you just wrote it as a science fiction novel. Put up a web page that shows the synopsis, the first chapter, any art that is associated with it, and links to all of the major sites that sell it (e.g., Amazon, bn.com, or Kobo). Create a Facebook page for the book and a Twitter account for you as an author, and link out to your book page prominently there. Get some good Facebook ads going on a budget of $10–$20 per day to gain more page likes. You might also put some money into promoting your Twitter page and some of your tweets. Every day on your Facebook page you would offer a paragraph or so on the nature of reality, Turing test theories, artificial intelligence, Buddhist philosophy as it relates to the plot, computer hacking, the semantics of hacker handles, Kung Fu articles, news stories that deal with any of these subjects, and so on. On Twitter, you would post questions to your followers about these same subjects. You'd follow actors from science fiction shows and engage with them. You'd try to find people who talk a lot about science fiction and have a lot of followers, and try to get them to notice you (refer to Chapter 13 for more information on that).

Know Your Audience Really, Really Well

You probably did some of this research up front before you wrote your book, but social media marketing requires more specific details and data. Who exactly is it that is going to buy your book? Who are the people who currently love your book? Who reads books that are similar to yours? Find out exactly who they are. Are they men? Are they women? Are they in the U.S.? Are they worldwide? Do they speak English? Do they speak other languages? Are they young or old? What other things do they like to do? Are they married or single? Do they like outdoor activities or watching TV? What kind of documentaries do they like? These are the kinds of things that you need to know. Grab a piece of paper and start writing down everything that you know about your target audience.

Write down everything you can about the vast majority of your readers. If you don't know anything about your readers at all (which may be the case for most fiction books), it might pay to do some surveys or research. Or, you can ask your audience directly. Simply ask on your website (as a pop-up), on your blog, and within your social media streams, "What's your biggest question about *x*?" where *x* is the topic or niche that you occupy. A tool that can help you is the Ask database (*http://askdatabase.com*). A dialogue gets started, and your credibility is established as an expert for answering the tough stuff.

Look to your blog comments for answers. Who are the people who comment the most? Who are the people who reply on Twitter? Have a look at those people, and then start looking for more people like them. You want to take some time to create great posts and content. Plan out what you're going to post and which days you are going to post it.

Search for relevant Facebook pages and Twitter profiles. You can also look up websites and blogs that are related to your market, your topic, the genre, and the kind of author you are.

You can also search for relevant blogs and podcasts on these web research sites:

- Quantcast (*http://quantcast.com*)
- Alexa (*http://alexa.com*)
- Compete (*http://compete.com*)

The data from these sites will give you a demographic profile of the sites you're considering. For example, if you went to Oprah.com (*http://oprah.com*), you would see the demographic profile of all of Oprah's audience. You can do that for relevant topics.

Also look for other books in your genre on social media. Are they on the four big networks? If you can find pages and sites for the most popular books in your genre, then you can see what's working. That's where successful authors are putting the most effort.

You can also search forums. Forums for all sorts of topics are all over the Internet. There are author-based forums (such as WritersNet (*http://writers.net*)), book-lover forums —forums for everything. If you are writing a history book, there are history buff forums. So find some forums and join them, then become an active member. Don't go in there just to spam your stuff. Go in and participate; be a part of the community. Read and look at the questions that people are asking. Can you answer them? If you can, that gives you a bunch of great stuff to use and publish on your social media sites.

Take a look at the people who are posting reviews for books in your genre on Amazon. Look at who is commenting on those reviews, and what they are saying.

Search for your topic or authors in your genre on YouTube, and click on the Statistics button next to the view counter (it's the little graphic of the bar chart). If public stats are enabled, you can see who is watching those videos.

Plan Accordingly

In the lead-up to your book launch, you're going to be stressed. You're going to be pressured. You're going to forget things. You're going to sit down at your computer to write some tweets or blog posts, and blast it all out like verbal diarrhea. That is the worst thing you can do. Instead, plan your posts so that they strategically leak tiny bits of information along the way. That's what builds this demand for your book and your posts. Your audience will want to hear what you have to say when you create great posts and content. That comes from planning.

Also remember that you're building a long-term audience. This is going to give you the biggest payoff. A long-term audience for an author is priceless because when you have people who like your stuff—if you've already written one great book—then they want to follow it. They want to see what you're going to do next. When your next book comes out, they are ready and eager to buy it.

You never know; a good blog can even become a book! Many writers have taken this route over the past decade, such as the authors of *I Can Has Cheezburger? A LOLcat Collekshun* (Gotham), *Barack Obama Is Your New Bicycle: 366 Ways He Really Cares* (Gotham), and *Stuff White People Like: The Definitive Guide to the Unique Taste of Millions* (Random House).

Don't feel pressured into reacting out of anxiety. Don't say, "Oh my God. My book is going to launch in a week. What do I do now?" If that is the case, there are a lot of strategies in this chapter that will still work in that timeframe and beyond.

Certainly, it is better to have more time. If you are planning to launch your book in the next 6 to 12 months, there are a lot of things that you can do now to make sure that your payoff is huge.

The Big Players

We've said more than once in this book "quality over quantity" when it comes to social media. To execute on that, you have to narrow down your social networks to those that are most effective for book promotion. The top four big-name sites for authors are:

- Twitter
- Facebook
- Pinterest
- YouTube

Of course, if you like a social media site that isn't listed here, then feel free to use that. The core strategies for the sites we talk about in this chapter should be just as relevant to other social networks.

No matter which social media sites you're on, you should customize them to the fullest extent possible. You can include contact information or book selling information in the design, either as part of the background graphic, or as text somewhere else on the page. Use your book cover, interior art, your author photo, and a theme or font that is relevant to the book. For example:

- *https://www.facebook.com/artofseo*
- *http://www.twitter.com/sspencer*

Twitter

For some reason, Twitter seems like a great medium for spam, but mindless self-promotion never works there or anywhere else. Also, make sure that you don't log into Twitter only when you want to tweet things about yourself, your book, or your book launch. Go to Twitter with the idea of sitting back and listening. Watch and read what others are posting.

Search for other authors and readers based on interest, keywords, topics, and names. Find and follow people who have interesting things to say on your topic, about being an author or about being a book lover. You might want to follow up to a few hundred people per day, depending on your topic. You can follow people automatically based on keywords and interests. By doing this, you will add a variety of cool people to your stream who you may not have found otherwise. You will be able to hear their conversations and see what they're tweeting about. You're going to get *involved*.

Begin by reading and following; sit back and just get the feel of Twitter. When you start posting, mix up your tweets so not everything is promotional. Endeavor to add value in every tweet. If you're at a loss for words, then describe something positive that's going on around you or in the world.

Include an auto-tweet option in the free chapter or PDF version of your book. When readers click that button, a tweet is created that might say something like: "I'm reading *Social eCommerce* by @sspencer et al. Get the 1st chapter free here:" and include a link.

You can also post pictures. Personal pictures are fantastic on Twitter.

Retweet the tweets of other relevant, ideal people in your market. Follow the market leaders in your genre; retweet their stuff, comment on it, and reply to it. When people tweet at (@) you, reply to them.

It's so powerful when people interact with one another on Twitter. That's the way to use Twitter successfully, not just pumping out your links one after another. Get involved in a conversation. Share other authors' books freely. This is such good karma. If another author is trying to promote her book and you like it (if you've read it), and it's related to yours or interesting to you, then share it. Retweet it and get it out to your followers, too. That author will be glad that you're helping her. You can comment to her and tell her how much you enjoyed her book. You want to engage with your audience. Reply, comment, and retweet often—that's the whole idea behind Twitter.

Use hashtags to your advantage. If you have free book promotion days through your publisher or Kindle Direct Publishing (KDP), you can tweet things like #BookGiveaway, #freeKindleBook, or #free to help get it out there so that new people will find it.

There are a lot of people who love free Kindle books; they will jump on every opportunity. Make sure that you include a clickable link for them to download your book, and ask them to leave a review. You can also communicate with and follow Kindle addresses such as Digital Book Today and Kindle Ebooks; search for other relevant Twitter accounts on your own, and engage and reply.

Free ebooks and giveaways are great for publicity, but your publisher may not want to participate, or even allow you to do this (via digital restrictions on ebook files). However, publishers usually allow authors to give away a free sample chapter, either as a standalone item or as something that can be published as an article on another site. O'Reilly Media has discount days for many of its authors, where books on certain topics or subjects are discounted. O'Reilly also hosts webinars taught by its authors and discounts are offered on that author's book during the webinar. No matter what's available to you in terms of sample or promotional content, you can and absolutely should link it from Twitter.

Facebook

First, activate subscriptions on your personal profile. This allows other people to follow you without being a personal friend of yours. When you post something that is public, they will see it in their News Feed. However, consider what you're posting on your personal profile. Understand that it's going out to fans and other followers who may not know you personally. If you publish any personally identifiable information, people can find you using that. Be careful and thoughtful about what you post on Facebook. In fact, it's best to have a professional public profile that represents you as an author, and a private personal page.

Regardless of your situation with your personal Facebook page, you should create an author and/or book page to help optimize for search. Author pages should be titled with your book-credited name and perhaps "author" as well, such as "Author Stephan Spencer." People can easily find that when they search for authors on Facebook. That page can be all about your book-related stuff.

Some authors like to have a book page just for the title of their book, especially if they're creating a book series. This is a fantastic way to generate interest when people are searching in Google or Facebook for your book title. Check out the Facebook page for *The Art of SEO* (*https://www.facebook.com/artofseo*) as an example.

Facebook landing pages are really effective. To take full advantage of them, create custom tabs and images for each book on your author page; this makes it much more interactive. When people click on that thumbnail image, they are taken directly to a page where they can read reviews, see your pitch, or go straight to your Amazon listing.

Create a basic content plan. If you have trouble following it, then schedule future posts for your profile and Facebook pages. By posting automatically, you don't have to remember to do it every day.

You definitely want to include some teaser photos of your work in progress. These are very popular. You can post a photo of your desk, your coffee mug, or the view outside your window when you're writing. Where is your computer? What is your inspiration? What is it that drives you? What are you working on today? Some authors will post pictures of their notebook or notes that they've written. They post pictures of things outside that have given them inspiration for their work. All of that is really important and should definitely be included in your Facebook updates.

You can also thank reviewers publicly each week and provide a link to the review on Amazon. So if Lucy posts a lovely review on your Amazon page, you can say, "I received this lovely review from Lucy in Oxford. Thanks so much, Lucy." Tag her in the post, and link to her Amazon review so that people can click and buy or download your book for free.

As with Twitter, you must avoid spammy self-promotion. Become a fan of other authors and contribute to their pages. Like their photos, videos, and comments. Comment as your author page. Now that you've created your own Facebook author page, you can comment as "Stephan Spencer, Author" on these other pages as long as your comment is not spammy or asking people to like your page. Your comment should add value to the post or photo. If you have free download days, share them and don't forget to ask for reviews.

Include a reason why people should click your link and download your book right now. Don't just say, "Here is my book," with the link. That's not going to get anyone inspired to action. You can add a quote from the book. You can add a question or topic from the book. It should be something that piques readers' interest or asks them a question. Then you can say, "Today is our free download day" or "Don't forget that tomorrow is our free download day." Bookbub is a popular site that notifies users of limited-time free book deals, and could be worth looking into.

Make a video trailer for your book. That's a really powerful way to help spread the message. A video trailer can help generate a lot of traffic if you publish it directly to Facebook. If you publish on YouTube, that's fine, too; there's more information about that in the next section.

Spend some money to promote this post and extend your reach, particularly if you have free downloads to announce. You can also create specific Facebook ads to announce a free download day. You can say, "For today only: a free ebook download. Click here to go to Amazon for the free download."

Inside your Ads Manager, you can make a page post engagement ad, target your ideal audience, and promote your post directly from your ads account. Now instead of just a percentage of your fans seeing it, you can extend the reach to include friends of fans, for example. Use smart targeting to find people interested in your topic or style of writing. Consider targeting pages of popular authors as well.

You can also use page post engagement ads to promote your author or book page. It's an effective way to build your fan base over time. Spending as little as $10 per day is enough to grow a steady, targeted fan base when you are a new author.

Facebook photo contests are a great way to promote your book after it's available. Ask readers to take creative photos and upload them to the contest app. Fans can then vote on their favorite photo to win a prize. However, be sure you use an approved Facebook app to run a contest on your page.

There are tons of pages of interest on Facebook that you can try to leverage. Search for them based on your topics and keywords. For instance, there is Amazon Kindle, Authors on the Cheap, Free Ebook Deal, Free Kindle Books, iAuthor, Kindle Korner, Kindle Tips and Tricks, and Reading Kindle, to name a few of the more popular ones. They are cool, interactive, vibrant pages that you can get involved in. Like them, get involved, and comment.

YouTube

Begin by searching YouTube for other authors and book trailers. Then make a video (or several) that works along the same lines, create a YouTube account in your name (as the author), and upload them.

There are lots of things you can make a video about (these topics apply generically to Pinterest as well): the topic of your book, your inspiration, your writing process, what you like to do in terms of writing, progress updates, book delivery, finding it in the store, book signings, people buying the book, cases of books, the book on a bookshelf, customers holding the book, or alternative book cover designs. You can explain some literary aspect of the book, or read an excerpt aloud with some related art—the cover, internal graphics, or promotional art. If you're looking for some high-end author video inspiration, check out these videos:

- My Formerly Hot Life (*http://www.youtube.com/watch?v=UXs7oPbGARU*)
- Kamikaze (*http://www.youtube.com/watch?v=sF1L3y4Ltyc*)

When you post your video, make sure you put a link to your site, landing page, or Amazon URL so that people can just click and buy your book directly from the video's About tab.

Whatever you create on YouTube, share it on your blog by embedding the YouTube code. You can also upload the same videos directly to Facebook for extended reach, but don't embed the YouTube code in Facebook; if you do, it will just come up with a tiny picture that can't be expanded.

YouTube isn't the most powerful way for authors to reach potential readers, but it definitely helps get to people who may not have known about you from your blog, Facebook, Twitter, or Pinterest accounts. Facebook is very personal; Twitter is like a newsfeed; Pinterest is more visual; and YouTube is visual and audio. Hitting all four gives you a well-rounded approach.

Pinterest

Unless you're publishing a children's book or a graphic novel, you probably wouldn't immediately think of Pinterest as a place to promote your work. If it's just words, what could you possibly show with graphics?

Photos don't have to be biographical—that is, they don't have to show the actual content of your book—they can also be topical. Pinterest boards are more effective as a subtle form of marketing rather than as a tool for direct sales. Some of the best boards are composed of the topics related to or in the vicinity of a specific subject.

Pinterest doesn't do file hosting, so you're going to have to upload your graphics to another site. Facebook is an excellent choice; hopefully you've already created an author and/or book page there and have already uploaded some graphics. So with Pinterest, take all of your photos from your Facebook author or book page, and pin them. Create a board or two to explain why these photos are relevant to your work.

Some photos can satisfy readers' curiosity about the author. For instance, take some photos of the desk and the office where you wrote your novel. Maybe you wrote an entire chapter while drinking margaritas at Captain Tony's Saloon in Key West, in the same dark corner of the bar where Ernest Hemingway used to hang out. Pin the photos!

If you have a particularly creative book cover, you can post a "making of" series of photos that shows how it was designed. This could include early sketches, photographs, models, or you or your graphic artist hard at work on the cover design.

If you're writing historical fiction, post photos and drawings from the era you're writing about. If it's a pre-photography period, perhaps you have some pictures of artifacts from that era that you can show.

And, of course, somewhere on your board, include links to your site without being annoying (a link to "Learn more," "Read the story behind this," etc.).

If you're out of ideas, browse Pinterest's "Film, Music and Books" category. Look for authors or book titles that are in your genre. Search for free ebook promotions; see what other authors are doing.

You can also repin relevant posts and pictures from the authors of the boards that you've followed. If you find something that you like or that you want to share with your audience or people who are following you, you can repin it.

Create an author profile and board for each book or each character that you have in your book.

Also consider creating an open board for projects that you're working on where you allow others to collaborate by pinning pictures of a location, an item, costumes, or period clothing. It becomes an interactive experience for your readers.

Literary Social Media

The big players aside, there are a few social networks that specialize in books, readers, and authors. Now that you have your baseline social media presence in place on the four major sites, you should shift your focus to niche social media.

Pixel of Ink

Pixel of Ink is similar to Kindle Nation Daily, which we've already mentioned. If you have the budget to advertise there, definitely do it. A lot of author traffic comes from these two sites.

SmashWords, KDP, CreateSpace, and ACX

A number of ebook publishing platforms for self-published authors exist, including SmashWords, Kindle Direct Publishing (KDP), CreateSpace, and Audible Creation Exchange (ACX). These are not social media in the traditional sense, but they do have a social component to the way they match books with readers. SmashWords, "the world's largest distributor of indie ebooks," can be the only way you publish, or it can be one of many different publishing platforms. As far as publishing platforms are concerned, Kindle Direct Publishing is for self-publishing ebooks; CreateSpace is for self-publishing print titles printed on demand; and Audible Creation Exchange (ACX) is for self-publishing audiobooks. Each ebook publisher has a different level of reach, so you may have to go with, for instance, both Kindle Direct Publishing and SmashWords, but this depends on your publishing agreement. If you sign up for KDP Select, you agree to make Kindle Direct Publishing the only ebook distributor for an autorenewing period of 90 days.

If you don't opt in to KDP Select, or you wait beyond your 90-day exclusivity agreement, you can publish for free on SmashWords and then write to KDP and inform it that there is a lower price available elsewhere. Doing this may reduce the Kindle price to match SmashWords—even if it's free.

Amazon AuthorCentral

Amazon AuthorCentral is a service in Amazon for authors whose books are provided on the site. AuthorCentral allows authors to create a central page about them hosted within Amazon—basically a central hub for all of their published works. Sign-up is free, and allows authors to claim the titles that they wrote in Amazon's catalog, and then displays those titles in every format they are available on Amazon. Although it is not a social network in the general sense, it does allow authors to post a biography, along with video and pictures (great for movie or book trailers) and link their other social media and blog accounts via RSS feed so that it pulls together all of the author's latest tweets and posts. Amazon customers can sign up to be alerted via email when new books from the author are released, which helps boost awareness of their latest publication date and then, hopefully, sales.

Goodreads

Goodreads is a social network for book lovers. The same basic Facebook friend/fan/like paradigm exists here, with some book-centric modifications.

You can set up an author page and "claim" your books listed there. Goodreads has an intricate recommendation system that uses your ratings of other books to determine what you might like to read in the future. This is second only to Amazon in terms of sites where you want people to post reviews. One positive review on Goodreads can attract a large number of potential readers.

Goodreads also offers book giveaways. You specify the number of books you have available to send out, where you are willing to ship, and what the timeframe for the giveaway is. There is no limit to the number of giveaways you can do. It may make sense, depending on how much it costs to do book fulfillment, to run multiple consecutive giveaways until you feel you've reached the outer limits of your market.

There is also a somewhat rudimentary ad system built into Goodreads. It offers decent targeting options, but it's easy to overtarget and get very few views while suffering a very high CPC.

Another cool thing about Goodreads is the review widget. You can paste a bit of Java-Script into your blog and it will show your Goodreads reviews, and link to your book page there.

LibraryThing

LibraryThing is like Goodreads, but there is more reader interaction. There are forums where readers can talk about books, and authors can interact directly with readers. However, you don't want to be a drive-by author and just dump your marketing message into the forum and leave. Instead, post an interesting article and then stick around for the discussion. Or join in the discussions in other threads, and become an active participant of the site. Rate and review the books you've read, talk to other authors, share stories with one another.

LibraryThing also offers giveways in the same way that Goodreads does, except it also has an ebook option.

Shelfari

Shelfari is Amazon's barebones social network for book recommendations. It is like a stripped-down version of LibraryThing. It's still worth claiming your book as the author and filling in as many details and trivia points as you can. Then rate and review other books and see if you can become part of the network of recommendations.

Get Reviews

Professional book reviews are hard to come by nowadays because few periodicals are willing to pay for them. The handful of major newspapers and magazines that do still publish them tend to publish reviews of the same already famous books.

The good news is, there are more book reviewers than ever, and many of them are just as skilled and educated—if not more—than the professionals they've replaced. You just have to know how to get in touch with them.

Amazon and other online booksellers may not be social networks in the typical sense, but the review system and the community of reviewers that exists on Amazon is definitely a form of social media.

Amazon Top Reviewers

Amazon publishes a list of its most prolific and highly rated reviewers (*http://www.amazon.com/review/top-reviewers*). If a reviewer has contact information in his profile, there's nothing stopping you from contacting him to ask for a review. This is a delicate situation, though, because the top reviewers get these requests frequently and are picky about what they will accept. Many of them do not provide contact information for this reason. A large number of them don't even review books.

Don't concentrate on the top 20 reviewers; they're too swamped with review requests as it is. Instead, take a look deeper into the Top 1,000 Reviewers list, and try to find people who write about your specific genre.

Another approach you can take is to look at the Amazon pages of the books and authors you're competing with (or are at least in the same genre), and contact the most highly rated reviewers who have posted reviews there. You already know that they are interested in books in this genre, so you'll have a much easier time getting their attention.

The Amazon Vine Program

This is an Amazon program that matches up prerelease books with experienced reviewers from the aforementioned top reviewers list. Books entered in this program are reviewed prior to their release so that on launch day, each participating book's product page already has a number of in-depth and meaningful reviews. The reviewers (sometimes called "Viners") are hand-selected by Amazon employees; they're all top-rated, prolific review writers.

Getting a book into this program from the author or publisher side is difficult, even if you're published through a big publishing house. If you're self-published, there does not seem to be a way into Amazon Vine. If you're a traditionally published author, ask your editor if she can have your book included in the program.

Other Reviews

Amazon is the clear market leader in online book sales, accounting for about a third of all bookselling revenue. If you've only got the time to concentrate on one site, this is it. If you have more resources to spend, there is also Barnes and Noble (*http://bn.com*), AbeBooks (*http://abebooks.com*), Books-a-Million (*http://booksamillion.com*), Kobo (*http://www.kobobooks.com*), and the Apple iBooks Store (*http://www.apple.com/ibooks*).

Ask Nicely and Publicly

And of course there is the general public. Every review counts, so don't be afraid to ask for them. Have a "Share this book" page on your website where you display a brief personal message about how grateful you are when people help you spread the word about your book. Have buttons for your key social networks right there ready to go, and ask people to "Share this."

Other Tips and Tricks

Still got more marketing juice left? Try these options.

Prime Lending Library and KDP Select

If you publish an ebook through Kindle Direct Publishing, you have the option to join the KDP Select program, which gets you into the Prime Lending Library and assigns you five promotional giveaway days. As mentioned in "SmashWords, KDP, CreateSpace, and ACX" on page 179, KDP Select requires digital exclusivity for 90 days, and will autorenew every 90 days (with five more promotional giveaway days) unless you specifically opt out.

Many people use all of the five days consecutively to try to reach the top of the Kindle charts for free books. However, you're perpetually competing against a huge array of public domain books, and everyone else who is running promotional days or who offers an ebook for free forever as a promotional trick for some other product or service. Instead, it could be a better strategy to stagger your five free promo days, perhaps one per week or one every other week. By doing this, you will be able to leverage social media more effectively. You can announce, "It's free again. Come quickly. This is our last free day." Then you can promote ads and tweets on that day with a link to the download.

Speak at an Industry Conference

As mentioned earlier in this book, there are many industry conventions and conferences that you can attend to learn more about social media and ecommerce.

If you're going to attend one of these conferences, make sure you have business cards printed with your book's ISBN and a friendly URL (one that is easy to remember and type into a browser), or perhaps a QR code. Hand them out to people as you meet them; it's a pretty standard business networking practice. Except now instead of contacting you later to talk about a business deal, they might buy your book instead.

The more prestigious among us don't just attend; we're on the speaking schedule. Having a nonfiction book establishes you as an expert on the subject you wrote about. Even if you're self-published, authors still carry a lot of prestige. If you're at a conference and think to yourself, "I could totally do one of these presentations or keynotes," then make it your mission to meet the conference organizers while you're there, and let them know you're a published author who would like to speak at next year's conference.

If you're proactively seeking speaking engagements, check out conference websites to see if there is a pitch form, and be mindful of the deadline (it's usually quite a long time before the conference opens). Make sure you have a speaker kit of your past engagements ready to send to interested conference organizers. Speaker kits are invaluable for establishing credibility and outlining qualifications. Think about adding sample topic ideas, past engagements, and even speaker scores and reviews. Figure 10-1 shows mine; you can download the full thing at my website (*http://stephanspencer.com*).

Figure 10-1. The introduction to my speaker kit demonstrates my credibility as a professional speaker and proposes several potential presentations

Show Off Your Writing Portfolio

If you have a significant body of work spread out across multiple publications and events, then you should establish an online portfolio. This makes it easier to find and review all of your work without doing a lot of searching. Some sites we like for writer and speaker portfolios are:

- clippings.me

- Muck Rack (*http://muckrack.com*)
- Contently (*http://contently.com*)
- Pressfolios (*http://pressfolios.com*)

Case Study: The Mighty Force of an Established Community

Chris Hurn of Mercantile Capital Corporation saw a great opportunity not just to write a book on a subject he's passionate about, but also to make money from it directly and indirectly. A good book that explained this process would help create demand for financing, which would turn the book into a lead-generating tool for his property financing business. As an added bonus, this would enhance Chris's credentials as an industry expert, and attract media attention for interviews, speeches, and article quotes.

Social media was part of Chris's go-to-market book promotion strategy from the very beginning—even before the beginning. Chris planned ahead, and already had an impressive community built by the time *The Entrepreneur's Secret to Creating Wealth: How the Smartest Business Owners Build Their Fortunes* was ready to launch. His company had accumulated more than 3,600 Facebook likes/fans, 15,000 Twitter followers, 1,800 YouTube subscribers, 165 Google+ connections, and 150 LinkedIn followers. Additionally, Chris's personal accounts on these sites had substantial reach. Combined, he had an audience of more than 43,000 potential readers.

Though there was a lot of traditional book promotion, Chris made sure that social media was involved wherever possible. When he or his staff posted a promotional video to YouTube, he made sure that a direct message was sent to his YouTube subscribers.

All of the book endorsements that Chris received were turned into social media posts. Many were posted before the book's launch date, and led to a landing page that allowed people to preorder. The rest of the endorsements were posted regularly after the book was released as part of an ongoing social media campaign. Chris started with endorsements that were general, and saved the more detailed endorsements for later when he needed to raise the stakes for people who'd been thinking about buying the book for a while, but weren't yet convinced.

Every time someone posted a review on Amazon, it was mentioned, excerpted, and linked to from all of the social media sites that Chris was using.

To push it over the top, one of Chris's staff members emailed some friends and associates who had large followings on Twitter, and asked them to mention the book. They even developed a book promotion kit to provide influencers and reviewers with content that could easily be posted to social networks, such as facts about the book, current endorsements, graphics, articles, and interview questions.

Chris also included literary social media, creating accounts and pages on Shelfari, Goodreads, and RedRoom.

So with all of that effort, did it work? Was it worth the time, money, and energy? When we wrote this case study, *The Entrepreneur's Secret to Creating Wealth: How the Smartest Business Owners Build Their Fortunes* had been on the market only a few months. According to Chris:

> We've seen results from the very beginning (the prelaunch of the book in early September 2012). Our investment has been considerable on many fronts (PPC ads, PR firms, book trailers, etc.), but the social media front has been minimal. Due to our slightly longer sales cycle (it's common for commercial real estate contracts to be written for 60 to 120 days to close), we've seen only a handful of deals directly from the book... but it only takes two average closings for us to recoup our entire investment. When the dust settles, I expect the ROI from this book to be about ten times the marketing cost.

Real-Life Q&A

Q: How is social media different for authors?

A: It isn't. It's exactly the same as social media for anything else. You want to engage your audience. You want to generate interest and participate, not just push your links out there to everyone. That is where you will generate the community and engagement from your audience.

Q: I got some great results with social media last time. I'm publishing another book in a few months. Do I do everything the same the second time around, or is there a different strategy I should take for a second book?

A: Hopefully, you've been continually engaging your audience since the first book, and haven't let it go stale just because you're not launching a book. If you let it rot, then you've got some repair work to do.

If you've kept your community going, then you will have that groundswell behind you each and every time you launch a new book. All you have to do is keep going, except now you're going to focus on the new book.

Q: I'm sure I could sell a lot of books if I could speak at an industry conference. How do you get invited to be a speaker?

A: Start by proving that you're a decent speaker. Make a video that shows that you can present an informative, intelligent, and entertaining talk. Then post it on YouTube and promote it a little. This gives you *social proof*, and supports your application to speak.

You can also reach out to satisfied clients and ask for recommendations. If they attend industry conventions, they may have the opportunity to tell the event organizers that they want you to give a presentation at next year's conference.

Before you hit the big convention circuit, you might want to build your speaking résumé by presenting at smaller or regional events. There are many industry or topical groups, such as Java User Groups (JUGs) and Linux User Groups (LUGs), that actively seek people to give short presentations at monthly local meetings.

Some conferences take public requests for speaker pitches. This usually has to be done far in advance of the actual conference date. To speak at Search Marketing Expo (SMX), for instance, go to the SMX website and fill out the pitch form. SXSW has a panel picker on its site.

Some conferences do not take open requests. If that's the case, contact the conference organizer and give your pitch directly.

Q: I have an Amazon Associates account. Can I create a link to my book with that and get a commission on my sales?

A: Absolutely. There is nothing wrong with doing this. Not only will you get a commission for your own book, you will also get affiliate credit for anything else that reader purchases from Amazon that day, even if he doesn't buy your book. The Amazon Associates cookie is valid for 24 hours.

Q: I suck at making videos. Am I doomed in terms of video promotion?

A: You are not doomed. Instead of making a fancy, well-produced video, you can do a live interview or webinar with a simple webcam in the lead-up to the book launch. You can do this as a Hangout on Google+, or by using a screencasting service. You can interview key experts that you used for the book, experts in the field whom you know, or you can have someone interview you. Take questions from your live viewers, and show video of your face. Then, later, you can promote the replays of these interviews for people who discovered you afterward. Or make an animated video (Figure 10-2), whiteboard video (Figure 10-3), or screencast (Figure 10-4). All three create easy opportunities for hooking in an audience.

Figure 10-2. Omid Malekan's animations receive millions of views because they are topical, witty, and informative

Figure 10-3. All it took for DiamondEnvy to make this video was a cartoonist and a few hours; the video is high quality, and is a solid addition to its video SEO strategy

Figure 10-4. Screencasts are easily recorded and make great quick promotional material

Summary

This chapter is a bit meta, isn't it? After all, the people who wrote this book are, by definition, authors. And if you're reading this, then you've almost certainly bought at least one of our books, so we must have done something right in terms of marketing it. The thing is, we don't necessarily know which channel reached you, and we don't know if you are an outlier. Give that some consideration, though: how do you find the books that you've bought and read? How can you get your book involved in the channels that would reach you or (more importantly) your target market?

All we can do is explain what we know *can* work, but different genres and markets can have dramatically different paths to success. Fiction, for instance, is an epic uphill battle in terms of marketing unless you are a major celebrity or have a lot of social connections, a huge marketing budget, and/or a big publisher that will put a serious marketing effort behind your title. Even if you have all of those advantages, there are still no guarantees. You can even have a really good book with a great cover, produced by a major publisher, and sink a ton of money into marketing and still not earn a spot on the bestseller list. Meanwhile, a low-brow pop culture novella about mopey teenagers is making a millionaire out of some no-talent hack. It's just not fair, is it? Sometimes a work of fiction, even if shallow and poorly written, touches a cultural nerve that creates a literary sensation in spite of itself. If anyone could reliably predict that bit of magic, then publishers would never take risks on books that *might* make it. We hope that you'll market your fiction in an affordable and sensible manner that will give it the best chance of catching that cultural wave, if it's destined to do so. While it may be discouraging to consider the odds, keep in mind the fact that an unmarketed book has about as much of a chance of being successful as an unpublished manuscript.

Nonfiction is a little more clear-cut. Know your market, find the channels to reach it, and get out there and convince people that the easiest path to their dreams leads directly through your book. Most of the successful authors we know are using their books as one part of a multifaceted career, as we showed in the case study. It's a lot easier to add to an existing infrastructure than it is to create one from scratch.

Head over to the *Social eCommerce* website (*http://www.socialecommercebook.com*) for more Q&A and to post your own burning questions! You'll also have access to exclusive offers, discounts, and coupon codes on various social media tools and services.

To get exclusive access to instructional videos related to the concepts in the chapter, simply send a text with your email address to *+1(213)947-9990* and we'll send you some awesome links!

CHAPTER 11

Event Promotion

Promoting events such as concerts, seminars, conferences, classes, and workshops requires a slightly different strategy from other ecommerce categories. For non–speaking events such as concerts, games, or tournaments, it's simply a matter of designing great ads, spending enough money on the campaign, and doing extra-fine-grained targeting.

Speaking and teaching events (conferences, classes, etc.) involve more work to prove the value and importance of the content. People are going to spend a lot of money not just to attend your event, but probably also to travel there. This chapter deals mostly with four kinds of events:

- Digital (virtual)
- Local
- Regional
- International

Each requires a different approach to ad targeting when you're trying to attract the largest audience.

Within the digital category, there are three subcategories that you should keep in mind when thinking of your marketing strategy:

- Automated (seems like it's live, but it's actually prerecorded)
- Prerecorded
- Live

Establish Thought Leadership

The first thing you need to do is show that the event is going to be worthwhile—interesting, engaging, and valuable. To do that, you've got to establish the thought-leadership status of the people who are speaking at the event. This is true even for virtual events.

Your speakers should be doing a certain amount of this (as well as promoting your event) on their own. Check with them to make sure that they're mentioning the event on social media, and ask if they can contribute an article or podcast that you can post on your event website. Podcast-type interviews are fairly easy to do; just send three questions relevant to the topic, and either ask the speaker to record them, or set up a call or video conference to record the answers. I taught a two-day SEO workshop for the American Marketing Association, and to promote it, AMA and I partnered on a short podcast that was marketed to prospective attendees. You can find that example at *https://cc.ready talk.com/play?id=9au7h*. You can also host a short panel-type discussion and record it as a podcast.

If you're hosting a panel discussion, you might want to concentrate only on the most well-connected panelists. Market your biggest names. If you aren't sure who the top people are, use the research tactics mentioned in Chapter 13.

Record a preliminary thought-leadership conference as a podcast in the style of a group conversation with one moderator. Create a transcript from it to use as promotional material later.

It's also helpful if you, as the event host, are known in the industry. Everything public you do creates thought-leadership status. So any articles, podcasts, videos, or other content you can post around the Web will help draw attention to and give relevancy to your event. Don't just post on your own pages and sites; try to get in as a contributor on prominent industry blogs and in magazines. Most commercial content sites will not turn down free content as long as it's excellent. You can also try to get invited as a guest speaker on other people's podcasts and radio shows. Two sites to look into for this are:

- *webmasterradio.fm*
- blogtalkradio (*http://blogtalkradio.com*)

If you have the time and speaking ability, you can even start your own regular podcast or online radio show. James Schramko uses his weekly podcast "SuperFast Business" to supplement his blog and business training course. His end result is around 23,000 subscribers.

Add Hashtags

Go to Twitter and Facebook and create relevant hashtags for your event. Use them whenever you post something about that event, and encourage your speakers to do so as well. See Figure 11-1 for a good example.

During the actual event, make sure you let all of the attendees know about your hashtags so that they can use them in their social media posts. Assigning someone the task of live-tweeting from the event is also a great way to get discussion going around your event. And if you plan to hold regular events, using the same hashtag for each can generate buzz around future events.

Create Virtual Badges

You can get some extra reach by creating graphical badges that speakers and attendees can add to their social profiles, blogs, and other sites. If you need some inspiration, a good example is the SES conference (*http://sesconference.com/badges.php*).

Establish a Basic Ad and Content Strategy

Your event ads should be *progressive*—they should build up to the event. Have a countdown series of ads for every major interval ("One month until," "One week until," "Two days until," etc.). Offer an early-bird price, with a hard date for a deadline.

In terms of ad design, use a photo of the location as the image in the ad. If the event is in Los Angeles, use a photo of a building in Los Angeles, and be sure to use the words *Los Angeles* in the ad or the title so that you can more effectively reach your demographic. People who view ads don't know that they are targeted specifically to view them.

Giving away tickets in the weeks prior is a great way to get a buzz going about your event. People will begin to envision themselves possibly attending the event, and if they don't win, they're more likely to sign up. Jairek Robbins had a great promotion for his Rapid Results Retreat (Figure 11-2). The promotion involved 7 possible ways to gain additional entries in a giveaway drawing for a free ticket to the retreat, a cruise that spanned 16 days and 7 countries. Additional vote opportunities included sharing the promotion on a social media platform.

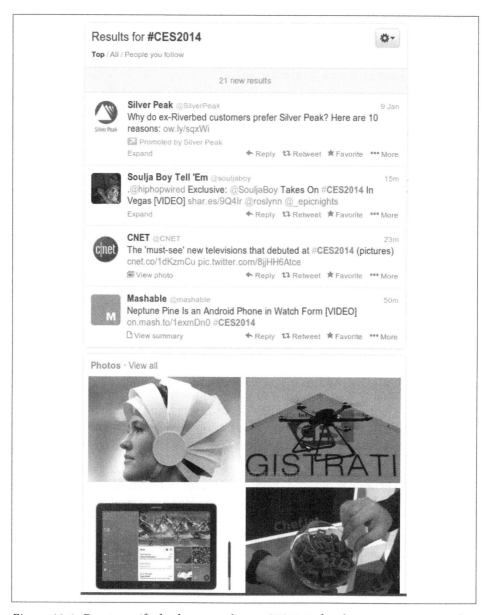

Figure 11-1. Event-specific hashtags, such as #CES2014 for the 2014 Consumer Electronics Show, are a great way for people to connect their experiences and content with your event

Figure 11-2. Robbins's contest saw huge success, with 1,190 individual entries

There are apps that will enable you to give people multiple giveaway entries if they share the giveaway on social networks. Definitely take advantage of this if you can. If you don't have the budget to use contest/giveaway apps like that, then at least ask entrants to share the event on Facebook or Twitter as part of their entry requirement. Similarly, you can give discounts for people who share the event on social networks.

Ask people to submit questions about the event and the content you'll be presenting at it. In the weeks leading up to your event, putting out a call for questions is a great way to get people thinking about the event, which increases the chances of them attending while also giving you ideas that you may not have considered. You can also livestream Q&A sessions from the event to give people a vested interest in coming up with questions or comments beforehand.

In addition, another successful tactic for event promotion, particularly for local events or "expert" events, is to find influencers in the local market who have large followings and offer them free attendance to the event in return for their promoting the event to their followers.

Leverage Social Networks

In this section, we discuss some tactics for specific social networks.

If you're having trouble thinking of good content, then lean on your speakers or presenters. Get some snippets from them that you can share on social media. Do they have previous content you can share? Leverage the existing fan base of the people who are speaking whenever possible.

If you're a one-person show, then use snippets from your event content. Give part of it away for free. Talk about related books and current events related to this topic.

Regardless of which networks you participate or advertise on, you must build an audience before you can announce the event—if you have time to plan, that is. Event promotion is a long-term strategy for a long-term business.

Multiple Events

If you run more than one event, then start a topic-based group on Facebook and/or LinkedIn so that you can maintain a list of people who may be interested.

Slideshare

Slideshare is a site for hosting and sharing PowerPoint-style slide presentations. In general, it is a great site for raising your professional profile as a speaker, presenter, thought leader, or manager.

If you can, create a virtual version of one of your event talks by uploading the slide deck and adding an audio voiceover. Then share the presentation on all of your social networks.

Lanyrd

Lanyrd is a social network entirely dedicated to conferences and speakers. It's practically a necessity to have an account here if you want to build your profile as a host or speaker for a technology-themed conference.

Regardless of your industry, having an active Lanyrd account with good content is a great way to build your online reputation as a speaker or conference host. A decent amount of engagement here is social proof of your speaking and organizing skills. Content on Lanyrd that is associated with you will also increase the volume of positive Google search results involving your name, your brand, and your company.

Portfolio Sites

If you have a significant body of work spread out across multiple publications and events, then you should establish an online portfolio. This makes it easier to find and review all of your work without doing a lot of searching. Some sites we like for writer and speaker portfolios are:

- clippings.me
- Muck Rack (*http://muckrack.com*)
- Contently (*http://contently.com*)

- Pressfolios (*http://pressfolios.com*)

AllConferences

AllConferences is a social network dedicated to conferences of all kinds. You definitely want to register here, and participate appropriately.

YouTube

If you have the resources to create a three-minute promotional video, then by all means do it and post it on YouTube. You can do an interview with some of the speakers, you can give away part of your presentation, or you can just talk for a few minutes about the event and how it will help attendees be happier, more successful, or more effective. For an example event promotion video, check out Next Level Experience (*http://thenextle velexperience.com*).

Use YouTube ads to promote this video to people who are fans of the event's topic or of the people who are speaking there. Share the video everywhere you can.

Meetup

You should have an account on Meetup (Figure 11-3) even if you're not promoting events. As explained in other chapters, it's a great way to network and to increase your search visibility. Meetups often feature speakers who have mastered a professional skill. Speaking at these can bolster your credibility in the local area, and even lead to partnerships or consulting gigs. In addition, if you are looking into giving talks at conferences, this is a great stepping-stone.

Create a Meetup group for your event. You can make this the main site for the event, if you want, or it can be a complement to your event website. This is particularly effective for local events, since Meetup is primarily a local service. Or, mention your event at a local meetup group that is relevant.

In the event description of your Meetup, be sure to use good keywords so that it's easily found through Google and the on-site search function. Don't do keyword stuffing, though; the description should make sense to a human reader.

Meetup has limited utility for international events, but if you have the resources to put into it, you can definitely attract a larger local crowd.

Figure 11-3. Properly used, Meetup can be a gateway to local colleagues, customers, and fans

Facebook

All of the previously explained tactics for Facebook apply. Create a page for your event, post good content, engage, promote, and so on. Certainly also create a Facebook event for your event and promote it to your fans, but make it clear to attendees that confirming their attendance on the Facebook event isn't sufficient to save their spot—they must register at your official event page to confirm their registration.

You're also going to want to create your own Facebook group dedicated to the topic that the conference covers, and leverage your Facebook fan base to participate in it.

Twitter

As already mentioned, create a custom hashtag (or hashtags, if appropriate to do more than one) for your event on Twitter.

You can take this one step further by using Twitter's API to create a custom widget for your site that displays tweets with this hashtag.

Create Your Own Social Network

It's possible to use a service to create your own social network. However, you or your event needs to be extremely popular, and you must dedicate a lot of resources to maintaining a custom social network and engaging with the participants. In most cases, it's better to create a Facebook group or Google+ community so that you can take advantage of an existing infrastructure with which your fans are already familiar. When existing networks don't have the features or control that your community needs to be successful, then you have a good business case for a custom social network. These are some services that we recommend:

- Crowdvine (*http://www.crowdvine.com*)
- Ning (*http://www.ning.com*)
- Presdo Match (*http://match.presdo.com*)
- Bizzabo (*http://bizzabo.com*)

If you take this route, you're going to want to promote your custom social network everywhere—Facebook, Twitter, and so on. Do whatever you can to get speakers and attendees to sign up here and participate on the site. Here are some examples of successful custom social networks:

- *http://ypo.crowdvine.com*
- *http://leanstartup2013.crowdvine.com*
- *http://events.bizzabo.com/eMetrics*
- *http://globaleducationconference.com*
- *http://community.blogpaws.com*

Case Study: Coaching the Coaches

Taki Moore is the creator and trainer behind Million Dollar Coach Intensive, a two-day bootcamp-style training intensive on Internet marketing for coaches run by his coaching and group consulting business Coach Marketing Machine. He teaches coaches to use webinars and automation to supercharge the sales funnel. To attract his clients, he uses a mixture of networking and social media/search engine marketing. Because they are so essential to interest client prospects, Million Dollar Coach Intensive places special importance in testing and running calculated and enticing Facebook ads. Below, Taki reveals a few of the insights he has found most valuable while testing targeted ads and landing pages. To learn more about Taki's Million Dollar Coach Intensive, check out Coach Marketing Machine (*http://CoachMarketingMachine.com*).

How do you use Facebook ads?

Taki: We use predominantly newsfeed ads with some retargeting (see Figure 11-4). Some is righthand sidebar stuff, but mostly its News Feed link post ads. The main reason for me is that eyeballs are on the News Feed. People have been trained to ignore the other stuff. You can actually get great click-through rates on the righthand side, but the News Feed shows up better on mobile. I'm pushing people towards content, so it just makes more sense that way.

Figure 11-4. One of Taki Moore's higher performing Facebook ads

Sometimes we use News Feed ads to promote blog content to create engagement. But most of the time we are sending people straight to an opt-in page, usually to a free report or checklist (*http://bit.ly/1kwlmNv*) (see Figure 11-5). We've gone straight to webinar (*http://bit.ly/1l4ekj4*), and our show up rate isn't as good. We've found really great show-up rates on the Facebook ads if they've clicked on the ad that day or the day before, but too much before that and it'll be about 20% show up, compared to our returning audience, which is around 50%–55%. For that reason when we go to webinar, we usually go to something else first, and make the webinar the Thank You page strategy.

Figure 11-5. One of Taki Moore's landing pages, built in LeadPages

Any surprising strategies you've found useful?

Taki: I typically think the more value that I can give people the better. I sent people to this killer video course, but our conversion on the landing page was lower. I believe in part it is because people think it will be valuable, but know they are going to have to sit through a bunch of video content to get the value. On our second video in the video series there was a 27-point checklist with a 3×3 grid of some steps on how to run a webinar that sells really well and how to market it. It turned out that the checklist was a hotter offer than the video course. So we just put that front and center and made the landing page just mail out the checklist. That page doubled our conversion rate, and in some cases almost tripled it. The video course was giving us around 11% conversion on the video course, depending on targeting; I think it ended up averaging around 28% for the checklist. People want it because the checklist is like a quick win or a magic pill, something that you can get big value from without having to work too hard for it.

How do you market differently for events?

Taki: We're doing a look-a-like audience on Facebook ads. We take our client base and upload them to Facebook. Facebook then looks for people who have six data points in common with our current clients. Then, we overlay that with the likes and interests that we are targeting, say "coaching and this person and that person." This creates a much more targeted list who are almost certainly the right type of people. Obviously, we've done custom audience, and we've done a look-a-like to our prospect list as well. We targeted LA, California, West Coast much heavier than we did East Coast because of travel time, because we are driving people to a live event.

We just had 58 people in the room this weekend, at least half from Facebook. The ticket price wasn't the big obstacle. The big obstacle is "I've got to get to LA and take two days out of my life. And maybe pay for accommodation." Upside, the room was nice and full;

we sold a lot of stuff. Downside, we managed to attract a few people who weren't my ideal, just because of the likes and interests we targeted. Of the 58 people in the room, we sold it to 18 of them at $18,000 a piece. We'll call the total between $270,000 and $329,000.

What do you use for landing pages?

Taki: We use LeadPages (*http://leadpages.net*). I love it because you can get a page up quickly and test things out. If something works out really well, but you want a little more control over how it looks, you can take your page to a designer and say "I want this, but *Like us!*" or something.

The great thing about LeadPages is that you can go to a page type like an "opt-in page" and then sort by conversion rate. The top 3 or 4 layouts are usually the ones we'll pick. Then we split-test them against each other and run them for a few days until it is statistically 98% guaranteed to perform better or worse than the other. Then we just ditch the loser. We've tested four different landing page templates with probably 40 different designs, and run Improvely (*http://improvely.com*) to then track the sales funnel.

Real-Life Q&A

Q: I've got some great material for a webinar, but I have no idea what software to use. Can you make some suggestions?

A: Sure. Here are some webinar recording and delivery services that we're aware of:

- Autopilot Webinars (*http://autopilotwebinars.com*)
- StealthSeminar (*http://stealthseminar.com*)
- Evergreen Business System (*http://evergreenbusinesssystem.com*)
- WebEx (*http://webex.com*)
- GoToWebinar (*http://gotomeeting.com/online/webinar*)
- Join.me (*http://join.me*)
- Google Hangouts (*http://plus.google.com/hangouts*)

In general, webinar software and services used to be very expensive, but they have reduced in price quite a lot, and continue to get cheaper with time. Google Hangouts, for instance, is an excellent tool for giving webinars, and not only is it free, it's also connected directly to a major social network (see Figure 11-6).

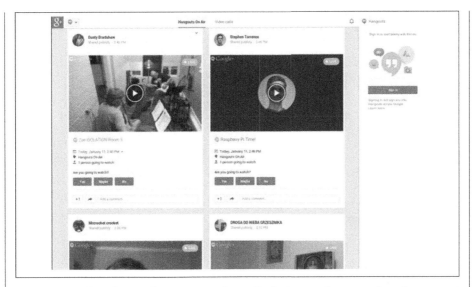

Figure 11-6. Google+ makes it easy to host, find, sign up for, record, and comment on Hangouts

Q: I had a whole plan for a traditional marketing campaign, but you've talked me into abandoning it all in favor of social media. Should I do that?

A: Maybe. If you have already had success with your previous traditional marketing efforts, then absolutely don't abandon them! Rather, select some of the things we've talked about in this chapter that you can easily add to that strategy, and see what happens.

Now, if you've seen rising costs and diminishing returns in traditional advertising, then you should think about cutting back on the parts of it that aren't working, and ramping up your social media efforts. The world in general is moving toward social media and away from old-style media.

For products and services that have a long or detailed sales process, or are very complicated and/or expensive, webinars tend to convert very well to sales, more so than a plain old landing page. Definitely go for the sale during the presentation, but don't show or provide the "buy" button until you get to the "bonuses" for fast-acting buyers.

The strategy for promoting a webinar is pretty universal, no matter where or how you're doing it. It's just a lot easier, quicker, and cheaper online if you focus on social media. When you're promoting your webinar, foster a sense of urgency and scarcity. There are only so many seats, slots, or tickets. Show a countdown timer, or show the exact (low) number of available free tickets. Offer people the chance to win something extra by signing up early ("The first 20 people to sign up get this extra"), such as a free ticket to another event, free access to bonus material or other recordings of expensive events, or free product giveaways.

LeadPages has premade templates for webinar registration pages that are incredibly quick to fill in (see Figure 11-7).

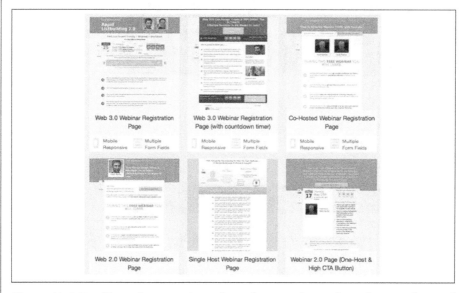

Figure 11-7. LeadPages has a variety of templates to choose from that are designed specifically to promote webinars

Q: In the beginning of this chapter, you said that there were three types of digital events. Why is that important?

A: It's just something to keep in mind for marketing purposes. A live event is going to generate more interest than a prerecorded event, so you're going to want to advertise that fact. You also don't want to mislead people; if you advertise something as live, but it is actually automated, it could backfire and generate a significant amount of negative buzz for future events if you're found out.

If your event is prerecorded or automated, that isn't necessarily a bad thing, but you're going to have to focus on a good value add. The recorded content is only part of the value. It may be prerecorded, but there is still someone there to field questions afterward, or there is some other interactive element to it that makes the fact that it's not live a nonissue. Or maybe the content is so good and so unique that you can do it live once and resell the recording a few times for people who couldn't attend the first event.

Another way to advertise or set up a prerecorded webinar is to tailor it for new customers or qualified prospects. Tell them that you have a webinar coming up in the near future, and then arrange to deliver it at that time. This can be done on an ad hoc basis, or you can schedule the events regularly.

Even though you're not going to lie about a webinar being prerecorded, you probably don't want to make it obvious that it is—you still want to give the appearance of it being live. Even if your attendees are aware that it's prerecorded, a well-configured presentation will still put them into the same mode of thinking as if it were live. For instance, if an attendee is late, don't let him start watching from the beginning of the presentation; make him miss the beginning and pick up where and when he joined, just as though it were live. The Q&A portion of the webinar should always look live, even if it's not. This may require you to handle the Q&A in a separate service or session. You can also allow new questions to come in during the prerecorded Q&A session from the original live event, and say at the end of the session that you will reply to all other questions via email. If you offer to do that, though, make sure you collect those questions and reply to them personally.

Q: I'd like to start a local LUG (Linux User Group), but I don't have any good promotion ideas. It's not something I want to spend a lot of money on, but I would really like it to be successful. What can I do for little or no cost?

A: First, make sure the event is worth going to. The launch event of a weekly or monthly group meeting has to have some spark and incentive in order to get off the ground. If you can affordably cater the event (offer free food), that will help quite a lot. In your case, one of the signature events of a LUG is an *installfest* where Linux experts help Linux newbies install a desktop distribution on their computer in a dual-boot configuration, or they set up a USB drive to provide an alternate boot option. If you can afford to cover the cost of pizza and soft drinks for the attendees, and offer to perform free data backups to DVD (bring a spool of blank DVD-R discs), those would be two excellent, inexpensive incentives that would drive participation.

Think about the subject of an installfest. You need people who know Linux, and people who want to learn Linux. Where would you find people who have interest on both sides of that operation? Computer repair shops, perhaps. Can you post a sign or flyer there? What about at computer stores? Perhaps the owner of a small local shop will even offer to cover the cost of the refreshments if he's allowed to bring some demonstration models and service flyers to the event.

It's possible that you can leverage an existing technology-oriented group on Meetup.com (*http://meetup.com*) as well. Search through the site and see if you can find related groups, then contact the group organizer and see if she's amenable to your hosting your own event through that group.

In general, local events have gotten a little tougher to promote because local periodicals have lost a lot of popularity and relevance. You can't take out an ad in the newspaper and expect results from it anymore. However, there's Craigslist—that's free, and has a lot of reach in the metropolitan areas that it serves. Post an ad there and keep it current right up until the actual day and time of the event. Then for the next meeting, post a different ad with photos and praise from the attendees of the inaugural event—social proof that this is a fun and interesting group that real people attend.

Also try to reach out to local bloggers; search all of the blogging services (e.g., WordPress, TypePad, Blogger) for people who are in your area and might have an interest in your event. For technical events, look for local blogs through Technorati.

Create a Facebook group for your meeting, and on the night of the event, take pictures and short videos and post them to that group. While you're among the attendees in person, go around with your smartphone or tablet and invite each of them to the Facebook group and ask them to post something and invite their friends. After the first event, you should have enough momentum to see a benefit from spending a little bit of money ($20–$50) promoting your Facebook group to continue to improve attendance. Remember: you're always looking for new members, even if you feel that you've achieved your attendance goals!

Summary

Events should definitely have a place in your professional life, even if you're not hosting them. We've explained in this and other chapters how attending industry conferences and relevant webinars can help keep you up to speed with a changing ecommerce landscape and put you in touch with powerful allies.

If you're just starting to venture into speaking or presenting at conferences, we've given you some excellent tools and tactics to get you on your feet. With motivation and practice, you will absolutely be able to work your way into major industry events and build your reputation as a speaker, industry expert, and author.

Head over to the book's website (*http://www.socialecommercebook.com*) for more Q&A and to post your own burning questions! You'll also have access to exclusive offers, discounts, and coupon codes on various social media tools and services.

To get exclusive access to instructional videos related to the concepts in the chapter, simply send a text with your email address to *+1(213)947-9990* and we'll send you some awesome links!

CHAPTER 12

Social Search Engine Optimization

So far we've concentrated on direct sales and customer interaction through social media. While social networks may be taking over the Internet at a rapid pace, traditional ecommerce websites are still where most online sales hapåpen. In fact, most *etailers* who are successful with social media are using it to eventually direct customers and prospects to a landing page on a corporate site or online store, so even if the method of getting there is new, the traditional website is still the focuså of ecommerce.

Traditional *search engine optimization* (SEO) may involve a number of different factors, from code changes and URL redirects on the server to getting people to link to your sites from places where search engines look. Hopefully, you already have a good SEO process in place. (If not, we recommend *The Art of SEO* [O'Reilly], which was coauthored by one of this book's coauthors, and is widely recognized as the definitive work on the subject.) Adding social media to your existing SEO strategy is both easy and inexpensive.

Beyond driving traffic to your site, you also want to be found in social network search engines. Google is pretty good about finding your publicly accessible social media profiles and pages, but what about the search engines that are built into the social networks? That's a whole different, and quickly advancing, kind of SEO.

 There are a lot of technical terms in this chapter. If you need clear definitions, you can find them in the Glossary.

Optimizing for Web Search

As long as Google remains the fastest route from point A to B, it will be the operating system of the Web, and the need for SEO will continue. Social networks offer just another venue within which searchers can conduct their queries. That means that large social networks like Facebook serve a dual purpose as search engines. As we've already mentioned, YouTube is the second most-used search engine. So optimizing for better visibility in search engines, whether Google or Facebook, isn't going away.

Use relevant keywords whenever appropriate, and post and engage with your followers regularly. By following these two simple rules, you are already well on your way to effectively optimizing your social media presence.

Using Photo-Sharing Sites for SEO

We have specific advice on Pinterest in the section "Pinterest for SEO" on page 213. However, there is one constant across all social photo sites: the SEO impact can be significant. Because most photo-sharing sites *nofollow* all outgoing links (meaning that search engines do not count those links toward rankings), there isn't usually a direct impact on the placement of search results.

While outbound links on photo sites probably won't directly impact your ranking, that doesn't mean these sites aren't useful for SEO. Google gives a lot of weight both to Flickr and to its own Picasa photo-sharing service, and so photos that you upload to these sites can rank well in Google and Google images. This can be particularly valuable for product images.

Google+ for SEO

Don't think of Google+ as a social network; think of it as Google's social interface to the Web. It's kind of like a mashup of every other social network—it's a little bit of Twitter, Facebook, and Pinterest all mixed together. The massive upshot is, if you post something to Google+ that ends up being +1'd and shared a lot, Google gives it more weight in web search results for logged-in Google users who added you to their circles. This is far more valuable than a generic link to a specific post on a different social network. Your content on Google+ is also indexed in a matter of moments, whereas other social networks will probably take longer.

If you have a local business, or any location to which customers will need to navigate, it is a strict requirement that you have a Google+ profile for your business. This is how your location will show up on Google Maps, and gives you the ability to customize your Google Local page. Additionally, you'll show up (and hopefully rank highly in) Google search results for your business name.

Google+ is also a great place to post live content, such as video demonstrations, interviews, and Q&A sessions. The recorded video can be stored and linked from indefinitely from YouTube, but the initial interaction and delivery happens through a Google+ Hangout. Most of this is valuable only after you've built a following.

So how do you build a following? More so than most other social networks, Google+ demands that you interact and engage with others to gain followers. You can't stand back and deliver content and hope for people to find and follow you—that is not a viable tactic. You have to find people and communities related to what you do or sell, and +1, comment, and share with them. Link back to people, mention them, ask them questions. After a few months, hopefully you'll find yourself in a significant number of circles. This takes a lot of work, and that work is ongoing, but for sustained influence on search results, it's a great investment.

Facebook for SEO

When properly optimized, your Facebook fan page can increase your business's online exposure without requiring a huge time investment (see Figure 12-1 for a great example).

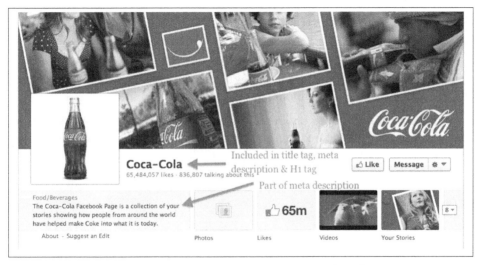

Figure 12-1. Coca-Cola's Facebook page is a great example of good SEO

Here are three important ways you can optimize your Facebook page:

Use descriptive keywords.
There are a number of places on your page where you should be including keywords that accurately describe your product or brand. It shouldn't take more than a few minutes to do this. Make sure you include them in your page name (particularly the first word), vanity URL, company description, and periodically in your posts (particularly within the first 18 words). Your page name and description are especially critical because they directly correspond with the title tag, meta description, and H1 tag on your Facebook page.

Post regularly and be engaging.

Likes, shares, comments, and check-ins are important for increasing your ranking in Graph Search. This means you should focus on regularly posting new content, and engaging with your fans. In addition, blog posts and articles that are linked to from within Facebook posts may receive higher search engine and Graph Search rankings when frequently liked and shared.

Make sure you've filled out every section of your page.

Facebook is more likely to move you to the top of Graph Search if you've filled out every section of your page. This includes your full address (especially critical for local search), phone number, product information, mission, overview, and about fields.

Twitter for SEO

Yes, tweets can rank in the search engines!

While Twitter links are *nofollowed*, Google does index tweets and profiles, and does take social signals into consideration. This means tweets that are retweeted are more likely to rank, and URLs within popular tweets may be weighted more heavily. However, tweets will not directly affect the search rankings of links to external sites.

As with all social networking optimization, keywords are of special importance. For instance, if you type "twitter reddit marketing" into Google, the first five results are for Twitter profiles and tweets, as shown in Figure 12-2.

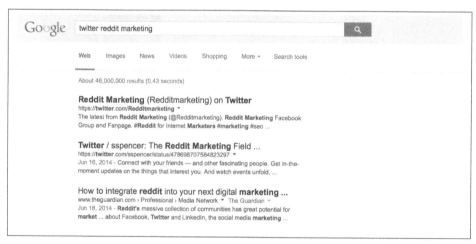

Figure 12-2. Tweets do indeed show up in Google, and can rank highly

Figure 12-3 is a screenshot of the second result in that list.

Figure 12-3. If you choose your tweet content carefully, you can rank highly for related search queries

This was favorited only twice, and not retweeted at all, yet this tweet ranks simple because it contains keywords relevant to the search query.

Here are some other ways to optimize your Twitter profile and tweets (some of which are illustrated in Figure 12-4):

- Include your keywords in your Twitter bio. Your bio will automatically be used as your meta description.
- Include keywords in at least some of your tweets.
- Tweet excellent content that gets retweeted to increase social authority.
- Optimize your Twitter lists by using keywords in the names of your list. These lists have unique URLs, so make the most of them.

Figure 12-4. An example of an SEO-friendly Twitter profile

LinkedIn for SEO

Google also gives a lot of authority to LinkedIn pages, so long as they are publicly accessible (that holds true for all social media profiles, though). To test the visibility and SEO friendliness of your LinkedIn profile, do a Google search for your name. If your LinkedIn profile is among the top results, you've got a good head start. Follow through by ensuring that your business page on LinkedIn is filled out, publicly viewable, and has a good URL.

LinkedIn profiles have three places where you can put in external URLs. There are several choices, the most obvious ones being Personal Site, Company Site, and Other. You can put any URL you want in any of these, but Other will also ask you for a description. This is your chance to use a compelling keyword phrase to connect to your ecommerce or business site. You can also customize the anchor text if you choose Other for your other links. You can put High-Fashion Blog or whatever pertains to your company. However, keep in mind that this is nofollowed.

YouTube for SEO

You can dramatically increase the chances your video will be found via YouTube search and in the search engines by following these tips:

Use descriptive keywords.
> There are a number of places you should include your keywords:

> *In your video title.*
> > Choose your top one or two keywords, and work with them to create a title that will be friendly to both visitors and search engines.

> *In your video description.*
> > Be sure to make these sound as natural as possible.

> *In your tags.*
> > Tags are how YouTube categorizes videos, so you should use words people are likely to use to find your video, including your brand name where relevant. To view a video's tags, either view the HTML source (incredibly tedious) or use the Chrome extension VidIQ Vision.

Upload a transcript.
> You can provide your own transcript or captions file, or you can rely on YouTube's automatic transcription. If you have the time, we suggest overriding the automatic transcription (as it is very inaccurate) and instead opting to manually transcribe your video. This is searchable content and you'll want to ensure the right words are being used. There are inexpensive transcription services available such as dotsub (*http://dotsub.com*), captionsync (*http://www.automaticsync.com/captionsync*), and castingwords (*https://castingwords.com*).

Upload foreign language translations.
> Again, it's searchable content and will help you rank for foreign language queries. And the translation appears in the video as subtitles.

Pinterest for SEO

Here are four ways to improve SEO with Pinterest:

Use relevant keywords throughout your profile and pins.
> This includes:

> - Your company username
> - In your About section
> - In your board names
> - In your pin descriptions

- In your pin filenames

Choose appropriate categories for your boards.

Because many people will go to the Pinterest categories section to find relevant pins, it's important to make sure you've listed your boards under the most relevant categories. To view a list of categories, click on the red button next to the search box at the top left of your screen (see Figure 12-5).

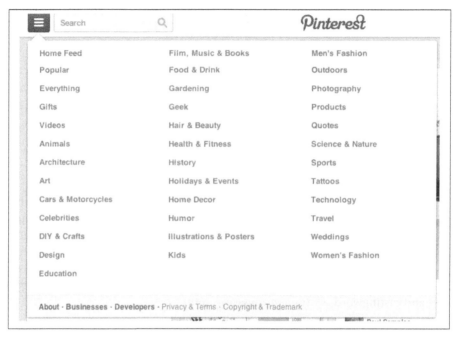

Figure 12-5. Ranking highly in a top category will give you a shot at increased traffic

Consider using the long-tail keywords.

For individual pictures, consider using longer, more descriptive keywords that won't be as difficult to rank for.

Include your city or region.

If you're looking to attract local search traffic, be sure to include your business's city name in your profile and/or your board names (Figure 12-6).

Figure 12-6. This vintage store has a large following, but still capitalizes on local traffic by listing its location

Optimizing for Social Search Engines

This is a tough subject to write about because most social networks are secretive about their search engines. In some cases, we suspect that they don't want to expose the limitations and primitive nature of their search capabilities; in other cases, they may have major flaws that would allow users to easily exploit the system and get to the top of the results. Social networks are extremely competitive with one another, especially when it comes to the quality of features—search being one of the big ones.

LinkedIn

If you're using LinkedIn to find clients, SEO for your business page should be one of your top priorities. Fortunately, improving your rankings on LinkedIn shouldn't take long, assuming you're already well connected and active on the site.

Here are a few tips for increasing your LinkedIn rankings (and your outbound SEO as well):

Fill out your profile completely.
 LinkedIn gives preference to accounts that have every section is filled in.

Use keywords.
 In your headline, description, products, services, and specialties fields.

Make connections.
 LinkedIn appears to give preference to profiles that have at least some connections, so even if you don't plan to use LinkedIn regularly, be sure to connect with at least a few people.

Join LinkedIn groups.
 By actively participating in LinkedIn groups, your profile activity goes up, increasing your social ranking.

Get recommendations.
 There is some evidence that profiles with more than 10 recommendations may receive improved rankings.

Facebook Graph Search

Facebook has put a ton of resources into its on-site search engine. There isn't much room for exploiting it, since you're limited as to what you can put into your profile and the Facebook admins are vigilant.

When you search Google, you're asking for relevant results from the widest possible array of sources; when you search Facebook, you're asking specifically to find people or some attribute that is normally associated with people. A Google search result will show you information in an anonymous manner, whereas Graph Search enables you to connect with the person, page, or group that you've found. So you could say that Graph Search is about who you know (or can know), whereas Google search is about what the Internet as a whole knows. By extension, Graph Search is also about who knows you. So if you have a relevant audience, then Graph Search will connect the friends of your friends with your business page.

The Graph Search result algorithm represents a mix of the following criteria: freshness, relevance, and closeness. There is also a geotargeting component to the algorithm, so if you have location data (both your business location and check-in locations), then you can rank more highly locally.

Here are some other general tips for increasing your visibility in Facebook's Graph Search engine:

Claim your page name.
Choose a good page name using your business name and/or location. Remember to keep it short and simple.

Choose your business category and subcategories.
Most pages can choose three subcategories.

Find the most relevant keywords for your business.
These can be your main SEO keywords, keywords from your AdWords campaigns, or even keywords from Google Webmaster Tools.

Provide detail and keywords in the About, Mission, and Company Description sections of your page and profile.
The more detail you can provide here, the better. Use strong, relevant keywords and URLs for best results.

Use relevant apps.
Apps for surveys, forms, menus, newsletters, ebooks, contests, and the like make it easy for fans to find your content. When you post only status updates, visitors get lost in a matter of days. By keeping your relevant information in an app, you ensure that most info is quickly retrievable.

Create your own version of a Facebook mini-website with an app.
Use it for lead generation, sales of top products, promos and giveaways, free downloads, and any other relevant content. You can get your app to appear as a tab/link next to Timeline, About, and Photos. See Figure 12-7.

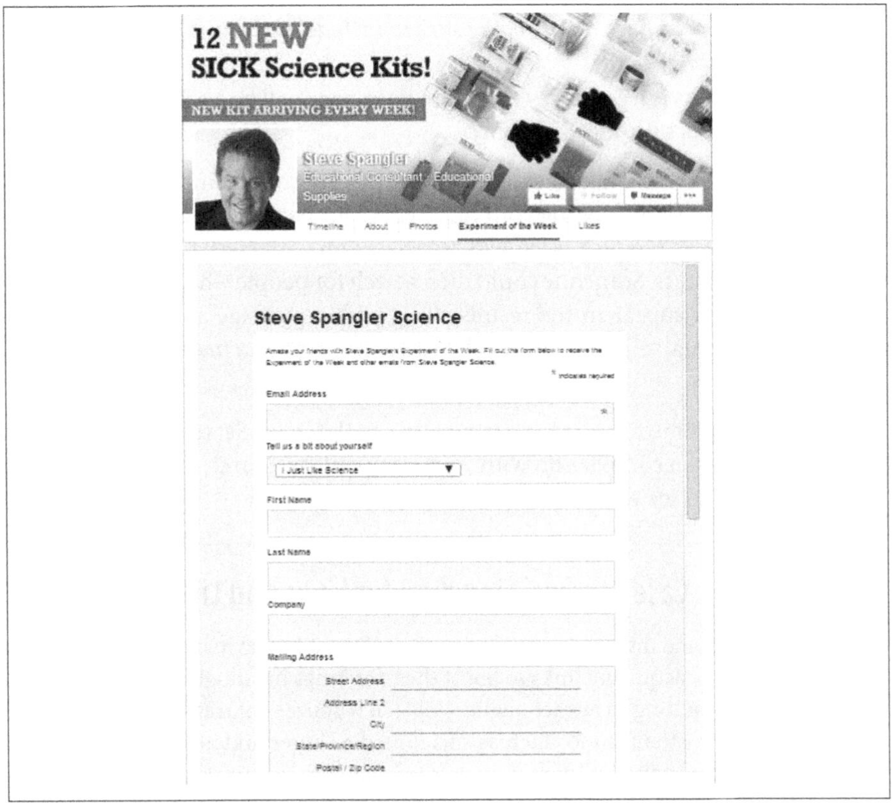

Figure 12-7. Steve Spangler's Facebook page has an "Experiment of the Week" tab and app

Develop an interactive, engaging, entertaining page-post style that suits your brand.
This is very important! Find your voice, and use it in your posts. Engagement is everything on Facebook, so it's worth investing some time in getting your message right. Regular, entertaining posts will keep users coming back for more.

Encourage content sharing.
Make it easy for people to share your content by posting plenty of photos and videos. Keep videos very short (under five minutes) and have them subtly branded with your company name and/or URL.

Discuss it.

Chat, reply, tag, and interact with your readers/fans regularly. Many big brands totally overlook this aspect of social media. Ignore this, and you will fail. Discuss hot topics, confront blunders head on, answer questions, and be fair, honest, and straightforward.

Tag photos with your page name, being sure to include your business name and location in the description.

Tagging photos is a great way to ensure your page will be seen when customers are searching for a business like yours.

Be careful what you click Like on with your personal account. Since you have liked your business page, you're associating your likes with your page and therefore your business. If you "like" racism, Graph Search will associate you with everything else you like, including your business. Someone could then search for people who like racism, and your business logo will appear in the results along with your page and profile. Find other examples at Actual Facebook Graph Searches (*http://actualfacebookgraphsearch es.tumblr.com*).

If you have some time to spend experimenting with Graph Search, you can get an idea of where you rank in comparison with your competitors. Search for your keywords and adjust the filters to see what the results are.

Case Study: Going Viral for Links and Likes

In early 2010, home improvement retailer BuildDirect had exhausted many of the traditional means of acquiring links to boost their rankings in Google. They needed a new strategy for continuing to attract quality links, new sources of traffic, and social signals that Google pays attention to, such as social media shares and activity. As a pure play ecommerce site offering building materials to both DIY consumers and builders/developers, BuildDirect traditionally pursued a content strategy focused around providing useful how-to and product feature information. Its then-Director of SEO, Content, & Social Media, Rob Woods (now an SEO consultant and content strategist), decided that what was needed was a new approach to the content strategy.

The approach Woods took was a multifaceted one. The first step was to conduct detailed research and build personas for those who were actually reading the content and driving the purchase process for their products. This allowed BuildDirect to understand that the true drivers of its success were not the (usually) men who were most often making purchases on the site but rather the (usually) women who were looking at how they wanted their homes designed and how they wanted their homes to feel, then finding the products that matched those wants and needs.

This led to Woods creating a strategy for content creation and promotion that focused much more on informing those female users about the latest trends and styles, and how

---

to achieve those in their own home. "One of the best strategies I found for getting started on a basic editorial calendar and getting ideas for what to write was actually going back to the traditional print magazine industry," Woods says. "I laid out several years of each magazine and you can really get a sense from that as to what the most popular topics are and when certain topics tend to be written about. The magazine industry has spent many decades perfecting what content to publish, when to publish it, and how frequently to rewrite and republish an article," states Woods.

While the creation of this type of content was meeting the needs of BuildDirect's actual readers and customers, it was intended to drive more engagement once users were on the site rather than driving new traffic. This led to the second wave of the content strategy: creating content designed to almost exclusively drive links and social shares to the site while still remaining somewhat on topic with the theme of the site.

The next step was to hold brainstorming sessions to come up with ideas for content that might have more entertainment value than educational value. In addition to their own internal team, Woods brought in two outside consultants, Brent Csutoras and Matt Siltala, who specialized in creating and promoting viral content. "Unless you have experienced viral content and promotion experts in-house it really is worth bringing in someone expert in the field, at least to get you started," says Woods. These consultants not only helped with coming up with ideas for viral content and developing processes for creating that content, they also provided access to *power users* on social media platforms to help with the promotion of the posts. Woods says, "Unless you have a vast social network of your own, it's vital to leverage influencers or power users who have the ability to give your content a kickstart in social media."

Even with a strong kickstart, you have to be prepared for many of your viral content pieces to fall flat and only a few to be stars. It's impossible to create content where every single piece you create goes viral. You have to experiment, test, and in some cases, even get a little lucky. "We tried several different ideas for humorous content. Not all of them worked, but we learned as we went. Our most successful content piece was one called *Redneck Home Remodels (http://bit.ly/1wr4eOs)*", says Woods (see Figure 12-8). "It connected on several of the factors that help contribute to a piece of content going viral. It was on its face humorous, showing ingenious and, to be fair, somewhat stereotypical, home renovations and hacks purportedly created by rednecks. It also, quite unintentionally, created controversy wherein many users thought we were making fun of poor people. We weren't, of course, but the discussion that followed in the comment section helped drive more views and shares of the piece. Our social media manager at the time, Rob Jones, made sure that we responded to all criticisms in a calm and professional manner," relates Woods. The article also had the good fortune of being seen and retweeted by Jason Alexander (George Costanza from *Seinfeld*). Being seen by someone so influential with a large following on Twitter (*https://twitter.com/IJasonAlexander*) gave the piece an additional bump in traffic after the initial spike had begun to wear off.

Figure 12-8. A clever content marketing campaign for a DIY home improvement ecommerce site

Video Search

No matter what you're selling, it will help you to have a video presence. Google Video Search still exists despite the fact that most videos are posted on YouTube and most video searches take place there. Video search is not sandboxed; if you're doing a normal web search, if there is a highly ranked video that is relevant to your query, it will show up in the standard search results.

Aside from YouTube, there are several other relevant (but substantially less popular) services that are worth paying attention to if you have some great videos:

- Vimeo

- Dailymotion
- Metacafe
- blip.tv

Instagram accepts videos as well, though they are time-limited to 15 seconds. You can also share videos through Pinterest. Twitter has its own 6.5-second looping, mobile video app called Vine (*http://vine.co*) that we've mentioned in previous chapters.

Facebook Graph Search takes tags into account, so whenever you link a video (or an image) on Facebook, make sure you tag it with your keywords. Also tag your own page in all of your photos and videos; this also impacts Graph Search.

Optimizing for YouTube Search

A YouTube analytics tool called Voot (*http://www.voot.net*) is a must-have for marketing on YouTube. It tracks your videos' YouTube search rankings as well as various engagement metrics like views, favorites, likes, and comments. Management icon Peter Drucker once said, "What gets measured gets managed," so put your analytics in place as soon as possible.

YouTube Insight (*http://www.youtube.com/my_videos_insight*) is also helpful for monitoring popularity metrics, but only for your own videos. You can also glean some insight into your competitors' videos simply by clicking on the graph icon next to the number of views—if the posters weren't savvy enough to turn that off. (Obviously you should turn this off on your own videos to keep it away from competitors' prying eyes.)

When you upload a video to YouTube, optimize the title, description, and tags (keywords). These all make a big difference when it comes to its ranking in YouTube—and for which keywords. Don't be too broad or too esoteric. Use YouTube's suggestion feature (autocomplete), Google Trends (*http://www.google.com/trends/explore*), and the YouTube Keyword Tool (*https://www.youtube.com/keyword_tool*) for keyword brainstorming. Google Trends has a great YouTube keyword research feature accessible by selecting the option "YouTube Search" instead of "Web Search". The title is one of the biggest factors in convincing a user to view the video, so give your videos keyword-rich yet catchy titles. And remember that YouTube has a title tag display limit of 62 characters. Don't go beyond that, but use it to your advantage. Append your brand name to your video titles in order to help build more prominence for that keyword in your channel.

Make copious use of tags on your videos, with all tags relevant to the content. Separate each tag with a comma, use adjectives as well as category descriptors to make your videos more visible to folks searching based on their mood, and don't use throwaway words like *and* or *to*.

Write unique descriptions that are optimized for SEO and differentiated from competitors. The words you use in the description of the video will make a big difference when it comes to where it ranks in YouTube, and for which keywords. Remember to use the words for which you are trying to rank. Don't be too broad (e.g., "construction video") but don't be too esoteric either. Make sure you add a URL before the descriptive text. That way, even when the "More info" option is collapsed, the user will still see the link and will be able to click it, provided you use a complete URL (including the *http://*).

In addition, make sure you have links back to your site so that people know where the video came from and calls to action in annotations. Make sure that the page to which the video links contains content that complements and enhances what the user experienced in the video so you are more likely to drive some links to your site as a result.

Make good use of thumbnails influence the searcher's click decision. The thumbnail is more important for clickthrough than the video ranking, so you want one that's eye-grabbing. Get in the habit of always creating a custom thumbnail where you've chosen a frame that piques the searcher's interest, ideally with graphics overlaid. If you are a verified YouTube user (meaning you supplied a mobile number to which YouTube texted a verification code), you can upload your own custom thumbnail (see Figure 12-9).

Figure 12-9. The Custom Thumbnail tab should be next to the video thumbnail options in the upload page

Videos longer than three minutes run the risk of not being watched to the end. Videos longer than five minutes are completed even less often. Whittle down your script until it's three minutes or less, if you want it to have a shot at going viral.

Allow users to view likes/dislikes on your videos. This encourages sharing and commenting. YouTube also uses ratings when calculating search result rankings. This is also a component to going viral, as lots of likes and views demonstrate "social proof."

Offer the option to embed your videos in other people's sites. This really encourages people to spread your video around, and makes it easier to share on Facebook and other social media sites.

Include a URL to your site or social media page within the video's description. YouTube will automatically make it clickable. The link will not help your search engine rankings because it's nofollowed, but you will get direct clickthrough traffic from it, and hopefully mentions in blogs and mainstream media.

Posting links via Twitter and Facebook, and embedding videos in blogs, can help with getting them indexed and ranking more rapidly.

Finally, annotate your videos with calls to action such as "Like this video," "Watch next video," and "Subscribe to our channel." It'll help drive engagement and, hopefully, generate more incoming links to your video.

Real-Life Q&A: The Searchers

Q: Should I promote my social media channels on my ecommerce site?

A: If it'll help drive sales, sure. Keep in mind, though, that social media is mostly for marketing—that is, for getting people to become aware of your brand and products. The destination is your ecommerce site, so the endgame is to get someone from a social network to your site and then to make the sale. It doesn't make much sense to send her back to social media once she's where you want her to be.

Having said that, in some cases it might make sense. If it's a tough sell, like if you are selling something that is expensive and a lot of visitors are interested but unsure about spending that amount of money, then it might make sense to embed a YouTube video showing a success story or a demo, or customer testimonials on Facebook.

Summary

Search is still the most complex and quickly adapting part of the technology that drives the Internet. There really are only four ways for people to get to your site: with a direct link from someone, with a shared post on a social network, with an ad that introduces it to them, and through a search engine. Social media has strong influence on all of those paths.

Search engines are always watching, so use your keywords everywhere you can, fill out all of your account information on every site, make sure your pages and sites are publicly accessible, and encourage sharing as much as possible. Links are still the most powerful factor in search results.

Head over to the *Social eCommerce* website (*http://www.socialecommercebook.com*) for more Q&A and to post your own burning questions! You'll also have access to exclusive offers, discounts, and coupon codes on various social media tools and services.

To get exclusive access to instructional videos related to the concepts in the chapter, simply send a text with your email address to *+1(213)947-9990* and we'll send you some awesome links!

CHAPTER 13

Influencer Outreach

You can't do social media alone. We've well-established the fact that you need to engage with your customers and followers. There's another kind of audience to reach, though —one that can provide a huge advantage: influencers. In SEO, they are referred to as the *linkerati*. The linkerati are social media mavens who command gigantic audiences and determine the virality of other people's content. If these people link to your site, you're going to get a lot of attention from humans and search engines alike. So you're going to want as many influencers to say as many nice things in as many places as possible as often as possible. Not only does this lead to more sales, it also increases your social media following and improves your SEO.

Back in Chapter 2 we described content marketing—an article or video that is designed to be popular and spread through social media like an aggressive virus through a willing host. You can create the best content piece in the world, but it won't go far on social media unless an influencer takes an interest in it.

Not only does social media provide another venue for searching, it also serves as an invaluable tool for acquiring links. Specifically, social media provides a venue to virally spread your content piece. One good article can put you at the top of Google search results, saving you a ton of money in PPC ad costs.

Of the three pillars of SEO—content, architecture, and links—it's the links pillar that's usually the weakest. Looking at sites individually, formulating your approach, sending personalized emails, picking up the phone to speak to webmasters—it's a hard slog. Yet without high-quality, relevant links, you won't be able to earn the trust, authority, and importance required to rank, and your optimization efforts will fall short.

Content marketing by itself isn't sufficient. You need to *seed* this content piece into social media and social news sites such as reddit and StumbleUpon, using power user accounts within those communities. In other words, you need to be (or be in good with) a social media insider who has wide-reaching influence within that site's social community.

Without a bevy of friends, followers, and fans, it's much harder to reach critical mass quickly enough. That's because the algorithms that determine what's new and hot within social news/bookmarking sites take into account the timespan within which the positive votes are acquired: 50 reddit upvotes in 10 minutes is entirely different than 50 upvotes over the course of a year.

The secret formula really is a formula. Think of it as an assembly-line process: viral ideas are generated, the chosen ideas are researched and written up as articles (or produced as videos), and then they are published to your website or social network page. Next, the articles are seeded into appropriate social sites by influencers within those sites' communities. The point is to reach the journalists or bloggers who will write about and link to your viral content.

Social news power users spend day and night monitoring various oddball news RSS feeds and other social sites for content. Once they find something, they quickly submit the URL along with a killer title and description before anyone else. This is how users move up in the pecking order within these social sites. The more stories they can get to the front page, the higher their status. If you're not a power user, you're nobody; your submissions have a very low probability of making the front page. On the other end of the spectrum, nearly everything that a top-ranked user touches turns to gold; it's not atypical for the majority of a top user's submissions to hit the site's home page.

Before you continue reading up on influencer outreach strategy, you must understand that this is a process that can succeed only if you already have an established following. You must have a social media presence, you must understand your marketing strategy, and you must have a decent-size audience. Without a solid social media foundation, it's going to be very hard to get the attention of major influencers.

We wish we could say, "this is a quick and easy process," but it isn't. It's going to take weeks or months to reach powerful influencers, but it'll be well worth the effort.

Nearly everything in this chapter is part or all of a process that journalists use to contact sources for news articles. Nothing here is underhanded or even particularly secret.

Build an Initial List

If you're active in social media, or if you are socially active in your industry, you should already have a good idea of who the big names are—the people who speak at conferences, the people with huge Twitter followings, the people who everyone circles on Google+. Start making a list of influencers, and use the names you already know as initial items.

Maybe you're just getting started in social media, or you're running a local business and don't go to a lot of conferences. In this case, you're going to have to identify influencers and begin following and interacting with them through social media. For instance, if you own a restaurant, follow all of the Food Network personalities like Rachael Ray and

Bobby Flay, and other celebrity chefs and related public personalities like Martha Stewart.

Fiction book list building can be difficult at first. If you're writing a science fiction novel, you could follow other science fiction authors, editors, agents, and publishers that publish science fiction. It would also be useful, though, to find news sources that report on topics like science, space exploration, medicine, and other topics that could be related to what you're writing about.

It's going to take several hours over the course of a few weeks to build a solid list. And by *list*, we mean the people you're following/friending/circling. Every major social network has a way of showing who you're connected to from your side; that's your list. Or, rather, over several networks there are several lists, but we refer to them as a single entity here for the sake of simplicity.

This list is going to be broad; it's going to cover an appropriately wide range of topics and people. At this point, don't pare down the list at all—make it bigger. Expand out as much as possible. Follow anyone and anything that might be related.

You should also expand out beyond social media a little. If you identify some extremely high-value influencers, subscribe to their blogs, RSS feeds, newsletters, and podcasts. You are not doing this so much to learn from these people (though there's almost certainly something to learn from them, no matter how much of a guru you are) as you are to get to know them better. Only after you know them are you prepared to interact with them positively.

Begin Interacting

As just mentioned, once you get to know some of the people you're following, you can begin interacting with them. If they ask a question, send them @ replies. If they post a link to something, comment on it. Retweet or reshare their posts. On Facebook or Google+, post thoughtful comments or links to stories with more information. Repin, tweet (with an @ mention), and comment on their Pinterest photos.

Don't ask them to link to you or repost your content at this point. Later on, you're going to contact these people directly and ask them to help share your content or write a review, but you're likely to fail if you make your request too early. You will have a much higher success rate if you're already somewhat familiar to them through social media. The whole point of this process up until now is not strictly "greater influence with the influencers," though that is one of the goals. The point is also to raise your own profile and build your own audience to the point that you are no longer a nobody on social media; you become a budding influencer yourself, which has the added benefit of making it easier to reach your customers and prospects.

Refine the List

By this point, you should either have a solid following, or you should be steadily building it and your target number should be in sight. While you're engaging your followers, begin to whittle down your initial list of influencers by using reliable metrics. How popular are their blogs and other domains? How much reach do they have beyond their social media followers and fans?

Instead of answering that question on your own, you may want to use a tool like Kred (kred.com), shown in Figure 13-1.

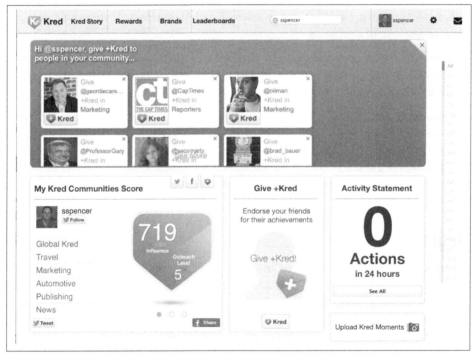

Figure 13-1. Kred shows you the most powerful influencers among those you're following on social media

Also useful is Klout (klout.com), which creates a composite Klout Score that shows your own influence (the more influential you are, the better your chances of getting the attention of a more powerful influencer), shown in Figure 13-2.

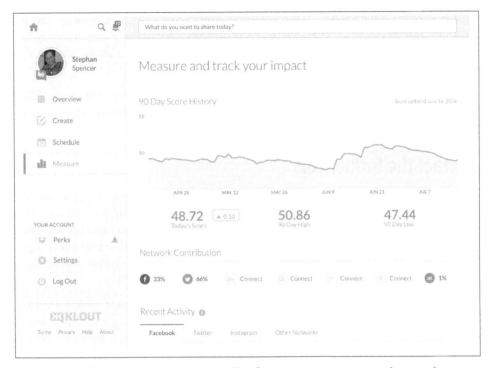

Figure 13-2. Klout shows you your overall influence across many social networks

Some other tools that you may find valuable for the purpose of gauging blogger's authority based on their proprietary metrics (which we have noted):

Open Site Explorer (http://www.opensiteexplorer.org)
  Measures mozRank and mozTrust

MajesticSEO (http://www.majesticseo.com)
  Measures TrustFlow and CitationFlow

LinkResearchTools (http://www.linkresearchtools.com)
  Measures Power*Trust

Followerwonk (http://followerwonk.com)
  Measure influence

All of these tools have their own algorithms to measure importance/authority/trust. Depending on your industry, product, and/or content, any of these tools may be more valuable than the others. It's important to note that Open Site Explorer, MajesticSEO, and LinkResearchTools analyze websites and web pages, not individuals.

Ultimately, though, this is not a numbers game; it's a quality game. If someone were to theoretically only have a dozen followers, but everything he posts goes massively viral, then despite the numbers he is a highly valuable influencer. That would be an unusual situation, but it's possible. There are some people who are on only one or two major social networks, such as YouTube or Google+; these people can be deceptively influential.

It's also not a numbers game in terms of how many influencers you must contact. Half a dozen really influential bloggers are more powerful than a thousand small-time bloggers.

Contact the Influencers

Cold calls are always difficult, even when they're emails. You want something, and you're contacting someone who is in a position of power and asking her to give it to you. This is not a role that anyone enjoys being in, but the most successful salespeople and marketers put that aside and master the art of initial contact. Think about how much you want social media success (or the business success that is on the other side of social media success). What are you willing to do to achieve that?

All you need to do initially is get your foot in the door with one good, solid influential mention on social media. Then you'll use that first big mention to get the attention of other influencers. Even among the top people on social media, everyone wants to be in with the cool kids. That first mention becomes the best method of obtaining mentions from others, so invest big in your first major influencer outreach effort. From that point forward, it gets easier.

Before you start sending emails, give serious thought to where you want to claim to be mentioned. On Twitter? On a famous blog? On Facebook? The social network or site where you want to be mentioned will help you narrow down your choices and customize your outreach message.

Pinterest Group Boards

If you are an active and established Pinterest user, you can use *group boards* to your advantage in contacting and participating with Pinterest influencers.

You can invite a mutual Pinterest follower (someone whom you follow, who also follows you) to be a contributor to one of your boards. This creates a group board. You will always be the administrator of that board, but you can add as many mutual followers as you like. By the same logic, one of your mutual followers can invite you to pin to one of his group boards.

If you can find a way to get a Pinterest power user to participate in one of your group boards, you could inherit a lot of his followers as a result. Similarly, participating in the same group board as an influencer gives you much more trusted and intimate access to him, and a much higher chance of getting a review, repin, or mention from him.

The Twitter Warmup

Why bother with a cold call when you can get more success with a *warmup*? Even if you're not targeting Twitter, if the influencer you're going after is active there, you've got to engage her there. High-value targets are almost certain to ignore a cold email, and will require a warmup on Twitter. If you make this effort to engage her with meaningful comments and retweets, it'll help her become more comfortable and familiar with you.

Tweet @ people. When the influencers you're watching say something that you can respond intelligently to, reply to them positively. Answer their questions. You can also thank people publicly for recommending something.

Watch their Twitter feed for a while so that you can be sure that they really are as wonderful and interesting as you think they are, and that you like what they're saying. You may discover that while someone seems to be influential, she mostly posts negative things about companies and products; that outreach effort could be a disaster for you.

Don't hide behind a brand account; use your full name (your personal account). Or, if you intend to have more than one person represent you on Twitter, you might create a public persona who virtually represents your company. This name will be your public face, and will get all the credit for your posts. It's not a good idea for an employee (or even a partner or cofounder) to use a personal account for Twitter outreach because if/when that person leaves your company, he'll take all of his Twitter followers with him and probably delete all of his tweets. All of the work that you've done to build up your outreach engine will be destroyed, or at least at the mercy of someone else. If you're going to create a persona, make it a woman; women (or female names, at least) have a much higher response rate in outreach email.

The Twitter warmup is not a one-time event; it is an ongoing effort that will take weeks to complete.

After you've successfully warmed up your target, you can ask for a link to your site or page via Twitter, but contacting her by private email is better.

Getting Contact Information

Certainly, if you can get someone's phone number and you're fairly certain he'd be receptive to a quick phone conversation, then give him a call and follow up at an appropriate time with an email.

Some people are more inclined to respond on-network (a message sent on the social network they participate in), and some are more receptive to email. Usually, email is better because it's more personal and is more easily noticed. Some influencers are so popular that they don't check their in-network messages at all—they get inundated with notifications and frequent messages from raving fans—but they almost certainly do check their email.

Getting someone's email address can be tough and time-consuming. If you find yourself spending an unreasonable amount of effort trying to get the email address of someone who has taken great pains to hide it from the public, then fall back to tweeting @ him on Twitter.

First, try looking on the influencer's blog or corporate site for an email address. Maybe it's in an obvious spot.

Do you have his business card from an in-person meeting at a conference or event? People usually put their email address on their business card.

Does his blog or corporate site have a Contact Us page? That goes to someone's email —if not your target influencer, then probably his assistant.

If you add someone on LinkedIn, you can get his email from there. The reply to the invitation comes from his email address. You can also send InMail.

As a last resort, do a whois lookup on the influencer's blog domain name (assuming it is a real domain name and not a subdomain on a public blogging site like Typepad, WordPress, Tumblr, or Blogger). Every domain has contact information for the domain owner; hopefully that will include the email address of the person you're trying to reach.

Paying for Reviews?

If you are trying to reach a product reviewer, be warned: some high-level reviewers may ask you for money in exchange for a review. Among journalists this is highly unethical, but bloggers and social media power users don't always fall into the "journalism" category. In the United States, anyone who posts a product review, whether she considers herself a professional reviewer or not, must disclose the fact that she received compensation (including a free product) for it. This is an FTC regulation; you can read about it at the FTC website (*http://1.usa.gov/1p3cJws*).

The FTC puts the responsibility for disclosure on the brand, not the publisher. That means you. So if you send a check with your review materials, or if you tell a blogger or journalist to go ahead and keep the review unit you're sending, you must check back and make sure that she has clearly printed an appropriate disclosure notice. This even applies to endorsements on Twitter.

The preceding paragraphs contain really important legal liability information about product reviews. Don't skip this stuff. Read it twice. We don't want you to get in trouble with the U.S. Federal Trade Commission.

Also, the following paragraphs contain really important information about following rules set by the world's largest search engine. It would be very bad if it decided to blacklist you, so please don't skip what's written next either.

Paying for reviews, or giving free products to reviewers or influencers, is an ethical grey area at best. Usually it's all right with disclosure if it's posted to someone's blog or social media page, but it could reflect badly on you depending on context. In some instances it is definitely unethical—for instance, book reviews or any product review on Amazon.com that is done on a for-hire basis is against Amazon's rules. Google also frowns upon paid links, so if you are paying a blogger for a review that includes a link back to your site or product page, that is technically in violation of Google's rules unless the nofollow attribute is applied to the link in the HTML.

Some social media power users offer expanded services for hire. For instance, a popular Pinterest user might solicit money to do a photo shoot with an in-depth review or interview. Food bloggers might offer to publish a recipe and high-quality photos and a review of the resulting product. This is not prohibited by Pinterest, but if you take this route, make sure any links are nofollowed and proper disclosure is printed.

Creating Templates

First, you need good unique content. A lot of social media gurus will tell you that you should try to build followers by linking to interesting stories. That will get you a small amount of success. If you want major success, though, you've got to be the source of interesting information, not just someone who links to it first.

Start with a pool of unpublished articles that can be customized somewhat. They should be mostly or completely written, but don't tell anyone about that. The point of your influencer outreach email is to ask for help or input on an article you're currently writing. You will, of course, quote or cite the influencer as a source. Quoting experts for articles is the best way to get them to link to you or mention you on social media.

The article you're customizing should be relevant to a topic that the influencer covers or is interested in. Don't publish it more than once; don't try to repurpose a published article unless it is more than three years old and can be rearranged and re-edited to be modern and relevant.

Don't mass-mail your target influencers. Personalization is hugely important. The message *must* be personalized. Absolutely do not send a generic message that starts with something like "Hello, fellow blogger."

Not only are impersonal messages likely to be ignored, they're also likely to be caught in a spam filter. The same message sent to many addresses on the same network (such as Gmail or Yahoo Mail) can be flagged as spam by the system. Not only will you have completely wasted your time, you'll also have associated your email address with spam. Your whole domain could get blocked.

This doesn't mean that you shouldn't have a standard message template that you start with. It does mean that the template must be customized significantly. To do that, read the influencer's blog and social profiles; write as if you are familiar with him. Since you've been following him and attempting to engage publicly with him for a while, most of this work should be done.

The template should not be long—fewer than 300 words or so. Busy people don't have time to read long messages from strangers.

Initial outreach

Make the influencer understand that you took the time to read his work; express genuine interest in him. Mention something he did in the subject line: "Just saw your <title of last blog post>"—that will get him to open the email. You can also try mentioning his name in the subject line, or using an actionable phrase like "Need your decision," "Need your feedback," "Can I quote you for this article?", or "One minute to read this upcoming article?"

For the message body, don't talk about yourself or your background too much. When you talk about yourself to a busy stranger, that's boring and skippable. Establish yourself in one sentence. If you referenced something he did recently, follow up that reference in the message body. Or talk about something else he's done recently and how it affected you. Talk more about him than yourself.

If you're writing to someone who consistently uses an online handle or persona, then go ahead and address him by his blog handle or persona first. If there's no response to the first outreach, make note of that and use his real name in the follow-up email. Most people use their real names today, but in the old days handles were more popular. People want the credit; they want to be more transparent about who they are.

Close with a request for a reply. You want to encourage more dialogue. Don't ask for more than that, though—never ask directly for something of value in an outreach email, such as a link or a review. Compliment or comment; ask a question or ask for advice, and ask for a reply or feedback; establish friendly contact; and then work from there.

The time at which you send your message can make a big difference. Each industry has different prime days and times. Look at the posting schedule if you can, and try to figure out the editorial calendar as well (if it's a big blog, the blogger probably plans out certain themes for content on certain days or during certain months). If it's a tech blog and you know that the blogger publishes three stories a week, try to get him the day before a story publishes (or the day after), but not on the day. Most of the responses you're going to get are early or late, when people check email. Very busy people typically check email on a schedule.

Many spammers send their email late at night, so try to be off-schedule from that. Send your email during the day in the afternoon to avoid the spam rush, but before the last email check of the workday in your influencer's time zone.

Follow-up

If you haven't heard back from your first outreach within three days, then you should send a follow-up. Following up is more crucial than many people realize. Michael Geneles, cofounder of outreach tool Pitchbox, asserts that following up increases your response rate by 60%. You should have a separate template for follow-up emails; don't send the same message you sent before.

It rarely pays to go beyond two follow-ups—don't send more than three emails to someone who isn't responding to you. If someone doesn't reply after the third attempt, there is a very low chance of a reply, and you're better off spending that effort on the next influencer on your list.

Before sending your first follow-ups, get reinvolved on Twitter to make sure you've got a solid connection.

Third attempt

If your first two emails didn't get responses, then the third probably isn't going to work, either. You're going to have to take a different approach with your third attempt. Is there a different email address for this influencer? Some people list a Gmail account as a technical contact or as part of a regular Google account, but they rarely check it. Look for an alternate email address for this person, and explain that you're trying to get in touch and wondering if you've got the right address.

You can also try to use in-network messaging through Facebook, LinkedIn, or other social networks in which this influencer participates. If you do this, come up with completely different content for your email; mention that you've tried to reach out and haven't gotten through, note that you love his work and want his advice on something, and ask for a reply.

Tracking Responses

The only way to improve is to measure. Keep metrics on what gets through and what doesn't. If a particular template or a particular kind of influencer is not working out, then change your strategy.

Was the response favorable? Was there a response at all? How often does the first follow-up work? The second? You may want to make a quick spreadsheet to keep track of this data.

Automating Outreach

Many of the techniques previously mentioned can be automated, or at least partially automated, to help save you time. As noted, it's never wise to fully automate your outreach, especially where you are reaching out to top influencers. There are, however, tools, systems, and techniques you can use to at least partially automate the outreach, responses, and tracking involved in reaching out to influencers, such as Pitchbox (*http://www.pitchbox.com*). A number of advanced techniques for outreach automation are laid out in an article by one of our authors, Stephan Spencer, called "Scaling & System-atizing Your Link Building" (*http://selnd.com/1wrdGkX*). While the article speaks specifically to building links, the techniques are equally applicable to reaching out to influencers in the social media world. As the final sentence of that article states: "Of course no tool, no matter how awesome, will ever eliminate the need for creativity in the creation of viral content, but with some systems and workflow in place, you will be able to achieve scale with your outreach in ways you never thought possible."

Offering Giveaways

If you're selling a product or service and hope to get a review from an influencer, you should consider arranging a giveaway as part of that effort. Regular product reviews are helpful, but in the grand scheme of things they aren't usually a major influence on sales. One thing you can do to easily enhance the impact of a product review is to add a giveaway. Not only does this encourage engagement with and sharing of the review, it also helps your influencer look good because she's enabling her readers/followers to get free stuff.

There are many ways to offer giveaways—social media apps, websites, desktop software programs, and the capabilities built into sites like Goodreads and LibraryThing. One site that we find particularly effective across multiple media and sites is Rafflecopter (*http://www.rafflecopter.com*). Configure a giveaway that will launch with the review, and pitch it your target influencers as an exclusive extra bonus that you're offering for their readers. You can create a different giveaway campaign for each influencer, if necessary. Don't forget to ask for reviews and social media mentions from all of the giveaway winners!

Using Other Approaches

If you totally strike out despite your best efforts, then try a more indirect approach. Try to get through to the people who your target influencer follows. These are her friends and close colleagues, and people she admires. Likewise, if you do manage to get a positive reply, ask the influencer who else she knows who could contribute to the article or provide a quote. Oftentimes you'll get names, phone numbers, and email addresses of other influencers—and with a personal referral!

Nothing establishes initial contact like actual in-person communication. Go to industry conferences and meet your influencers in person. Have coffee with them. If they are not accessible in person, then build relationships with their friends; they will become your references. Take a long-term strategy. Or play golf with them—or whatever social activity is appropriate to the industry.

Watch for Mentions and Links

If you were successful in getting a positive response, then keep a close eye on the networks that you're targeting. Watch for links and mentions that involve you or your company. This might not happen immediately. Often an article costs you a lot of money or time, so don't wait too long to see if it gets published or mentioned. If you get an agreement, follow up after a week and see if there's anything else you need to provide. If you don't get a publication date, ask nicely for one.

Twitter is the hub for monitoring what's new on the Internet, so that should be your place to watch for mentions. It may not come in the form of a hashtag or an @, so watch your target influencer's feed closely. Social media monitoring will be infinitely easier if you use one of the many social listening tools out there, such as Trackur (*http://www.trackur.com*) or Radian6 (*https://login.radian6.com/*).

Tread Carefully on reddit

reddit seems like a gold mine for outreach because whatever becomes popular there will be popular everywhere else. All you need is upvotes, and you've got it made, right? Wrong. While it may be OK to solicit follows and friend requests on other sites, soliciting upvotes on reddit is a good way to get yourself downvoted, attacked, and blacklisted.

reddit is quirky and aggressive. Outreach to influencers on reddit (moderators, top posters, top commenters, people with a lot of karma points) will likely prove more harmful than valuable. Anyone soliciting reddit interaction via upvotes or submissions is almost always seen as a spammer, and treated harshly.

Every once in a while, a reddit influencer (typically a moderator of a significant subreddit) is publicly exposed (and humiliated) as being corrupt or as a shill for some site or company. As a result, it's difficult to appeal to reddit influencers without looking like a selfish spammer. There is no reliable strategy for influencing reddit moderators or power users. All you can and should do on reddit is try to participate normally and submit your viral content along with a lot of other people's great content to the correct subreddits without the appearance of self-promotion.

Establish Yourself on Google+

Google+ can be a good platform for outreach, but it requires a lot of work. While it is growing rapidly, it's still tech-heavy. So if you're doing outreach for clothing, it could possibly be worth it to get established there and connected to influencers in that industry who are there, but right now that effort will probably be better spent on Facebook or Twitter.

However, Google is forcing Google Account logins for everything it does now, so you're probably already using Google+ without knowing it. It's worth it to set up a presence there and circle your influencers. If they seem to be in a ton of circles and have a lot of engagement, then give it a shot and track your progress.

Case Study: Influencing the Influencers

A prominent etailer who wishes to remain nameless wanted to generate critical mass for a content marketing campaign. The company sells premier designer swimwear brands and styles, many of which have been featured on celebrities and in leading fashion magazines. Since the company's launch in 2000, it has established itself as the go-to place for fashion-forward swimwear.

It was successful enough that it reached the limits of what traditional ecommerce techniques, such as email campaigns and banner ads, could provide. At the same time, the influence of traditional media was declining and consumers increasingly began to rely on social media for information and trustworthy recommendations. The company decided that social media was a must-have marketing channel, for several reasons:

- Increasingly, it's where consumers were going to find out what's new and what to buy.
- Content on social media sites could help build credibility and loyalty. People choose which brands they want to follow, and trust the brands they choose.
- Relationships with authoritative brands would drive traffic to the company's own website, boost its domain authority, and improve its search engine rankings.
- Exposure via social media could help offset shrinking publicity opportunities in traditional media. With declines in advertising revenues, the company was finding fewer traditional media outlets and the outlets that remained had less editorial space

---

than before. And with fewer opportunities, the competition for placements had intensified.

The Initial Content Marketing Strategy

The company's social media strategy was to offer high-quality content to influential bloggers and independent media outlets. It quickly realized that traditional marketing/public relations techniques were entirely unsuited to this new channel, which left it with no established tools to use or methodology to follow.

The world of independent media is a classic *long-tail* market; instead of a few key influencers with wide reach, it contains vast numbers of outlets. There are a handful with huge audiences, and many more with fewer but highly loyal followers. Because this world is fundamentally based on social relationships, the company couldn't simply blast out one-size-fits-all content to everyone. It had to cultivate relationships and develop trust with influencers, and create content that was unique and tailored to each opportunity. The company started with a seat-of-the-pants approach: come up with content ideas, Google search to find some blogs that look good, poke around on the sites to find contact info, send emails pitching the ideas, and see what came back.

That approach seemed to work at first, but once the company tried to scale up past the first 15 or 20 opportunities, the process quickly became impossible to manage. Hundreds of responses to its outreach were coming in, often days or weeks after the initial email had been sent, and many arrived from email addresses different from the one the company had originally sent the message to. When it ran new searches to identify more placement opportunities, the problems compounded; someone had to check these leads against ones already in the pipeline to be sure they didn't overlap. With all of these administrative challenges, the campaign wasn't scalable. It wasn't a question of how many opportunities were out there, it was a question of how many opportunities the company could manage. It was putting in more and more effort, and costs were rising, but results weren't following.

Cutting back wasn't an option because independent media campaigns must reach critical mass to be successful. A mention here or there doesn't create momentum. The buzz starts when consumers—and influencers—start seeing your name pop up everywhere.

Stopgap Measures

Next, the company tried setting up Excel spreadsheets that contained lists of contacts and related information, such as the initial and last contact date for each. Even with this higher level of organization, it still took a lot of time to manage these spreadsheets—time that would have been better spent cultivating relationships, pitching ideas, and creating content. As time went on, the pipeline began to clog. Opportunities stalled, and in each case the company had to go back and figure out why. Was the ball in the company's court, or the influencer's? Did the contact owe the company feedback? Had the contact gone dark and nobody had noticed? Soon, the company found itself creating more spreadsheets and other ad hoc systems to try to keep up with these issues.

A CRM (customer relationship management) system seemed like the next reasonable step. The company looked at several, but the logic and the language were a poor fit because CRMs are set up for sales, not for media outreach. For example, most are built around deals—how much a sale is worth, how far along it is, who the decision makers are, and so on. That logic doesn't work for a media campaign. Similarly, CRMs didn't have metrics for social media, such as Klout scores or domain authority, or a good way to track and report results.

Automating the Outreach Campaign

In 2013, the company became a beta tester for a new prospecting and relationship-building platform, Pitchbox, that automated most of these administrative tasks (Figure 13-3). What appealed to the company was that Pitchbox wasn't just a repurposed CRM. It was built specifically around the tasks involved in social media outreach. For example, it starts with a search function that looks for new opportunities on a scheduled basis, and then strips out contacts that are already in the pipeline. It ranks the opportunities by influence—using criteria that the user can define—which helps the company prioritize its efforts. It automatically identifies contact info and allows the company to reach out individually (for the most important contacts) or using templates to scale. Then it follows each opportunity through the entire pipeline—from initial contact through placement. Along the way, it flags stalled opportunities, shows where the campaign stands overall, and guides the user to the next step.

The automation of these administrative tasks revolutionized the company's outreach efforts. Using the same resources as before, the company saw placements go from approximately 10 per month to 50 per month. Administrative tasks were no longer throttling the campaign, and the amount of time spent on these tasks declined from approximately 75% of total hours to 15%. That freed up time for staff to spend on high-value activities: cultivating relationships, coming up with ideas, and creating content. In addition, the retailer was better able to forecast results, allocate resources, and hit goals. For example, it can look ahead and see how many placement opportunities it is likely to have in upcoming months, so it can allocate resources to create the content needed to fulfill those opportunities. Or if the company sees that it needs more opportunities in the pipeline to meet its goals, it can deploy more resources toward outreach instead of content creation.

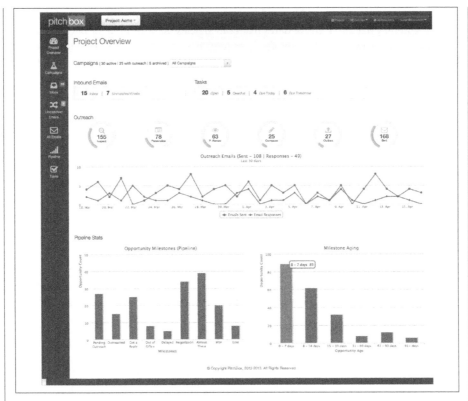

Figure 13-3. The Pitchbox dashboard

Achieving Critical Mass

Automation is critical to any long-tail business because long-tail markets have too many events happening to manage individually. The same principle holds for social media campaigns. They need to scale—reaching hundreds or thousands of influencers in a highly fragmented market—in order to reach critical mass. And to be scalable, they need tools and techniques to help manage these events. Enter, Pitchbox.

Real-Life Q&A: Reach Out and Touch Someone

Q: This whole thing makes me nervous. I'm nobody. The person I need to contact is somebody. Why would he reply to me? Is this even worth my while?

A: Become somebody first by building up your own social media presence; that makes you somebody. Before starting outreach, you must be established. The more followers you have, the better your response rate will (probably) be.

Old or infrequent content can be a problem for someone investigating your social media worth. You may need to remove dates from old articles on your blog, or backdate them to show a longer history of established content. If you're trying to bring attention to your blog, then you're going to need to host it on your own domain name (not as a subdomain of *WordPress.com* or *blogspot.com*). You don't want to look cheap and amateurish.

Q: What happens if I don't get a response? How many times should I contact someone without being a pest?

A: Three is the outside figure, over a period of a week or two. People are busy, especially entrepreneurs.

Q: How do I make my list?

A: Search for your keywords on social networks and see who's most active for those terms or hashtags. There are some people who write about different stuff each week, and some people who specialize in one topic. You can do a Twitter hashtag search or a Facebook page search. Twitter searches are good because you can search by keywords (not just hashtags) on people's profiles. You can also try LinkedIn, especially for anything related to B2B. Look for people who are speaking at conferences in your market.

For Google Blog Search (*http://blogsearch.google.com*), you won't want to use search terms like "fashion blogger" or "fashion blog"—look for the subject "fashion," or something more targeted, like "winter fashion," and then find bloggers therein. For a Google web search, "fashion blogger" or "fashion blog" are fine. Specific long-tail keywords are better than broad keywords. When you're writing your articles for outreach participation, focus your content on issues and subjects that apply to these targeted bloggers. The bloggers who write about broad topics are swamped by a lot of junk content, so it's harder to get through to them.

Q: This is way too much work for me. Is there a way I can spend like an hour on this instead of weeks or months?

A: There are firms that do this for you. There are also products that make the whole process much easier and provide a single interface for everything. Pitchbox (*http://pitchbox.com*) is a great example of this chapter's entire process folded into one web application.

Summary

If you're just starting out in social media from a commercial perspective, it can feel a lot like you're at the foot of Mt. Everest with no guide or equipment. If you want to climb that mountain, you have to be a positive contributor at base camp; you have to make friends with the experienced guides and knowledgeable climbers; you have to pull apart the term *social network* and be social and network with those above you in the hierarchy.

Influencers are people who spend a lot of time, personally and professionally, on social networks. If you're a successful entrepreneur, then you don't have time to be an influencer yourself, but you should always make time to try to build a relationship with one. Don't think of this as one-sided; you are providing something valuable, and so is the influencer. Your goal is to align interests.

Head over to the *Social eCommerce* website (*http://www.socialecommercebook.com*) for more Q&A and to post your own burning questions! You'll also have access to exclusive offers, discounts, and coupon codes on various social media tools and services.

To get exclusive access to instructional videos related to the concepts in the chapter, simply send a text with your email address to *+1(213)947-9990* and we'll send you some awesome links!

CHAPTER 14

Affiliate Marketing and MLM

More than anything else, the key to making money off of affiliate and multilevel marketing (MLM) sites is by gaining social proof through social networks. In either case, you're a middleman, so you've got to show that you, above all the other middlemen, are the most trustworthy and interesting.

In the past, an affiliate or MLM marketer would simply have to build a small website, buy some ads targeting relevant keywords, and, if she could successfully optimize her site, she could receive a decent amount of traffic and earn a decent amount of money.

Unless you were going door-to-door or in some other way leveraging your local community, social proof was largely lacking. That was great for many affiliate marketers; you could be a relative nobody, and because you were ranking highly for your keywords, people would find you and potentially buy based on your recommendations.

That's all changed. People now rely heavily on social media for product recommendations, reviews, and social proof. This is not a limitation—it's an opportunity. To succeed long-term, you need to look at social media as a key part of your master plan, not simply as a quick way to make sales.

Think about it. Would you be more likely to buy a product promoted by someone who had 10 fans on Facebook, or 10,000? Would you rather buy from someone who spends all his time spamming on Twitter, or someone who is constantly expanding his number of followers by building authentic connections and dialogue?

The way you engage with people on social media, along with the number of people who follow or like you, says a lot about you and your brand as an affiliate or MLM marketer.

Affiliate Marketing

Some merchants offer commissions for sales and/or leads that you deliver to them; this is affiliate marketing. Credit for affiliate sales is typically given through a special tracking code in the URL, or through a browser cookie that must be persistent in the visitor's browser from his visit on your site all the way through to the final checkout page on the destination site. An example of a well-known affiliate program is Amazon Associates.

If you're willing to really invest in your affiliate marketing efforts, social media is an excellent tool for establishing credibility and increasing sales.

Start by building your reputation. Without a solid reputation, you'll have a very difficult time being successful at affiliate marketing. People want to buy from those they trust, and trust isn't built overnight.

Create valuable content that establishes you as an expert. Having a solid content marketing strategy is key, because nothing says "expert" like someone who is consistently providing valuable content in the form of blog posts, ebooks, and whitepapers. Creating high-quality content, and then sharing it via social networking sites like Facebook, Twitter, LinkedIn, and Pinterest, is a surefire way to drive traffic to your site, build your reputation, and in the long-term, drive conversions.

Create Themed Content

A large percentage of your content, whether it's on a blog or social media, should be about topics, not products.

Let's say you're promoting a weight-loss product. Rather than creating reams of content about the product you're promoting, offer unique, high-value information based on the general theme of weight loss.

Within that strategy, you can most definitely include content about your affiliate products, and promote it however you see fit. Just keep in mind that shamelessly promoting a product to the exclusion of everything else (i.e., providing great content) will surely damage your reputation and sales in the long term.

Disclose All Affiliate Links

Whether you're promoting affiliate links on your website or social media, it's always a good idea to include a disclosure. Many affiliate marketers like to use a shortened URL on Facebook and Twitter (particularly on Twitter due to space limitations), but in some cases this can damage your reputation in the long term.

There's nothing wrong with using a shortened URL. Sometimes it's necessary, but be aware that you may take some flak for it, especially if you don't disclose the fact that you are getting compensated. If you truly believe in the products you're promoting, and are willing to stand behind them, then this shouldn't be a big deal.

Multilevel Marketing

Multilevel marketing is similar to affiliate marketing, except you are directly selling goods and services for a merchant. You are the middleman between a wholesale or specialty manufacturer and an individual customer. Some examples of MLM companies are Avon, Pampered Chef, Mary Kay, Amway, Scentsy, Thirty-One, WorldVentures, and Cutco.

Most MLM or network marketing companies encourage you to write up a list of friends and family members who might be interested—a warm market. But if you are not comfortable doing that, or that list has already been fully explored, a Facebook presence may be just the thing you need to get your business going.

First and foremost, you need to have a business Facebook page that is separate from your personal account. There is a tendency for people to simply use their personal account, but remember: this is a business. A Facebook page will give you a variety of marketing and advertising tools.

Before we get into specifics, let's talk about your overall Facebook strategy for this business model. Basically, you need to concentrate on relationship and credibility building. You also have to be enjoyable to follow.

Choose Pictures Wisely

The first thing people will see on your Facebook page will be your profile picture. Many business owners make the mistake of putting a picture of their product as the profile. You're smarter than that. You know that Facebook is a social experience and people will want to connect with you, not a picture of your product, so make sure you have a great profile picture of you smiling into the camera.

You will also want to use the photo album available on your business page. Use this to post interesting photos (and most of them should have you in them).

Be Multidimensional

Show that you have more to offer than simply your product. Whatever field you are in, strive to become a thought leader, and display your expertise on your Facebook page.

If you sell a product associated with cooking, post helpful tips, tricks, and recipes. Think about this: Food Network star Rachael Ray didn't have to strongly push her line of cookware to her devoted followers. Her fans grew to like her and trust her over time, and when she had a product to sell, they trusted her and went out to buy it.

If you are selling something for the home, offer weekly tips or tutorials on home decoration. Nutritional products? Offer the latest studies along with your thoughts or analysis on the topic.

The more varied (but topical) information you post, the more you are setting yourself up as an expert in your niche. Concentrate on becoming a thought leader first, and then you will find natural ways to encourage sales of your products when the moment presents itself.

Network

Become socially active on Facebook by using your business page. Commenting on other pages and responding to comments left on your page will foster that sense of community. Comments should be upbeat and valuable without any product pushing. As you consistently produce quality content, people will look to you as a leader or consultant, not a salesperson. This is an important distinction.

Here's what the Facebook business page specifics could look like for someone selling makeup products:

Profile picture
> This should be a photo of you smiling into the camera.

Album pictures
> Your album should include a variety of pictures of you working with clients.

Videos
> Provide a collection of how-to videos that take people step-by-step through common product applications.

Posts
> Your posts should be varied in content, but all pointing back to you being an expert. If you see a great article related to your product, post it on your Timeline with an extra tip or two. Make your posts interesting and conversational. Try to incorporate a bit of your personality here because you want people to be able to relate to you.

Facebook Ads
> This will be a little tricky, but worth your effort. Facebook is not known for liking MLM or affiliate ads, but the more you offer valuable content on your Facebook page, the greater your ad approval chances will be.

For an MLM business model to be effective of Facebook, you'll want to strive to be respected, trusted, and enjoyed by your fans and potential clients.

Case Study: A Sneak Peek into a Super Affiliate's Facebook Ads

Zac Johnson, "super affiliate" and long-time Internet marketing blogger at *ZacJohnson.com*, loves the potential for easy profit in affiliate marketing. He has understood the incredible value of social media and Facebook ads to create affiliate revenue since very early on, and continues to benefit from his knowledge of multivariate testing and interest targeting to optimize click-through and conversion rates for an impressive sales rate.

Typically, Johnson looks for offers that can be associated with an interest or hobby that are likely to be liked on Facebook. He then uses those interests to target users with that interest for the ad. Because he can target a concrete, directly-related interest, the potential for clickthrough becomes so much higher. In one case, Johnson found an eBook and online course through ClickBank that teaches how to do skateboarding tricks that seemed to be a winner. As an affiliate for the offer, he would earn 50% commission on all referred sales, which comes out to $7.78 basically just for referring quality traffic to their site.

For the skateboarding course offer, Johnson chose to target men age 25-35 who currently live in the United States and are interested in "skateboarding" and/or "Tony Hawk". The end result targeted around 2 million current users on Facebook.

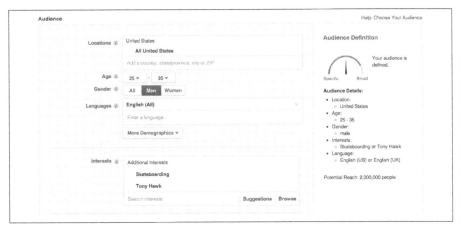

Figure 14-1. Johnson used demographics to feasibly scale the ad's reach

He then set up the ad. The key was to make sure he was never paying more to get a click-through than the profit margin of the campaign's sales and commissions. The tactics he had set up first worked, to a good extent. The click-through rate was fantastic, and it was definitely making sales. However, Johnson was not yet turning a profit.

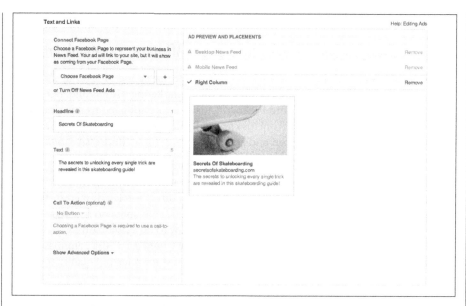

Figure 14-2. Johnson's initial ad

Here's where he finds the value of multivariate testing. If you have an ad that you believe is not yet reaching its full potential, multivariate testing makes it easy to see the formula that your ad campaign needs. Upon monitoring the clickthrough rates of several campaigns, one can generally gauge which one is most cost-effective and converting. Most commonly, the higher the clickthrough rate on your ads, the lower the cost per click.

Ad Name	Status	Bid	Type	Clicks	Impressions	CTR (%) ▼	Avg. CPC	Avg. CPM	Spent
Secrets of Skateboarding 3	Active	$0.05	CPC	1,026	202,264	0.507%	$0.05	$0.24	$49.38
Secrets of Skateboarding 4	Active	$0.05	CPC	459	97,804	0.469%	$0.06	$0.29	$28.73
Secrets of Skateboarding 2	Active	$0.05	CPC	227	53,197	0.427%	$0.08	$0.34	$18.15
Secrets of Skateboarding 1	Active	$0.05	CPC	70	17,393	0.402%	$0.10	$0.40	$6.99
Trick Secrets Exposed 20	Active	$0.05	CPC	322	109,905	0.293%	$0.11	$0.31	$34.24
Trick Secrets Exposed 19	Active	$0.05	CPC	300	103,648	0.289%	$0.11	$0.32	$33.08

Figure 14-3. This shows the variation one can see through testing various ads. The top ad has the highest clickthrough rate and lowest cost per click.

Secrets Of Skateboarding
secretsofskateboarding.com
Are you the best skateboarder in CA? See
the top tricks for skateboarders in your area!

Figure 14-4. Johnson's updated ad after multivariate testing

One strategy Johnson found effective was to make the copy more personalized. Instead of targeting "United States" in general, he started making separate campaigns for skateboard enthusiasts in a particular state or region, and then mentioning the specific state in the copy. As a result, and after a few additional tweaks, he finally found a formula that achieved profit.

Real-Life Q&A

Q: The competition in this space is huge. I get the feeling there are companies a lot bigger than mine that are able to put a lot more time and money into this than I can. Are there any secret weapons for smaller MLM sellers?

A: It depends on what you're selling. If you're with a huge MLM provider, then there's going to be a ton of tough competition. However, that in itself creates a new market that you might be able to sell to. Surely, there are many things you've learned about MLM success; you can sell these tips to people with less experience via webinars, training courses, and other gated content.

This might not be the answer you're looking for. However, if you've already exhausted your ability to develop creative ads and social media pages, then it's time to consider a different approach. If you're not selling to the long-tail of the MLM market, then perhaps the solution is to look at emerging and niche social networks where there will be less competition.

Q: I've been trying to test an affiliate offer with Clickbank using a redirect, but my ad continues to get rejected. Are redirects not allowed?

A: It depends on the offer. Clickbank stuff can be tricky sometimes. We use redirected traffic in client ads every day.

Summary

It can be tough to make a living solely off of affiliate or multilevel marketing. If that's your goal, though, you've got to be a social media hard-charger. Build an audience and a following at all costs, and then slowly work your sales pitch into your regular routine.

We wish we could validate the promises that a lot of MLMs make about being independently wealthy by merely leveraging already established contacts, but it's never as simple as that. Like any business, you have to get out there and make it clear that you are the person to buy from. Product quality is a baseline; personality and relationships are what makes the sale in this realm.

Head over to the *Social eCommerce* website (*http://www.socialecommercebook.com*) for more Q&A and to post your own burning questions! You'll also have access to exclusive offers, discounts, and coupon codes on various social media tools and services.

To get exclusive access to instructional videos related to the concepts in the chapter, simply send a text with your email address to *+1(213)947-9990* and we'll send you some awesome links!

Glossary

+1 (Google)

The voting paradigm on Google+, similar to Favorite on Twitter and Like on Facebook.

Ad network

A company that connects advertisers to websites that want to host advertisements.

Ads manager

The page on a business Facebook account at where you can view and manage ad campaigns, as well as view performance reports.

Affiliate

A promoter of a merchant's products or services who receives compensation for delivering sales or leads to the merchant or merchant's website.

Affiliate marketing

Performance-based marketing that rewards an affiliate for bringing in clients through the affiliate's marketing efforts.

Aggregator

An application or service that collects information from many disparate sources. Usually refers to an RSS aggregator, which collects links and excerpts from multiple news sites and blogs via an XML news feed.

API

Application programming interface, a set of behind-the-scenes entry points and interfaces to a service or program. For instance, the Twitter API enables you to build applications that embed tweets.

App

An application or program, though the term usually refers to a program that runs on a mobile or web platform.

Astroturfing

A fabricated grassroots effort. This is a *black hat* tactic whereby you make it look like anonymous people on the Internet are enthusiastic supporters of your products.

Avatar

A graphical representation of your profile. This can be an icon, drawing, photo, or in some cases an animation.

Badge

An icon that is assigned to a profile to represent an achievement. This is a part of *gamification*, wherein a process is made into a game; a badge would be a form of reward for accomplishing a certain task or achieving a certain goal.

bit.ly

A service that shortens URLs for use in social media, SMS, and email.

Black hat
> A disfavored tactic. Typically, this is against the laws, rules, or terms of service of a given platform or site.

Block (Facebook)
> An act that unfriends a party and prevents it from seeing your profile, tagging you, inviting you to any events, and contacting you via the medium.

Blog
> Short for *weblog*. This is a personal journal, or a topical publication that contains mostly personal opinion and observation. In some jurisdictions, a blog may be considered true journalism. In the corporate world, a blog is often a place for company representatives to post informal (but vetted) comments and insights.

Blogosphere
> Where a *blog* refers to a personal journal or topical publication outside of a corporate site, it is part of the *blogosphere*; that is, popular bloggers are typically connected to one another through RSS feeds and social media.

Blogroll
> A list of blogs that you publicly recommend, usually on your own blog's sidebar.

Boost post (Facebook)
> A Facebook Ads option that allows you to pay to promote a certain post to a limited audience. You boost a post directly from your Facebook page versus the Ads Manager.

BRB
> A social media abbreviation meaning "be right back."

Buzz
> The perception of popularity, as measured by word-of-mouth referrals.

Campaign
> In Facebook Ads, this is a collection of ads that share a common audience. In general marketing terms, a campaign represents a single concerted effort to accomplish a sales goal.

Check-in
> A basic social action that a mobile user can take to indicate his participation in an event or an arrival at a location. You might "check in" at Starbucks at Penn Station, for instance, and that may put a pin on a map in your newsfeed.

Circle
> A Google+ paradigm for grouping certain users according to what you would like to share with them.

Citation flow
> An algorithmically derived score created by Magestically SEO that estimates a domain's importance to search engines.

Clicks
> The number of times that users clicked through on an ad to the ad's landing page.

Commenting
> The act of posting a comment on someone else's posted content.

Connection
> A LinkedIn paradigm for identifying people you have recognized as professional connections.

Core product
> The main product you are selling in a sales funnel.

Cover photo
> The banner photo that sits atop a Facebook profile. Its dimensions are 851 pixels by 315 pixels.

CPC
> Cost Per Click. This is how much you are charged each time a visitor clicks on one of your ads.

CPM
> Cost Per Mille. This is how much you are charged for every 1,000 people who view one of your ads.

Creative Commons

A popular set of licensing schemes that make it easy for others to share your content while you retain the copyright.

Crowdfunding

A method of collecting donations from fans or supporters to contribute to an otherwise cost-prohibitive project such as a movie, game, album, or consumer product. Indiegogo and Kickstarter are examples of crowdfunding sites.

Crowdsourcing

A public request for input, comments, or solutions to a (usually very difficult) problem or question. Quora is an example of a crowdsourcing site.

Cyberbullying

A motivated effort to cause emotional harm or publicly lower someone's status on social media.

Delicious (formerly deli.ci.ous)

A social bookmarking site that allows users to store, organize, and share posted links through tagging.

Digg

A social news aggregation site that allows users to vote content up or down to influence its rank.

Disclosure

To reveal, uncover, or go public with a piece of information.

Dislike (YouTube)

A negative rating marker.

DM

Direct message. Also called *InMail* or *PM* (private message), depending on which site you're on. Each social network has its own way of sending direct, nonpublic messages to other members, though the rules and costs associated with this are different for each service.

Domain authority

An algorithmically derived score created by Moz that estimates a domain's importance to search engines.

Double opt-in

A sales process in which users fill out a form to subscribe to services or notifications and then confirm subscription through email or text.

Doxxing

Short for "dropping documents," doxxing refers to outing a reddit user's real-life identity.

eCommerce

The business of selling things online.

EdgeRank

Facebook's algorithm for determining what posts appear on each user's News Feed, and the order in which they are presented.

Embedding

Integrating external content, such as a video or a tweet, into your page.

Emoji

A graphical emoticon used in text messaging, online forums, and social media.

Emoticon

A pictorial representation of a facial expression created by a combination of keyboard strokes used to establish mood or tone in text messaging, online forums, and social media.

Engagement

A measure of how many of your fans or followers are interacting with your content through comments and shares.

Events

A Facebook feature that enables invitation and attendance tracking for real or virtual events that occur on a specific date and time; for instance, a concert, class, or webcast.

Facebook

A profile-based social media site that centers on posting updates, which are then seen by Facebook "friends." Originally developed as a way for college students to connect.

Fan

On Facebook, a person who has clicked Like on a page (not a profile).

Favoriting

A tag added that both gives a positive rating to the original poster and stores the favorite post into one accessible folder.

Filter (Instagram)

An overlaying light effect added to a posted photo on Instagram.

Flash mob

A sudden, planned (but secret to nonparticipants) assemblage of people in a particular (usually public) place as performance art.

Flickr

The first major photo-sharing site. Now owned by Yahoo.

Follow

Opting in to receive updates from a party.

Follower

A user on Twitter who has chosen to follow your account.

Follow Friday

A Twitter tradition of recommending accounts to follow on Twitter every Friday. This is usually (but not necessarily) accompanied by the #ff or #followfriday hashtag.

Forum

An online message board. Usually it represents a place to discuss a certain subject, or it contains in-depth discussions pertaining to a particular community.

Foursquare

The first major check-in site for mobile users. Users sign into FourSquare while at a business location to notify friends of their location and to potentially unlock deals from the business.

Friend

A Facebook user who has clicked Like on your personal profile.

Friend request

A request from a user of a social network to be part of your circle of connections.

Friendly URL

A web address that is easy to remember and has meaning for users. This is opposed to a *dynamic URL*, which makes little sense and contains no indication of what it leads to.

FTW

A social media abbreviation meaning "for the win."

Gamification

Applying game-style thinking to a non-gaming application or situation.

Geotag

Geographic metadata embedded in digital photographs. Most social networks and photo sharing sites are able to read geotag information provided by the phone or camera a photo was taken with.

Geotarget

A marketing method of using geographic metadata to determine a user's geographic location and then delivering customized content to that user determined by the location.

Google+

Google's social interface to its many integrated services, though it is usually thought of as a social network in its own right.

Graph Search

Facebook's powerful multidimensional search function.

Grey hat

Considered ethically questionable, but is not yet considered spam or black hat.

Group blog

A collaborative weblog that has more than one author.

Group (Facebook)
: Discussion forums within Facebook. These can be public, private, or secret.

Guest blogging
: To have an article or post hosted on another's blog or on a multiauthor blog.

Guest post
: To publish an article or blog post on another's blog or on a multiauthor blog.

Handle
: A nickname that typically applies only to a certain service.

Hangout
: A video conferencing feature built into Google+ that allows quick and easy real-time video sharing among your circles.

Hashtag
: A discussion topic, denoted by a pound symbol (#). Originally applied only to Twitter, it now applies to most major social networks.

Hat tip
: In blogging, this refers to a mention or a link to the blog or website in which you originally found the posted material that you are reposting.

iFrame
: An HTML element for embedding the contents of a web page within another web page.

imgur
: An online image-hosting service closely associated with reddit.

Impressions (Facebook)
: The amount of times an ad is displayed and viewed, regardless the amount of times it is clicked.

Inbound marketing
: An online marketing paradigm that involves producing good, helpful content that leads back to your site in some way.

Index
: A collection of data, stored in a manner that is easily sorted and retrieved.

Instagram
: A photo-sharing site that is specific to mobile devices, and is extremely popular among teenagers.

Instant messaging (IM)
: A service that sends text messages between two (sometimes more) recipients. Examples are AOL Instant Messenger, Yahoo Messenger, and ICQ.

Karma (reddit)
: The total score of your rating of your comments and links.

Klout
: A social media monitoring service that attempts to assign a score to your online presence as represented on major social networks.

Landing page
: The destination for an ad. Usually this is customized for the particular ad or campaign, but it could also be your home page, product page, or Facebook page.

Lead box
: An opt-in button that leads to a popup or overlay to fill in contact information.

Lead magnet
: A free informational item given to prospects in hope of obtaining contact info and drawing them towards a sale.

Lead page
: An opt-in page for filling out contact information to receive a given item or piece of information.

Like
: A Facebook action that indicates that you like, enjoy, or agree with content hosted on the site (such as a post, picture, or page).

LinkedIn Open Networker (LION)
: A term for a LinkedIn user with a very large number of connections and who accepts most friend requests.

Liveblogging

A blog post that aims to present rolling contextual coverage of an event or situation as it occurs.

Livestream

To show as a live video or audio feed online.

LMAO

A social media abbreviation meaning "laughing my ass off."

LOL

A social media abbreviation meaning "laugh out loud."

lolcat

A popular meme based on images of cats with humorous captions in lolspeak.

lolspeak

An abbreviated form of communication popular in text messaging and online forums.

Lurker

A visitor, reader, or user who is present and paying attention to the conversation without participating or engaging in any way.

Man Crush Monday

A social media tradition in which men post a picture of or announce their "man crush" on Monday.

Mashup

A site composed of feeds and streams from other sites; an aggregation site.

Mayor (Foursquare)

On Foursquare, the person who most frequently visits a particular establishment or venue—typically a very influential and well-connected person in the community surrounding this place.

Meat Puppet

A false identity injected into a discussion or forum with the sole purpose of swaying consensus. It is similar to a sock puppet but not automated.

Meetup

A social network for creating real-life meetings of people with similar interests.

Meme

A viral, cultural catchphrase, amusing idea, or witticism that is easily modified to communicate a new perspective. Typically, a meme manifests as a photo with a standardized caption, such as Confession Bear, Good Guy Greg, Scumbag Steve, and Courage Wolf. Quickmeme.com (*http://quickmeme.com*) is the most popular site that enables quick meme creation and sharing.

Metadata

Literally "data about data." If data is raw information, metadata is the description and organization of that information. For instance, the audio recording of a phone call is data, but a list of incoming phone call times and numbers is metadata.

Microblogging

Blogging in a highly limited fashion. Twitter is the most popular microblogging site; it limits each post to 140 characters.

Mobile

Anything related to smartphones and tablets.

Moblog

Mobile blogging. This is how you publish to a blog or website using your mobile phone.

Moderation

Curation of user-supplied content. Typically this is in a forum setting where a moderator ensures civil, on-topic communication among participants.

Moderation queue

A moderation queue is a series of unpublished comments or reviews on a website that require action on the part of the moderator.

mozRank

An algorithmically derived score created by Moz that reflects the importance (through popularity) of incoming links to one's site. Approximates Google's PageRank score.

Newsfeed

A newsfeed is a tool to format updates that are made to a website or blog to make it easy for users to see the updates.

Notification

An alert received when a party you follow has an update on a social media platform.

Offers

An offer on a website refers to a task that's needed for the site and is either rejected or accepted.

OMG

A social media abbreviation meaning "oh my god."

OpenGraph

OpenGraph is a platform on Facebook that gives you APIs and tools provided to third-party developers, enabling them to create applications that are hosted outside of Facebook but operate inside a Facebook session.

Opt-in

Opt-in refers to joining an email mailing list. Platforms and programs that use opt-in tools require the subscriber to click on a link to confirm she wants to be a part of the mailing list. A double opt-in requires a sign-up and then a confirmation of sign-up.

Opt-out

Opt-out refers to removing yourself from an email mailing list. Subscribers can do that at any time through a link that takes them to a website where they can change the settings and stop emails from coming from that organization.

ORM

Online reputation management, a way to monitor and take action to control the reputation of something or someone on the Internet.

Page

What you cite or post on the Internet. Most websites have multiple pages or links.

Page authority

An algorithmically derived score created by Moz that estimates a web page's importance to search engines.

Page post engagement ad (Facebook)

An advertisement that displays in the News Feed of a targeted audience demographic.

PageRank

An algorithmically derived importance score calculated by Google and assigned to every web page on the Internet. It is the foundation of Google's ranking algorithm.

Pandora

A music website that creates personalized online radio content based upon a selected artist or song.

Permalink

The URL on a website. It points to a specific blog post or web page.

Photoblog

A way of sharing and publishing photos in a blog format. The main difference between a blog and a photoblog is that blogs generally focus on text, while photoblogs emphasize photos.

Pinboard (Pinterest)

An organization folder for your pinned images and videos.

Pins (Pinterest)

Pins are the images or videos you put on boards created in Pinterest. You *pin* an image so it stays on your board and creates a link.

Pinterest

Pinterest is a website that allows profile owners to share photos and videos collected via the Internet or personally.

Pitchbox

A prospecting and workflow platform that helps the user find and initiate relationships for marketing, PR, and link building through targeted, automated outreach.

PM

Personal message. (See DM.)

Podcast

A digital file that's created when a radio show or other audio is recorded and provided on the Internet for others to listen to.

Poke

A tool on Facebook that enables you to say hi, what's up, or otherwise draw another person's attention to your presence on Facebook.

Post engagement

Direct participation with a social media post. This could be through likes, shares, comments, retweets, clicks, or replies.

Post (generic)

On a blog or social media site, a post is the way you share the information you want others to read.

Power Editor (Facebook)

A tool created by Facebook that works within the Google Chrome browser to manage multiple Facebook ad campaigns at once. It is tailored to bigger advertisers.

Power*Trust

An algorithmically derived authority and trust score created by LinkResearchTools and comprised of over six third-party authority and trust metrics.

PPC

Stands for "pay per click." A type of online advertising where the advertiser pays for each click received.

Privacy policy

A privacy policy on a website protects the owner regarding the content she posts. It also discloses certain things on the site, such as posts added with the intent of making money.

Profile

What you create when you make an account on sites like Facebook, Twitter, or Pinterest. It shows your name and any information you want to share or is required by the site.

Profile picture

Your avatar, or a picture that is symbolic of your social media profile, used to distinguish it from others.

Profit maximizers

The final stage of your sales funnel. These are for only the most interested prospects, as what is featured as a profit maximizer is usually a very large amount of money, and thus a more difficult sell.

Promoted page (for personal posts)

Advertising in Facebook to get more likes to your page.

Promoted post (Facebook)

Refers to paying for an increased likelihood that a larger audience will see your message or post. Promoted posts are done from the Ads Manager or Power Editor.

Promoted tweet

An advertisement tweet that is visible on the Twitter feeds of a targeted audience demographic.

Proxy

An intermediary for requests between internal hosts and untrusted or external hosts. Web proxies are used by Internet surfers wishing to anonymize their Internet surfing.

Push notification

Delivers notifications from servers of third parties to phones.

Reach

The number of people who see your post.

reddit

A social bookmarking site. Catorgized by means of subreddits, or subpages that users may search for.

Remix

A remix can refer to a blog or article that's been rewritten. It can be totally different or just a different angle or belief.

Repost

To post on social media something that you have already found on social media.

Retweet (RT)

When you post something someone said on Twitter to your profile, telling your readers it came from that person and not you.

RSS

Really Simple Syndication, an XML format used to push website or blog articles to remote readers. It helps ensure that subscribers always have the most current content.

RSS reader

An RSS reader enables you to see updates from the websites you include in your account. You'll only see when they're updated, and you'll be able to easily see the specific change.

Sales funnel

A chart that visualizes the steps of initial contact to opt-in, to purchase, to upsell.

Screencast

A recording of actions taken on your computer screen usually with audio voice-over. It's a video that's easily viewable on a computer.

Scribd

A tool that enables users to post documents in many different formats and embed them on a website page using an iPaper format.

Second Life

A virtual online world in which users use avatars to interact with others.

Selfie

A picture one takes of oneself and then posts on social media.

Selfie Sunday

A social media tradition in which people post selfies on Sunday.

Sentiment

The way you view something or your opinion on an event or situation. This is visible in blog posts, articles, and website content.

SEO

Search engine optimization, techniques and strategies for improving a URL's position in search engine results.

Share (Facebook)

To repost on Facebook with a link to the original post.

Skype

A video chat service that is downloaded to the computer.

SlideShare

SlideShare is similar to YouTube, but it's for slide decks rather than video. SlideShare allows you to upload PowerPoint, PDF, Keynote, and OpenOffice files privately or publicly and then, with the help of slide decks, they can be viewed on websites or handheld devices.

SMH

A social media abbreviation meaning "shaking my head."

Snapchat

An app that enables users to take temporary photos or record temporary videos, add text, and add drawings, and then send them to recipients included in a controlled list.

Social bookmarking

A way to keep websites you're interested in organized in one place. It enables you to see what others have bookmarked as well, which helps you discover sites you may not find otherwise.

Social media

A way to interact with others. You use websites such as Facebook and Twitter to communicate with others, learn about businesses or topics of interest to you, and share your business or knowledge.

Social media monitoring

An observation of content in social media sites like Facebook and Twitter, blogs, and discussion forums. It allows you to see overviews of the topics or opinions on these sites.

Social media optimization

The use of several social media sites to raise the awareness of a product, event, or business. These social media sites include tools like RSS feeds and social bookmarking and sites like Twitter, YouTube, and Facebook.

Social network

A group of people who are connected in some way. Usually the connection has to do with a business or purchase that was made, but it can also be through friends or family members.

Social news

The ability to submit and vote on stories submitted by others. News stories are not hosted on social news sites; they contain only links out to other sites, votes, and comments from readers.

Sock puppet

A false automated identity found online and used to deceive others.

Spam

Commercially oriented email or other content sent without the request or knowledge of the recipients. Sometimes refers to repetitive notification messages or other unwanted content, even if it is not of a commercial nature.

Splog

Short for "spam blog," this is a blog that's for spam only—that is, where the author promotes affiliate website links only to make money.

Sponsored post (on a blog)

A blog post wherein the blog owner is paid for making it.

Squeeze page

A landing page where the primary goal is to get the user to opt-in to an email list.

Status update

Usually referring to Facebook or blogs, it is an update of a situation posted to social media.

Story

A series of snapchats that are chosen to be available to be rewatched as many times as desired within a 24 hours of being posted.

Stumble

The action of browsing through suggested sites on StumbleUpon.

StumbleUpon

A social bookmarking site where users recommend other sites to visitors.

Subscribe

To opt in to receive information or periodic updates from a chosen party.

Tag

A nonhierarchical keyword related to posted content, often on a blog.

Tag (Facebook)

Associate a Facebook user to a piece of content such as an image or a status update.

Tag cloud

A section of a website that contains keywords from the site. These are generally found on blogs, on the sidebar.

Technorati

A search engine specifically for blogs.

Terms of service (TOS)

The list of things that one must agree to and follow in order to use the site, purchase the product, or use the service.

Thread

Usually found in a forum or on Twitter, a thread contains an entire conversation between two or more people.

Throwback Thursday (TBT)

A social media tradition in which people post an old photo of themselves on Thursday.

Timeline

On Facebook, a Timeline puts all of the posts in order based on the time. You can also add specific events to the Timeline such as a wedding, the birth of a child, or a job change.

TL;DR

A social media abbreviation meaning "too long; didn't read."

Trending topics

Used on Twitter, trending topics show the keywords or hashtags that were popular and used most at any given time.

Tripwire

A low-cost item offered to prospects in the hope that it will lead into their buying a more expensive product from you.

Troll

A person who publishes posts and starts conversations with the intent to cause disruption or to start an argument.

Trust flow

An algorithmically derived score created by Majestic SEO that estimates a web page's trustworthiness to search engines.

TrustRank

Similar to PageRank, but instead of starting with a random seed set of sites and calculating outward from there, the calculation starts with a trusted seed set (e.g.. Harvard, Cambridge, and Oxford University websites).

Tumblr

A tool used to post text, images, videos, links, audio, and more to your tumblelog. This platform is similar to a blog.

Tweet

The formal name for a post made on Twitter.

Twitter

Twitter is a way for anyone to tell a story or share information in 140 characters or fewer.

Twitterverse

The term used to describe those users who have and use Twitter accounts.

TY

A social media abbreviation meaning "thank you."

Unfollow

To opt out of receiving updates from a given party on social media.

Unfriending

Removing a friend from your Facebook friends list.

Unsubscribe

To opt out of receiving news from a given party.

URL shortener

Enables you to turn a long URL into a shorter one. This is especially valuable on Twitter since you're limited to 140 characters per post.

uStream

An online livestreaming video hosting service that allows viewers to feed or watch live video.

Views

The number of impressions on an ad, or number of times that users watched a video.

Vine

An app owned by Twitter that allows users to create short, looping videos that can be hosted on Twitter.

Viral marketing

Using buzz to market your business through social networks. This process enables you to share what you offer virally or virtually.

Vlog

A video blog, shared through YouTube, websites, RSS feeds, and other platforms, that enables others to watch with ease.

Wall

Your Facebook wall is where your posts and friends' posts are displayed for you and others to read and comment on.

Webcast

A video broadcast posted and viewable on the Internet for anyone you choose to watch and listen to at any time.

Webinar

A seminar held online through the Internet.

White hat

Refers to following the major online services' (e.g., Google's or Facebook's) suggested guidelines and rules, focusing on the audience's needs and wants, and not taking unethical, inappropriate, or risky shortcuts.

Widget

A software application comprising portable code.

Wiki

A website created by many contributors. It allows users to add or edit the content.

Woman Crush Wednesday

A social media tradition in which women post a picture of or announce their "woman crush" on a Wednesday.

Word of mouth marketing

A marketing and advertising strategy that relies upon word-of-mouth and social media referrals as their main method to obtaining prospective customers

WTF

A social media abbreviation meaning "what the f***."

YouTube

A video-sharing service owned by Google. YouTube is the number two search engine in the world.

Index

We'd like to hear your suggestions for improving our indexes. Send email to index@oreilly.com.

Desktop News Feed ads (Facebook), 120–125
deviantART, 17
DiamondEnvy, 186
Dickson, Tom, 9
digital content marketing, 71–84
    engaging vs. selling, 73–75
    on Facebook, 78
    The Fortune in You case study, 80
    good products for, 73
    on MySpace, 78
    on Pinterest, 78
    strategies for, 71–73, 76
    on Twitter, 78
    on YouTube, 79
digital fulfillment, 74
direct messages (Twitter), 2
disclosure rules for paid reviews, 232
Disqus, 13, 34
Dogster, 17
Dollar Shave Club, 133
DoubleClick, xxii
    giveaways vs., 74
doxxing, 14
driving directions, 92–95
    correcting, 93
Drucker, Peter, 221
ducttapemarketing.com, 160

E

e-mail addresses, acquiring, 231
eCommerce Expo, 162
eCommerce, categories of, xxv
Elance, 43
elevator pitch, 4
eMarketer, 102
employees social media access, 145
The Entrepreneurs Secret to Creating Wealth:
    How the Smartest Business Owners Build
    Their Fortunes (Hurn), 184
eTail West, 162
ethics, 26–29
ethnicjewels.ning.com, 199
Etsy, 47
events, promoting, 191–206
    ad strategies for, 193
    badges, creating, 193
    creating social networks for, 199
    on Facebook, 198
    with hashtags, 193

    in social networks, 195
    on Meetup.com, 197
    multiple, 196
    portfolio sites, 183, 196
    thought leadership for, 192
    on Twitter, 198
    on YouTube, 197
Evergreen Business System, 202
Experian Hitwise, 10
eyes in ads, 117

F

Facebook, 3–4
    account suspensions, 146
    ad approval process, 120
    ad testing/design, 105
    Ads Manager, 117
    book promotion on, 174–176
    buying fans/followers/friends, 26
    check-in deals, 88
    digital content marketing on, 78
    event hashtags, 193
    event promotions on, 198
    Graph Search, 216–218
    offers, 129
    physical goods, marketing on, 53
    for SEO, 209
    service marketing on, 89
    storefront marketing on, 89
    trolls on, xxiv
    unpublished posts, 114
Facebook Ads Power Editor, 113
Fast Company Magazine, xx
Federal Trade Commission (FTC), 232
FedEx, 107
Ferriss, Tim, 107, 115
fiction books
    influencer lists for, 227
    promoting, 82, 169
filtered reviews on Yelp, 92
5 Data Insights into the Headlines Readers
    Click, 41
Flay, Bobby, 226
Flickr, 47
    Google search results for, 208
Flipboard, 39
flooding the feed, 47
Followerwonk (Moz), 229
Followgram, 57

Huffington Post, 41
Hurn, Chris, 184
Hyundai, 107

I

I Can Has Cheezburger? A LOLcat Collekshun
    (Gotham), 172
IBM, 35, 170
ideavate, 43
images in advertising, 117
imgur, 15
Improvely, 202
impulse buy, 74
In-N-Out Burger, 107
in-network messaging, 235
Inbound Marketing Summit, 162
influencers, 225–243
    attracting, 233–237
    building lists of, 226–227
    contact information for, 231
    contacting, 230–237
    e-mail addresses, acquiring, 231
    follow-up on, 235
    on Google+, 238
    interacting with, 227
    links, monitoring, 237
    mentions, monitoring, 237
    metrics for, 228–230
    offering giveaways to, 236
    outreach to, 234
    on Pinterest, 230
    Pitchbox case study, 238–241
    on reddit, 237
    refining lists of, 228–230
    reviews, paying for, 232
    tracking responses from, 236
    Twitter warmups, 231
infographics, 129
InMail (LinkedIn), 7
InMobi, 103
Instagram, 16
    physical goods, marketing on, 55–58
    service marketing on, 89
    storefront marketing on, 89
    video content on, 221
introverts, marketing strategies for, 38
inventory, 24
iPads
    as giveaway prizes, 128

in Will it Blend campaign, 9
IRCE Focus, 162
Irvine, Robert, 95–97
iVillage Live, 9

J

Javi the Frog, 97
job openings on LinkedIn, 6
Johnson, Zac, 249
Join.me, 202
Jones, Rob, 219

K

Kamikaze (Kuwahara), 177
KDP Select (Amazon), 182
    Smashwords and, 179
Kern
    Frank, 72, 116
key performance indicators (KPIs), 114
keywords, 109–112
    in Meetup descriptions, 197
King, Zach, 3
Klout, 228
Kmart, xx
Kobo, 170
Kred, 228

L

landing page, 119
    for books, 175
Lanyrd, 196
LeadPages, 76, 202, 202
    webinar templates on, 204
Li, Charlene, 160
LibraryThing, 17, 180
    giveaway capabilities on, 236
like/follow buttons, 31
likeable.com/blog/, 160
LinkedIn, xxiii, 5–7
    e-mail addresses, acquiring, 232
    groups, creating, 129
    Premium subscriptions, 7
    reputation management on, 147
    searching in, 215
    for SEO, 212
LinkedIn Open Networkers (LIONs), 6
linkerati, 225

About the Authors

Stephan Spencer is the author of *Google Power Search* and co-author of *The Art of SEO* (O'Reilly). Stephan founded Netconcepts (*http://www.netconcepts.com*), an SEO and interactive agency in the 1990's. The firm was acquired in 2010 by Covario (*http://www.covario.com*).

Stephan is a highly sought-after SEO, content marketing, and digital strategy consultant to retailers large and small. His clients post-acquisition have included Zappos, Sony Store, Quiksilver, and Chanel, to name a few.

Stephan's newest venture is ScienceOfSEO.com, a video-based SEO training and coaching program.

Stephan is the inventor of the pay-for-performance SEO technology platform Gravity-Stream, now part of the Rio SEO toolset.

Stephan is a Senior Contributor to Practical eCommerce (*http://bit.ly/1pf8cpJ*) and to MarketingProfs.com, and a columnist for Search Engine Land (*http://selnd.com/1mIzUcJ*), Marketing Land (*http://mklnd.com/WJgW0i*), Search Engine Journal (*http://bit.ly/1pfbEAD*), Lifehack (*http://bit.ly/Uv68kO*), Multichannel Merchant (*http://bit.ly/1kXKbSE*), and The Huffington Post (*http://huff.to/1z7rrbK*). He's also been a contributor to DM News, Catalog Age, Catalog Success, Building Online Business, Unlimited, and NZ Marketing magazine, among others.

Stephan is a frequent conference speaker on SEO and other online marketing topics for the Direct Marketing Association (DMA), American Marketing Association (AMA), Shop.org, Internet Retailer, SMX, IncisiveMedia (Search Engine Strategies), O'Reilly/TechWeb, PubCon, ECMOD, IQPC, and IIR. His hundreds of speaking gigs have taken him around the globe—everywhere from Berlin, London, Toronto, Santiago, Sydney and Auckland, to New York, Chicago, San Francisco, Los Angeles, and places in between.

Stephan is an avid blogger. He blogs at Stephan Spencer's Scatterings (*http://www.stephanspencer.com*), NaturalSearchBlog.com, BusinessBlogConsulting.com, ChangesForGood.org, and Google, I Suggest... (*http://googleISuggest.blogspot.com*). He's also been a contributor to Searchlight (part of the CNET Blog Network) and the Shop.org blog.

Stephan is on the board of Impact Network (*http://www.impactnetwork.org*) and on the advisory board of CrowdGather (*http://crowdgather.com*).

He holds an M.S. in Biochemistry from the University of Wisconsin-Madison.

If you are looking to hire Stephan to help you take your online presence to a new level, he can be reached in the following ways: me@stephanspencer.com (email), (608) 729-5910 (phone), @sspencer (Twitter), stephanspencer (Skype), stephanspencer (Facebook), and stephanspencer (LinkedIn).

Jimmy Harding is an author, advisor, speaker, consultant, and entrepreneur. He is the CEO and founder of Jimmy Harding Consulting and the creator of Game Changer Talks, a podcast dedicated to bringing you high-level strategies to take your business to the next level. In 2013, Jimmy's proprietary marketing programs helped his clients increase their profits by $20M. He is an expert in creating marketing strategies and systems that combine traditional advertising with direct response marketing and the most up-to-date and effective digital media and social technologies. His consulting and marketing agency helps business owners develop, plan, and execute growth strategies to not only completely dominate their marketplace within 12 months, but also position themselves for longterm sustainable growth and market share.

Jennifer Sheahan, founder of FB Ads Lab, has for many years helped entrepreneurs and business owners to acquire the skills and knowledge they need to market their products, services and business in this dynamic environment. She is well-regarded in the online business community; she is a well known and sought-after public speaker who travels extensively throughout the world in both a learning and teaching capacity.

Colophon

The animal on the cover of *Social eCommerce* is a greater adjutant (*Leptoptilos dubius*), member of the stork family (*Ciconiidae*). The name *adjutant* comes from their stiff military gait when walking.

The greater adjutant is huge—57 to 60 inches in height. With an average wingspan of 99 inches, these are the largest of living storks. They have a massive wedge-shaped bill, which averages about 12.7 inches in length, bare head, and distinctive neck pouch.

The adjutant feeds mostly on carrion and offal, sometimes feeding on vertebrates when the opportunity presents itself. They used to be found in large numbers in Asia, but numbers have been declining to the point of being endangered. This is thought to be due to improved sanitation. Drained wetlands, pollution, and disturbance has led to loss of adjutant nesting and feeding habitat. This, paired with hunting and egg collection, has caused massive declines in population. In 2008, the population was estimated at less than 1,000. The IUCN Red List of Threatened Species lists the greater adjutant as endangered.

Many of the animals on O'Reilly covers are endangered; all of them are important to the world. To learn more about how you can help, go to animals.oreilly.com.

The cover image is from *Cassell's Natural History*. The cover fonts are URW Typewriter and Guardian Sans. The text font is Adobe Minion Pro; the heading font is Adobe Myriad Condensed; and the code font is Dalton Maag's Ubuntu Mono.

Have it your way.